Tackling Unemployment

Tackling Unemployment

The Legislative Dynamics of the Employment Act of 1946

Ruth Ellen Wasem

2013

W.E. Upjohn Institute for Employment Research
Kalamazoo, Michigan

Library of Congress Cataloging-in-Publication Data

Wasem, Ruth Ellen.
Tackling unemployment : the legislative dynamics of the Employment Act of 1946 / Ruth Ellen Wasem.
pages cm
Includes bibliographical references and index.
ISBN-13: 978-0-88099-452-1 (pbk. : alk. paper)
ISBN-10: 0-88099-452-5 (pbk. : alk. paper)
ISBN-13: 978-0-88099-453-8 (hardcover : alk. paper)
ISBN-10: 0-88099-453-3 (hardcover : alk. paper)
1. Full employment policies—United States. 2. Employment stabilization—Law and legislation—United States. 3. United States. Employment Act of 1946. I. Title.
KF6055.W37 2013
344.7301'20424—dc23
2013000724

© 2013
W.E. Upjohn Institute for Employment Research
300 S. Westnedge Avenue
Kalamazoo, Michigan 49007-4686

The facts presented in this study and the observations and viewpoints expressed are the sole responsibility of the author. They do not necessarily represent positions of the W.E. Upjohn Institute for Employment Research.

Cover design by Alcorn Publication Design.
Index prepared by Diane Worden.
Printed in the United States of America.
Printed on recycled paper.

To the memory of
Jessie McCullough Wasem and Charles Terry Wasem

Contents

Figures

Tables

Illustrations

Acknowledgments

Growing up in the Upper Ohio Valley, where the local economy had until recent decades depended on mining and steel, provided me with a rough education in the vagaries of employment. The boom time of the 1950s and 1960s gave way to decades when, for many, unemployment always lurked around the corner. The book is dedicated to my parents, Charles Terry Wasem and Jessie McCullough Wasem, who lived most of their lives in eastern Ohio. I would further acknowledge my brother, Terry Denton Wasem, and my lifelong friend Jackie Hawk Dunlap, both of whom live in eastern Ohio today, for their moral support as I was writing this book.

The kernel of this book was a dissertation begun during the recession of 1982, the last time U.S. unemployment had reached 10 percent before it briefly topped out at that number in November 2009. The Institute for Social Research's Center for Political Studies at the University of Michigan funded much of my graduate studies and enabled me to work with many outstanding researchers. The Harry S. Truman Presidential Library and Museum also provided research funding, and the Horace H. Rackham School of Graduate Studies gave tuition support. Considerable credit is due to my dissertation chair, Jerome M. Clubb, and committee members Maris A. Vinovskis, John E. Jackson, and Terrence J. McDonald for holding me to high academic standards while providing the encouragement necessary to complete the dissertation in 1989.

Fast-forward two decades to 2009, when the nation was in the midst of the Great Recession. Joyce Vialet and her husband, John Vialet, became the catalysts for this book. Joyce had been my mentor in immigration policy at the Congressional Research Service and recalled that I was completing a dissertation on employment policy when we began working together in the late 1980s. Had it not been for the Vialets' interest in discussing this subject during a stormy weekend in 2009 at Newport, Rhode Island, this book may never have been written.

Soon all of my free time was devoted to researching the Employment Act of 1946 anew. As we walked our dogs together, neighbors Tad and Susan Cantril guided me to the public opinion data from the 1940s that formed the basis of Chapter 3. Survey research experts (and former classmates from the University of Michigan) Celinda Lake, Barbara Smela, and Fran Featherston provided valuable comments on that chapter. Labor economists Linda Levine and Gerry Mayer, as well as Joyce, Barbara, and Fran, reviewed the first draft of the manuscript.

I am grateful to Kevin Hollenbeck of the W.E. Upjohn Institute for Employment Research, who expressed early interest in the book and suggested key revisions to the manuscript. Benjamin Jones of the Upjohn Institute has been an energetic and thoughtful editor of the book. Erika Jackson typeset the manuscript, including the tables and figures. Any flaws and shortcomings, of course, are mine.

The views and conclusions of this book solely reflect those of the author and not those of the Congressional Research Service, the U.S. Library of Congress, or the Upjohn Institute for Employment Research.

1
The Employment Act in Historical Perspective

As the United States approached the middle of the twentieth century, it was undergoing a considerable change in its conception of the role of government and of the government's responsibility for maintaining the economic well-being of its people. The Great Depression had shaken the country's economic foundation and posed a threat to the social stability of the United States. The activist programs of the New Deal intervened and, many say, prevented a complete national collapse. What the New Deal did not do, ramping up for the nation's entrance into the Second World War did: end the economic depression. Direct federal spending for World War II, which stimulated wartime production, lifted America out of the Great Depression.

At the leadership level, many concluded that the wartime spending had validated the theories of John Maynard (Lord) Keynes, a British economist who advocated, among other things, deficit spending during economic downturns and depressions. Some policymakers further argued that it would be reckless if the government did not establish Keynesian economics as formal policy. There were quite a few leaders, however, who thought the New Deal had gone too far and who certainly opposed any effort to further strengthen the federal role in the economy.

Though the American public knew little of Keynes and his theories on compensatory spending, they did know that they wanted no more depressions. Many people, idle during the 1930s and working overtime during the war, were realizing that they were part of a national economic system and thus were vulnerable to its fluctuations. Moreover, the socioeconomic composition of the population was undergoing change, and the fact of social and economic interdependence was now obvious. The result was a redefinition of the role of government and government responsibility.

The push to enact full employment legislation was a pivotal step in this process. An examination of the debate on full employment policy offers an opportunity to identify the forces in this contest, to see how these forces lined up, and to clarify the issues that distinguished these forces from one another. Full employment legislation provides a case study that enables us to gain a better, albeit incomplete, understanding of the dynamics of redefining government's tasks.

As originally introduced, the proposed Full Employment Act of 1945—hereafter referred to as the full employment bill—mandated a dramatically new role for the federal government in the economy. It was the first piece of seriously considered, comprehensive economic legislation from the perspective of the consumer and working person. More sweeping than protective labor legislation such as workmen's compensation and minimum-wage laws, the bill stated that all persons able and willing to work were entitled to employment—an employment bill of rights. It also would have established a permanent system for national economic planning and would have required compensatory federal spending in periods of recession.

The legislation that was ultimately enacted became the foundation of economic policy for many years. It provided the justification for compensatory spending, tax cuts, job-creation tax credits, and other Keynesian tools, which the many subsequent administrations used to buoy the U.S. economy. It established the President's Council of Economic Advisers and the congressional Joint Economic Committee—key structures intended to conduct national economic planning. Indeed, it placed the ultimate responsibility for maintaining the nation's economic well-being upon the federal government.

A history of the Employment Act of 1946 is especially pertinent today, as many of the world's developed economies teeter on the verge of a major economic recession, perhaps depression. The U.S. Congress and the president are again debating the role of the federal government in alleviating unemployment and stimulating job creation. Although full employment is not a common phrase in the current lexicon, the twentieth-century debate over full employment offers lessons for our times. The parallels will emerge as the history unfolds.

USAGE OF UNEMPLOYMENT AND FULL EMPLOYMENT

Unemployment. The term still prompts images of the gaunt faces in the breadlines of the 1930s, although today we are more likely to see depictions of statistical trends in the graphics shown on the news. To the affected individuals and families, it is an ego-shattering experience that places the basic requirements of food and shelter at risk. To the society as a whole, it is indicative of a troubled economy when it rises above the level of frictional unemployment—i.e., unemployment that occurs when people are naturally moving between jobs. Some researchers, moreover, associate unemployment with increases in personal problems such as divorce, substance abuse, and mental health problems, as well as community-wide problems such as delinquency and violence (Strom 2003).

Unemployment is a concept that grew alongside industrialization. It is an integral, if unfortunate, aspect of free enterprise capitalism. It occurs when an individual's job depends on persons or forces beyond his or her control or when the person lacks the skills needed to perform the job at hand. It appears that originally the term "unemployed" was used literally to refer to those who were not working. This earlier definition thus encompassed children as well as elderly persons. Before the 1850s, the use of "unemployed" to describe adults connoted laziness and incompetence (Keyssar 1986, p. 3).

The contemporary definition of unemployment derives directly from the idea of involuntary idleness. As the United States was experiencing the depression of the 1870s, the word "unemployed" began to be limited to those forced out of work. The term "unemployment," referring to both the condition of persons and the condition of the economy, began appearing in print in the late 1880s. The 1911 edition of the *Encyclopaedia Britannica* was the first to include an entry on unemployment (Garraty 1979, pp. 139–140; Keyssar 1986, pp. 3–5).

Full employment, like unemployment, is a modern concept. As countries around the world were experiencing the Great Depression of the 1930s, full employment became a focal point of policy debates. Though Keynes did not originate the term, he certainly fostered its discussion. More importantly, Keynes, as well as American economist Alvin Hansen, advocated full employment as a policy alternative for free market economies that countered the fascist and socialist remedies for unemployment (Klein 1947, pp. 153–159).

Full employment means somewhat different things to different people. In his 1944 *Report on Full Employment in a Free Society*, William Henry (Lord) Beveridge defined full employment as "having always more vacant jobs than unemployed men" (Beveridge 1944, p. 18). Leon Keyserling, an original member of the Council of Economic Advisers, said that full employment is simply no unemployment—when everyone who wants a job has a job.[1] Generally, economists describe full employment as the condition of the economy when the only unemployment is frictional—i.e., the rate of unemployment that normally results from people changing jobs. The rate of unemployment that economists have considered acceptable in a full employment economy has ranged from less than 1 percent to 5 percent (Dornbusch and Fischer 1981, pp. 7–8, 376; Garraty 1979, p. 229).

This book defines full employment as the condition of the national economy when all who are able and willing to work are employed. This definition is based upon popular usage of the term during the late 1930s and 1940s and is derived from the Keynesian view of full employment as a function of national income or the gross national product. This economic equilibrium, through forecasting and planning, can be achieved with private enterprise and investment; however, the federal government is expected to use compensatory spending and other fiscal tools to raise the national income when the private sector falls short of the investment sufficient for full employment. Thus, this usage implies a proactive role for the federal government and a promise of employment for the labor force.

HISTORIOGRAPHY OF THE EMPLOYMENT ACT OF 1946

The researchers of postwar domestic policy, as well as the biographers of Harry S. Truman, almost uniformly agree that the full employment bill, ultimately enacted as the Employment Act of 1946, is one of the major pieces, if not *the* most important piece, of domestic legislation during the Truman years. Alan Brinkley (1996, p. 264) characterizes it as the "last great battle for the New Deal." Alonzo Hamby (1973,

p. 60), in his thorough account of American liberalism following World War II, *Beyond the New Deal*, ranks the legislation's importance highly: "More than any other measure, this bill seemed essential to the future of postwar America," he says. Truman biographer Robert Donovan (1977, p. 166) labels the legislation as the "landmark in the Truman administration." A retrospective volume edited by Francis H. Heller (1982, p. 211) with contributions from major figures in the Truman administration describes the act as "fundamental." James Sundquist (1968, p. 54), characterizing it as the "legal mandate for fiscal activism," documents its seminal role in policymaking throughout the years from Presidents Eisenhower to Johnson. And in *Unemployment in History*, John Garraty (1979, p. 231) concludes, "Its passage was a landmark in the history of national economic policy, and also of American political history, for it set up a Council of Economic Advisers, the influence of which on public policy was to be enormous."

Some scholars extend the importance of the Employment Act beyond American domestic policy. William Appleman Williams (1972, pp. 231–239), for example, considers the fear of economic depressions and the desire for full employment as essential aspects of the American "open door" view of the world. He presents then–assistant secretary of state Dean Acheson's testimony before Congress in November of 1944, during which Acheson states, "We cannot have full employment and prosperity in the United States without foreign markets" (p. 236). Williams links the goal of full employment with expansionist foreign policy and the escalation of the Cold War.

Beyond recognizing the importance of the Employment Act, the scholarly research conveys a consensus of opinion on the circumstances surrounding its enactment. Four common themes emerge from the literature.

A major consensus in the literature is that the original full employment bill clearly grew out of Keynesian economic theory. Margaret Weir (1992, pp. 27–58) opens her discussion of employment policy in the United States with a discussion of Keynesian principles, such as compensatory spending, that were embodied in the full employment bill. As Hamby (1973, p. 60) observes, "Fundamentally, the bill was an attempt to write into law the economics of Keynes and Hansen by requiring enough compensatory government spending to wipe out unemployment." In an edited volume on the policies of the Truman administration, Barton Bernstein and Alan Matusow (1966, p. 47) state, "The intellectual origins of the Employment Act of 1946 can easily be traced to the economic theories of John Maynard Keynes and the famed Beveridge Plan in Britain." Likewise, Sundquist (1968, p. 61) maintains, "The discussions leading to the 1946 Act centered upon Keynesian concepts and techniques for planning and influencing of aggregates—the 'national production and employment budget,' the 'aggregate volume of investment and expenditure,' and so on."

The literature, second, offers a unified voice on the importance of the bill to the liberal community, largely because liberals saw Keynesian policies as the solution to unemployment and its ensuing problems. Brinkley (1996, p. 260) describes how progressives in the labor movement as well as those from the National Farmers Union and the Union for Democratic Action "lobbied vigorously and effectively" for full employment legislation. "Their long-range hopes for stability focused upon a daring new piece of legislation, the full employment bill," he writes. Hamby (1973, pp. 60–64) says, "It demonstrated the way in which Keynesian economics had captured the allegiance of liberals during the war." The full employment bill became the centerpiece of the liberals' postwar agenda and the focal point of legislative lobbying efforts. Donovan (1977) characterizes the bill as "the liberals' dream" (p. 122) and recounts their aggravation with compromise versions (p. 169). The dismayed reaction of the liberals to the modifications of the "crucial full employment bill" is more fully described by Hamby.

A third point of consensus among scholars is that President Harry S. Truman offered weak support for the original bill and was partly responsible for its dilution. The only notable exceptions to this view are those expressed by people who were part of the Truman administration. Bernstein and Matusow (1966, p. 47) present Franklin Roosevelt as the champion of full employment in his 1944 campaign and characterize his successor as giving only a formal blessing: "Despite Truman's open endorsement, the bill received wavering support from the administration." Hamby (1973, pp. 63–64) argues that the White House acquiesced to compromises that weakened the bill. Donovan (1977, p. 122) describes negotiations between the House committee responsible for the legislation and the administration, portraying Truman as willing to water down the measure so that it would be reported out of committee. Weir (1992, pp. 52–53) credits Truman as a supporter of the legislation but concludes he was unable to command party loyalty or generate public pressure for the legislation.

Fourth and finally, consensus exists on the congressional treatment of the bill. Throughout the debate on full employment, the liberal Senate leaders are seen as pushing the original bill only to be stymied by the conservative House, particularly the Southern leadership. Donovan (1977, pp. 122–123) explains how the bill "floundered" in the House Committee on Expenditures in the Executive Departments, a committee he describes as being dominated by ideological conservatives, especially committee chairman Carter Manasco (D-AL). Hamby (1973, p. 64) quips that this committee rewrote the original bill to offer a "version so weak that Washington wits said it had been 'Manascolated.'" Brinkley (1996, pp. 263–264) describes the "evisceration" of the legislation by the coalition of Republicans and conservative Democrats.

A consensus in the literature on these four themes surrounding the Employment Act of 1946 is not surprising, because the legislation became the textbook case for a generation of college and university courses on the U.S. Congress—literally. In 1950, Stephen Kemp Bailey wrote an award-winning book on congressional behavior. Innovative for its time, *Congress Makes a Law: The Employment Act of 1946* was a study of legislative policy formation that highlighted the importance of congressional staff and interest groups. Bailey analyzed the support for the legislation by looking at the biographical characteristics of the members of Congress and at the socioeconomic traits of their districts. His method is unsophisticated by current standards but was a major step toward the systematic analysis of legislative behavior. Bailey (1964, Vintage paperback edition) concluded by advancing the theory that the House of Representatives was more conservative than the Senate because it consisted of a more rural, provincial group of people, and that this provincialism led to policies less supportive of a strong federal government.

The four common themes of the literature discussed in the preceding paragraphs all emerged in Bailey's work. The book opens with the Keynesian origins of the legislation. Bailey proceeds with a discussion of how the liberal community championed the idea of full employment and placed it at the fore of its agenda. He describes key senators who advocated the bill and the instrumental role their staffs played in crafting the legislation. On the other side of the aisle, Bailey delineates the conservative House members who obstructed the legislation. Bailey portrays Truman as weak, ineffective, and offering support that was too little, too late. His implicit conclusion is that a critically important piece of legislation was diluted by players who behaved less than responsibly in the political process. Most scholars who have come after Bailey share his affection for the original full employment bill and echo his theme that the Employment Act of 1946, albeit a landmark, fell far short of what was called for at that time.

VANTAGE POINT OF HISTORY

This book concurs with many of the interpretations of the full employment bill presented in the literature. In fact, this research reinforces the picture of a dramatic departure from previous policies that the initial legislation offered and the importance of this bill to the liberal community. The Keynesian underpinnings of the proposal and the view that wartime spending validated the buoyant effect of compensatory spending are also accepted without dispute. The important role of the economic planning apparatus that resulted from the Employment Act, notably the Council of Economic Advisers, is implicit in this research as well.

The points of departure with the current historiography, however, are considerable. Foremost, this research does not agree with the prevailing interpretation of congressional behavior on the full employment bill. Specifically, it challenges the conclusion that the proposal split members of Congress along North-South and urban-rural lines and that opponents were "provincial" in their thinking. Instead, it offers a more nuanced analysis of the economic, demographic, and political factors that drove support for and opposition to full employment, drawing parallels to the populist and Federalist-versus-Anti-Federalist traditions in American politics.

This research, moreover, counters the conclusion that Truman responded limply on the full employment bill. It refutes arguments about his alleged willingness to compromise the "full employment" language, and it challenges the view that Truman was detached from the negotiations. As it turns out, Truman was more engaged in the legislation than President Franklin Roosevelt had been before his death in 1945. A significantly different interpretation of the Truman administration's strategy emerges.

Finally, this research does not treat the full employment bill as a single proposal that, when modified, proved ineffective. The bill, rather, is presented as a package of legislative proposals offered as a comprehensive strategy for achieving full employment. By studying the various elements that made up the full employment bill, one can observe that, just as some elements were diluted by the legislative process, others were strengthened. The legislative dynamics of the Employment Act of 1946 are considered within the broader tensions over the role of the federal government in the American economy.

There are four central elements of the full employment bill to examine as we track its course through the legislative process. First and foremost is the stated responsibility of the federal government to ensure full employment when the private sector falls short, primarily through compensatory spending. A second key element is the apparatus or structure to implement that responsibility. Third is the concept of national economic planning, which likewise forms a core element of such a proposal. And the fourth feature, equally as important as the previous three, is the strength of the commitment—the guarantee of employment—that the federal government is making to the American people in this proposed policy.

Whenever Congress debates legislative proposals, it is difficult to foresee the long-term importance of the action. Grandiose claims about the far-reaching effects—both positive and negative—are all too frequently made during the process. From the vantage point of history it is often easier to appraise the significance of what came to be and what might have been. The long-term significance of the full employment bill lies directly in what it proposed to achieve and how members of Congress responded to its purpose and plan of action. This book studies anew the full employment bill and the resulting Employment Act to explore how the government's response to high levels of unemployment redefined the federal role in job creation.

Note

1. Leon Keyserling, oral history interview by the author, August 11, 1982.

2
Federal Role in Employment Stimulation

The ideas that the federal government should engage in employment stimulation and should ensure full employment are rooted in the experiences of the Great Depression. During the Depression, people were searching for solutions to the hard times that were occurring in America and elsewhere. The New Deal set the stage for the debate because it established the precedent for an activist federal government. But whereas many of the ingredients for a federal role in job creation were formulated during the New Deal, confidence in the federal government's capacity to achieve full employment grew out of the war mobilization efforts of World War II. Indeed, the performance of the U.S. economy during the war validated the idea of compensatory spending and made full employment a realizable objective.

SOCIOECONOMIC TRANSFORMATION

The economic and demographic changes that America experienced during the first half of the twentieth century are well known, as the nation became more urban and industrial, better educated, and ethnically more diverse. Scholars have theorized about—and in many cases documented—the social and political consequences of these changes. This socioeconomic transformation did much to shape the debate on the federal role in job creation as America approached midcentury.

America was growing. The U.S. economy had grown from a gross national product (GNP) per capita of $1,001 in 1900 to a GNP per capita of $2,342 in 1950. The Great Depression affected economies worldwide, and America's GNP growth rate exceeded those of other industrialized Western nations such as Germany, England, Italy, and Canada for the same period. Disposable personal income in the United States grew dramatically, from $71.5 billion in 1920 to $206.9 billion in 1950 (U.S. Census Bureau 1975, p. 224).[1]

The population was growing as well: in one decade alone, it grew from 76 million in 1900 to 92 million in 1910. Half of the 16-million-person increase during this decade, an estimated eight million, came from a continuing flow of immigrants. By 1950, the population of the United States had reached 151.7 million people; that is, in 50 years' time it had doubled (U.S. Census Bureau 1975, p. 11).

As the population grew, areas that had once been rural became more densely populated. Towns evolved into midsized cities, and suburbs formed around major cities. Many people left rural areas to live in metropolitan centers, and most of the new immigrants settled in cities as well. The result was that the nation shifted from being predominantly rural in its residential characteristics to being urban. The percentage of people living in urban areas rose from 39.7 percent in 1900 to 59.0 percent in 1950. The pivotal year was 1920, when, for the first time, just over half of Americans were living in urban areas (U.S. Census Bureau 1975, p. 11).

During this same period, the educational attainment of Americans was rising. In 1900, only 6.3 percent of the population over 17 years old had graduated from high school. By 1925, this percentage had risen to 24.4 percent, and by 1950, some 57.4 percent of the population over 17 years of age had a high school diploma. The percentage of those aged 5 to 17 years who were enrolled in school, moreover, increased from 78.3 percent in 1900 to 92.3 percent in 1950. Conversely, the percentage of the population that was illiterate dropped from 10.7 percent in 1900 to 3.2 percent in 1950 (U.S. Census Bureau 1975, pp. 380–382).

This period also witnessed a steady change in the composition of the workforce, as illustrated in Figure 2.1. This change is most evident in those occupations considered working class. In this instance, "working class" refers generically to those people that are employed in blue-collar or low-paying white-collar occupations, such as clerks, laborers, skilled production workers, and those employed in low-paying service jobs. The manual and service occupations, always a major portion of the labor force, grew from 44.9 percent of the workforce in 1900 to 51.6 percent in 1950. Even more striking than the growth in blue-collar employment was the increase in low-paying white-collar employment. The number of persons employed in clerical and sales jobs expanded

Figure 2.1 Occupational Distribution of the U.S. Labor Force, 1900–1950

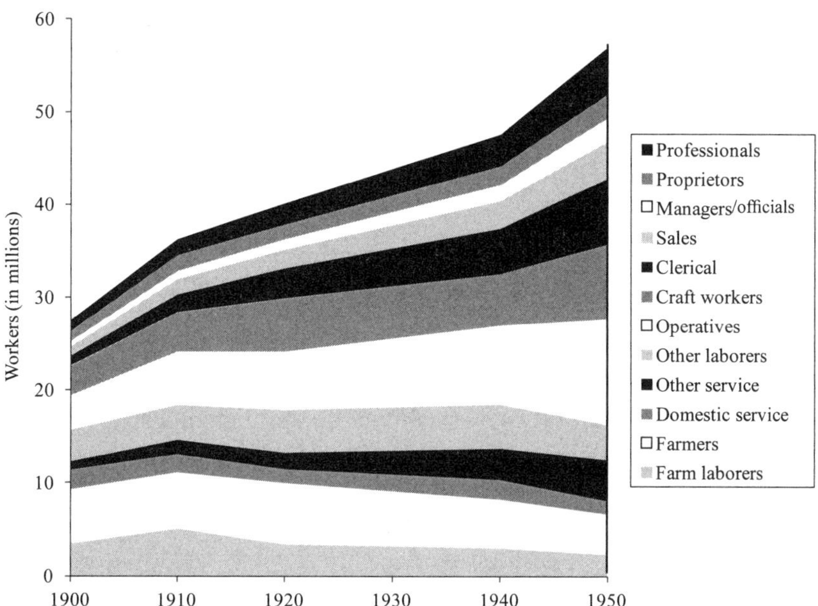

NOTE: The 12 occupational categories listed in the legend are represented by four shades (black, dark gray, white, and light gray) repeated three times from top to bottom. These bands are identified in the small squares next to the category names.
SOURCE: U.S.Census Bureau (1975).

from 7.5 percent of the labor force in 1900 to 19.3 percent in 1950, for an overall growth rate of 157 percent. Meanwhile, the portion of people engaged in agricultural labor shifted from 7.1 percent in 1900 to 1.6 percent in 1950. These figures display an important change in the socioeconomic composition of the United States, as the proportion of working-class Americans grew from just over half (52.4 percent) of the population in 1900 to well over two-thirds (70.9 percent) by 1950 (U.S. Census Bureau 1975, pp. 139–145).

This change in the socioeconomic mix of the United States did not produce a uniform result across the nation. Some areas experienced considerable population growth, while others did not. In 1940, the percentage of the population living in urbanized areas ranged from

89 percent in Massachusetts to 20 percent in Mississippi. New Mexico, Florida, and Nevada had experienced the highest rates of growth in urbanization, ranging from 15 to 20 percent increases from 1920 to 1940. Massachusetts, Pennsylvania, and Rhode Island had the largest proportion of their populations in working class occupations in 1940, each with greater than 85 percent. On the other hand, North and South Dakota and Mississippi had less than 60 percent of their populations in working class jobs, the lowest rates in the nation (U.S. Census Bureau 1975, pp. 25–39).

The Great Depression affected the income levels of almost all Americans, but not necessarily equitably. State unemployment statistics in 1939 ranged from a high of 14.4 percent in Pennsylvania to a low of 4.0 percent in South Carolina. In that year, 4.0 percent of the families in the United States reported that they had no income or financial resources. The rates of those who fell under this destitute status ranged from lows of 2.0 percent in Delaware, Rhode Island, and Utah to highs of 6.4 percent in New Mexico, 6.8 percent in North Carolina, and 7.2 percent in Mississippi (U.S. Census Bureau 1975, pp. 25–39).

The partisan composition of the electorate was shifting as well, manifested most clearly in the political realignment that took place during the Great Depression. In 1900, the Republican presidential candidate received 51.7 percent of the popular vote. In the early elections of the twentieth century, the Democratic presidential candidate never obtained 50 percent or more of the popular vote until 1932, when the New Deal realignment forged a Democratic majority that brought the working class, ethnic, and urban voters into the political mainstream (Austin 1986; Lubell 1965, pp. 43–68). The Democratic coalition gained its strength, in part, through the changing socioeconomic composition of America.

On the whole, the American public was well educated, ethnically diverse, and predominantly working class. The socioeconomic mix of the population was changing in ways that accentuated the interconnection of economic and social phenomena and the dependence of the individual on national and sometimes international forces. Although the American people had faced upheavals, they managed to preserve America's culture, political institutions, and economic system in the face of awesome challenges presented by the Great Depression and World War II.

EXPERIENCES OF THE GREAT DEPRESSION

Prior to the Great Depression, unemployment and the hardships that ensued were seen as local rather than federal problems. "Poor farms" existed for the disabled and the feebleminded, and unsupported women and children were often at the mercy of local charities and orphanages. In those days, unemployment compensation for the able-bodied man frequently was a night in jail and a train ticket out of town.

Following the stock market crash of 1929, the number of Americans who were unemployed grew at an alarming rate. In New York City, for example, 60,000 people had registered with the municipal Free Employment Bureau by the beginning of 1931. Though the actual figures of unemployed defied enumeration, the phrase "twelve million unemployed" echoed the despair of the 1930s. In 1932, *Fortune* magazine estimated that more than one out of every four Americans was a member of a family that lacked a regular, full-time breadwinner. The Bureau of Labor Statistics (BLS) estimated that 1933 was the peak year for joblessness, with unemployment levels reaching 24.9 percent (Bernstein 1985, pp. 276–277; Bird 1966, pp. 22–51; Blumberg 1979, p. 22; Degler 1970, pp. 383–384). Figure 2.2 presents the percentage and number of persons unemployed over the Depression years.

Many people who remained employed nonetheless experienced a decline in salary, a reduction in hours, or employment in jobs well beneath their skill levels. By the end of 1932, the hourly wage rate for industrial workers ranged from an average high of 30 cents to an average low of 20 cents. Women fortunate enough to find jobs often faced pitifully low wages, as evidenced by Chicago data indicating that one-fourth of women working in that city earned less than 10 cents an hour. Findings from a longitudinal study in Oakland, California, reveal that a majority of families averaged more than a 50 percent loss in income between 1929 and 1934 (Elder 1974, p. 61; Freidel 1965, pp. 1–20).

The Great Depression severely affected rural America, particularly since the agricultural economy already had been turbulent through the 1920s. During the Depression, an estimated one-fourth of all family farms were lost to drought and foreclosure. As a result, many former farmers became homeless migratory workers in search of gainful employment. The Select Committee to Investigate the Interstate Migra-

Figure 2.2 Number and Percentage of Persons Unemployed, 1929–1941

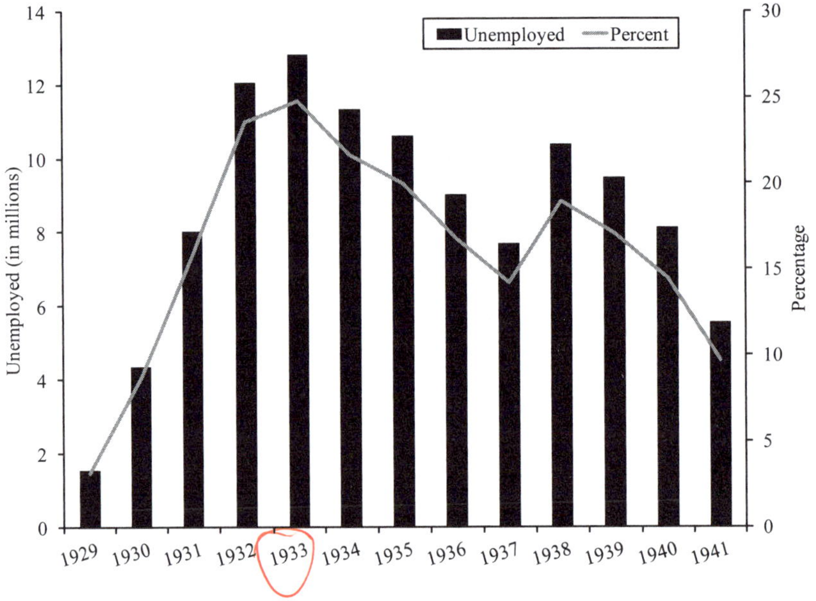

SOURCE: U.S. Census Bureau (1960, p. 70).

tion of Destitute Citizens estimated that in one year alone—1937—one million people connected with farming and four million nonagricultural persons were migrants. John Steinbeck's Pulitzer Prize–winning novel *The Grapes of Wrath* conveyed elements of truth in its fictional account of the Joad family's desperate struggle as Okies migrating to California in search of a sustainable life during the Dust Bowl drought of the 1930s (Bernstein 1985, pp. 1–15; Freidel 1965, pp. 2–6; Steinbeck 1939).[2]

Those who were industrial workers living in rural areas were acutely hard hit by the Great Depression. The conditions in the coalfields of Harlan County, Kentucky, became well known, as First Lady Eleanor Roosevelt visited the area. There were entire towns in Harlan County where no one had income, and people reportedly lived on dandelions and berries. When journalist Martha Gellhorn went to a rural industrial region in South Carolina, she compared the work of federal relief to the desperate job of removing the wounded from the battlefield so they could die quietly in the hospital (Gellhorn had covered war, including the D-day landings). Yet she marveled at the resilience of the people.

"If anything, these people are a sad grey," Gellhorn wrote, "waiting, hoping, trusting" (Bernstein 1985, pp. 306–307; Bird 1966, pp. 26–27).

The institution of the family also faced crises during the Great Depression. Legal claims of wives who had been abandoned rose 134 percent from 1928 to 1932 in New York municipal courts, and there was reason to assume that embarrassment and lack of resources prevented many more desertion claims from being brought forward. Hospitals and agencies that served infants and children reported notable increases in the number of abandoned babies. Even among those families that stayed together, there was evidence of considerable stress. Glen Elder's research disclosed that the psychic costs of status loss included such effects as restricted social activities outside the home and heavy alcohol consumption by the father (Blumberg 1979, pp. 22–23; Elder 1974, pp. 60–63).

There were other casualties of the Great Depression. Suicides rose dramatically from 1930 to 1933. Despite President Herbert Hoover's insistence that "No one has yet starved," deaths from starvation were reported in the rural backlands of America as well as in major metropolitan areas. The New York City Welfare Council listed 29 deaths from starvation and an additional 110 from malnutrition in 1933. Authorities in Los Angeles, referring specifically to young men and boys who had "hit the road" from communities across the country and had wound up in Los Angeles, estimated that at least 25 percent of them needed medical care when they arrived in the city. When sociologists Helen and Robert Lynd returned to "Middletown" (their fictional name for Muncie, Indiana, in their published studies) during the depths of the Depression after having first studied it in the 1920s, they were struck by how the Depression had almost universally affected rich and poor alike, concluding that "it has approached in its elemental shock the primary experiences of birth and death" (Bird 1966, pp. 22–51; Degler 1970; pp. 383–384).

As late as 1931, Hoover disagreed with those people who thought that the government could legislate policies to pull the nation out of the Depression. "Such views," quipped Hoover, "are as accurate as the belief that we can exorcise a Caribbean hurricane." Hoover instead emphasized that voluntarism was the best solution to the woes of the Depression, though he supported self-liquidating public works projects. He engaged in highly visible campaigns to help charities and private philanthropic groups raise money for the needy (Degler 1970, p. 391; Leuchtenberg 1963, p. 335; McElvaine 1983, pp. 72–94).

In 1931, Sen. Robert Wagner (D-NY) introduced the Employment Stabilization Act, which proposed a board for planning public works, a system for collecting unemployment statistics, a federal employment service, and an unemployment insurance program.[3] Hoover vetoed this public works bill following the bitterly cold winter of 1932. He only reluctantly signed a diluted version of the legislation, the Emergency Relief and Construction Act (known popularly as the Garner-Wagner Bill), in July 1932. This law was a meager response to a major problem, yet it signaled the growing support for federal intervention (Degler 1970, p. 391; McElvaine 1983, pp. 72–94; *Time* 1932).

Although Hoover's ineffective responses to the worsening economy resulted in his overwhelming defeat in his 1932 reelection bid, the assessment of his presidency today is less harsh than public opinion of him was in 1932. Some historians credit Hoover with rejecting policies that would have given unprecedented power to business, thus preventing the formation of an oligarchy. Barton Bernstein maintains that Hoover was the first of the "new" presidents and argues that, although he was restricted by his constitutional scruples, he did more than any previous president had done to combat a depression. Robert McElvaine characterizes Hoover as a transitional president who rejected the "old economic fatalism" and used governmental power to urge business to act cooperatively to stimulate recovery. In any event, the failure of Hoover's voluntary approach opened the door for Franklin Roosevelt and his package of federal programs known as the New Deal (Bernstein 1968, pp. 265–267; McElvaine 1983, p. 69; Williams 1961, p. 428).

LEGACY OF THE NEW DEAL

The U.S. economy had collapsed by the time Franklin Delano Roosevelt took office in 1933. Under his leadership, the federal government almost immediately offered a variety of programs, some at odds with others, to deal with the severe economic situation. The New Deal programs addressed problems in all sectors of the economy, including industry, agriculture, banking, and investments. And, most importantly for the discussion at hand, the federal government under the New Deal formally assumed responsibility for relieving the unemployed.

The Federal Emergency Relief Act (FERA) of 1933 removed public assistance from local jurisdiction because state and municipal governments were unable to deal with the magnitude of unemployment brought about by the Great Depression. This act, along with public works programs such as the Civil Works Administration (CWA) and the Public Works Administration (PWA), both enacted in 1933, and the Works Progress Administration (WPA), enacted in 1935, placed the federal government in charge of alleviating unemployment. Throughout the New Deal, the emphasis was to create work and only provide relief as an emergency measure of last resort.

Another major piece of employment-related New Deal legislation was the Fair Labor Standards Act (FLSA) of 1938, which established the first federal minimum wage level. Roosevelt had championed the call for minimum wages, maximum hours, and restrictions on child labor during the 1936 campaign. Most proponents offered the humanitarian argument that these provisions were aimed at reducing poverty rather than the Keynesian argument that the FLSA would lead to increased purchasing power. The FLSA set a wage floor of 25 cents per hour and a workweek ceiling of 44 hours. Under the law, over a two-year period wages would rise to 40 cents an hour and the workweek ceiling would fall to 40 hours. The law also banned child labor. In order to garner enough votes in Congress to pass the legislation over conservative opposition, however, major portions of the labor force were exempted from the law.

The New Deal showed innovation in its efforts to solve the economic problems of the Depression. One interesting example is the National Industrial Recovery Act (NIRA), which was administered by the National Recovery Administration (NRA). This program merged three concepts: 1) fostering cartelization and self-help among industries, 2) expanding public works activities, and 3) increasing the employment and purchasing power of workers by shortening the workweek without reducing pay. NIRA, ultimately declared unconstitutional, was generally probusiness—with one important exception: section 7a, which asserted the rights of employees to bargain collectively, with representatives of their own choosing and without interference from management.

The New Deal's vehicle for economic planning, however, was not the NRA, but rather the National Resources Planning Board (NRPB). Established in 1933 as the National Resources Board, it was transferred to the Executive Office of the President in 1939 and became the hub of long-term economic planning. The administrative structure of the NRPB facilitated the flow of ideas among government, the business community, and academia because it made extensive use of committees organized by subject matter and staffed by bureaucratic and nongovernmental experts. The NRPB brought in many specialists as part-time consultants and thus reduced the lag that often exists between the development of an idea within the intellectual community and the consideration of the idea by the government bureaucracy.

The NRPB became the center of Keynesian policy analysis within the government. The major work of Keynes, *The General Theory of Employment, Interest, and Money*, was published in the United States in 1936. It provided the intellectual framework for the government to control unemployment as it managed a free economy. "After Keynes," John Garraty points out, "full employment seemed a realizable goal of public policy." However, the initial reaction of most economists and policymakers in America was skeptical at best. Advocacy of long-range economic planning, Keynesian fiscal practices, and full employment policy increased the NRPB's visibility as well as heightened the controversies surrounding it (Garraty 1979, p. 221; Warken 1979).

Roosevelt and his New Deal team subsequently have been criticized for not embracing Keynesian economics. James MacGregor Burns (1956, pp. 400–404) concluded that Keynesian economics offered the perfect middle solution between individualistic capitalism and socialism. Roosevelt's reluctance to commit wholeheartedly to deficit spending, Burns argued, prevented the New Deal from ending the Depression.

The Roosevelt administration never fully embraced Keynesian economics, writes Ellis Hawley, because the administration was caught in a dilemma between the benefits and practical necessities of large corporations and the simplicity and opportunity of competitive individualism. Hawley (1966, pp. 276–280) sees a shift in emphasis from central planning and corporate cooperation in the early years of the New Deal to an antitrust phase in the later years. Hawley notes that the recession of 1937 was pivotal in terms of the growing acceptance of Keynesian economics within the Roosevelt administration.

In 1938, President Roosevelt did express several ideas in his annual message to Congress that corresponded with Keynesian concepts about employment and the economy. At one point Roosevelt discussed the importance of increasing the purchasing power of the farmers and the industrial workers; he held that this increase would stimulate the purchasing power of the remainder of the workforce and that, as a result, the national income would be raised. He also addressed the matter of a balanced budget, making it clear that while he wanted a balanced budget, there were certain conditions that must be met. "The first condition is that we continue the policy of not permitting any needy American who can and is willing to work to starve because the federal government does not provide work," he said (Roosevelt 1941a, p. 8).

Congress gave a lukewarm reception to Keynesian economics and its component of full employment. This reception was due, in part, to the growth of the conservative coalition in Congress. Having gained strength in the election of 1936, this alliance of conservative Democrats and Republicans, though not always voting as a solid bloc, effectively stymied many of Roosevelt's later New Deal programs. The congressional conservatives' hostility to those who advocated full employment led them to muster sufficient support to suspend the NRPB's appropriations in 1943, and thus to let the NRPB expire (Patterson 1967, pp. 325–337; Warken 1979, pp. 228–245).

It is impossible to know whether the Depression would have lasted longer without the onset of the war, but William Leuchtenberg (1963, p. 347) notices marked gains in the economy before the wartime spending had any appreciable effect. "It is conceivable," he argues, "that New Deal measures would have led the country into a new cycle of prosperity even if there had been no war." Leuchtenberg further points out that one of the major unsolved issues of the Great Depression—whether to establish federal safeguards against inflation and unemployment—was addressed following the war by the enactment of the Employment Act of 1946.[4]

More recent economic analysis of the Great Depression points to several positive factors that were fostering an economic recovery before the onset of World War II. Current Federal Reserve chairman Ben Bernanke observed that the public had lost confidence in the "self-correcting powers" of the financial system in 1931–1932. Bernanke (2000, pp. 41–65) concluded that extensive government involvement in the financial system was the major New Deal program that succeeded in promoting the economic recovery: "Only with the New Deal's rehabilitation of the financial system in 1933–35 did the economy begin its slow emergence from the Great Depression," he wrote.[5]

Christina Romer, former chair of the Council of Economic Advisers, analyzes the business cycles and the GNP during the Great Depression and finds that monetary policy was "crucial" in the recovery. She further offers that fiscal policy was of little consequence in the recovery until 1942. Instead, her analysis suggests that the trend toward recovery was in motion before fiscal spending for the war began in earnest. She concludes "that aggregate demand-stimulus was the main source of the recovery from the Great Depression" (Romer 1992, p. 783).

ACCOMPLISHMENTS OF THE WAR YEARS

In the minds of most Americans, World War II brought America out of the Great Depression. Many previously idle persons were put to work in war production or enlisted in military service. Necessity forced the government into deficit financing of the war, and the resulting effects on the American economy validated the idea of public investment and compensatory spending. Many economists and policymakers converted to Keynesian thinking in response to the performance of the wartime economy.

The NRPB in 1941 circulated a draft of a proposal for postwar planning that proved to be seminal. This report, published as *After the War—Full Employment* in January 1942, was written by Alvin H. Hansen. Hansen had received his doctorate in economics from the University of Wisconsin in 1918 and was critical of Keynes during his early academic career. But by the time he became president of the American Economic Association in 1938, Hansen had embraced Keynes' analysis of the Great Depression and compensatory spending. Hansen now wholeheartedly advocated the vital role of the federal government in the maintenance of full employment (Barber 1987).

In *After the War—Full Employment*, Hansen (1942, pp. 1–7) voices fears of a postwar depression or inflationary boom, yet is optimistic that the nation can maintain business prosperity and full employment by means of an expansionist economic program. “Private business can and will do the job of production. It is the responsibility of Government to do its part to insure a sustained demand,” he writes (p. 3). He dismisses the opinion that the United States cannot finance its own production: “Costs and income are just opposite sides of the same shield. We can afford as high a standard of living as we are able to produce . . . But we cannot afford idleness” (p. 5).

Hansen describes how the public debt differs from an individual’s personal debt and how retiring the public debt could cause deflation, depression, and unemployment by lowering the national income. He adds, however, that it would be likewise irresponsible to raise expenditures, lower taxes, and increase the public debt if there is a tendency toward an inflationary boom. Hansen (1942, p. 7) summarizes his thoughts by saying that the public debt is an “instrument of public policy” because it is a “means to control the magnitude of the national income and, in conjunction with the tax structure, to affect income distribution.”

Hansen (1942, pp. 15–19) goes beyond a discussion of economic theory to offer pragmatic policy options. He outlines a model of output potential to deal with the expected postwar gap between potential and performance and, in turn, proposes six wartime measures to narrow this gap:

1) High corporate-income and excess-profits taxes
2) Sharply progressive estate taxes
3) Broadening the individual income-tax base together with steeply graduated surtax rates
4) Sharp increases in excise taxes on commodities competing with the war program
5) Partial payment of wages and salaries in defense bonds
6) Qualitative shifts in the components of consumption

Recognizing that the postwar economy would function differently from the wartime economy, Hansen (1942, pp. 18–19) also proposes six policy measures to ensure full employment during the reconversion. The suggestions can be summarized as follows:

1) Retention of a progressive (graduated) tax structure and a broadened tax base, with a major emphasis on the individual income tax and less reliance on the corporate income tax
2) A sharp reduction in defense consumption taxes
3) Adequate plans by private enterprise for private investment projects in manufacturing plants and equipment, in railroads, and in public utilities and housing
4) Adequate programs of public improvement projects, including nationwide development of national resources, express highways, urban redevelopment (involving, among other things, outlays in terminal facilities and reorganization of urban transportation), and a reorganized public housing program (including the setting up of a housing research laboratory designed to reduce construction costs and thus enlarge the scope of private housing construction)
5) Expansion of public welfare expenditures such as federal aid to education, public health, old-age pensions, and family allowances (This proposal would expand federal social service programs and, in turn, provide a means of reducing state and local property and consumption taxes, thereby stimulating private consumption expenditures.)
6) International collaboration to pursue internal policies designed to promote active employment, to explore developmental projects in backward countries, and to implement ways and means of opening outlets for foreign investment, of promoting world trade, and for the effective worldwide use of productive resources

With this report, Hansen had spelled out the economic elements and programmatic features of full employment policy. Some of Hansen's ideas, most notably on tax policy, were woven into President Roosevelt's 1944 State of the Union address.

The president delivered the speech in a live radio broadcast to the nation, as well as in a written message to Congress, and in doing so introduced what was to become the most contentious element in the debate over full employment—the right to employment. Roosevelt's

"Second Bill of Rights," later called the "Economic Bill of contained the following (Roosevelt 1950):

- The right to a useful and remunerative job in the industries or shops or farms or mines of the nation
- The right to earn enough to provide adequate food and clothing and recreation
- The right of every farmer to raise and sell his products at a return which will give him and his family a decent living
- The right of every businessman, large and small, to trade in an atmosphere of freedom from unfair competition and domination by monopolies at home or abroad
- The right of every family to a decent home
- The right to adequate medical care and the opportunity to achieve and enjoy good health
- The right to adequate protection from the economic fears of old age, sickness, accident, and unemployment
- The right to a good education

Before he concluded, Roosevelt drew a patriotic illustration to emphasize these rights. "Our fighting men abroad—and their families at home—expect such a program and have the right to insist upon it. It is to their demands that this Government should pay heed rather than to the whining demands of selfish pressure groups who seek to feather their nests while young Americans are dying." President Roosevelt chose to read the Economic Bill of Rights as the excerpt of his speech filmed for the newsreels that were shown in movie theaters across the country.[6]

The President echoed this famous Economic Bill of Rights speech as he campaigned for reelection in 1944, making the right to employment an integral part of the rhetoric of the postwar employment policy. Roosevelt's Economic Bill of Rights offered an antidote to the disgust many Americans felt over charges that the "dollar-a-year" executives—who were volunteering for government service in a show of patriotism—were also ensuring that their businesses were profiting from the war. Some of these businessmen who were volunteering as executives to oversee war mobilization were accused of redirecting scarce commodities to their civilian industries.[7] With this emphasis on working people, Roosevelt was returning to the roots that fed his early campaigns.

CONGRESS LOOKS FOR ALTERNATIVES

In 1943, Senate Resolution 102 established the Special Committee on Post-War Economic Policy and Planning, chaired by Sen. Walter George (D-GA). The senator's opposition to the New Deal had prompted President Roosevelt to back an unsuccessful challenger to George in the 1938 Democratic primary. Some observers of the day credited George with engineering the demise of the NRPB. The Senate's Special Committee on Post-War Economic Policy and Planning also included Alben Barkley (D-KY), Arthur Vandenburg (R-MI), Carl Hayden (D-AZ), Warren Austin (R-VT), Joseph O'Mahoney (D-WY), Robert Taft (R-OH), Claude Pepper (D-FL), Albert Hawkes (R-NJ), and Scott Lucas (D-IL).[8] They held hearings, conducted fact-finding, and issued a series of reports. Senator George made it clear that this committee, often referred to as the George Committee, intended to take the lead in setting reconversion policy.[9]

The fourth in the series of George Committee reports was particularly noteworthy because it focused on the role of Congress in dealing with the problems of postwar employment. The report clearly stated that the goal must be full employment, because full employment played the central role in ensuring prosperity. The committee, however, was explicit in stating that "full employment does not and cannot mean that everyone willing and able to work is gainfully employed at all times." The committee also strongly opposed the use of public works merely to provide jobs for the unemployed. Most importantly, the committee argued in the report that Congress's role in achieving full employment was to stimulate confidence in business (U.S. Senate 1944).[10]

In June 1944, the George Committee concluded its report with the following four recommendations to Congress (U.S. Senate 1944)[11]:

1) Establish an Office of Demobilization to coordinate reconversion of the economy to peacetime.
2) Terminate war contracts expeditiously.

3) Sell surplus war property promptly.
4) Start public construction—e.g., roads and dan possible.

It is interesting to note that the only federal spending that the George Committee recommended was for public works—i.e., projects perceived as popular in the home state but viewed as "pork barrel" by cynical observers.

The committee also recommended that Congress study revisions in unemployment compensation, problems of workers who migrated to "war boom" areas, and ways for the prevention of monopolies and trade barriers. The topics of price controls, rationing, taxation, investment, the budget, and foreign trade also made the list of areas that the committee thought warranted further attention (U.S. Senate 1944).[12]

The George Committee attempted to redefine full employment in classic economic terms that were decidedly probusiness. This semantic game suggested that the committee recognized the potential popularity of the phrase "full employment" and sought to capitalize on it. Thus, the George Committee was seizing on the term "full employment," but not on the Keynesian approach to achieving it.

Meanwhile, the House of Representatives established its own Special Committee on Post-War Economic Policy and Planning in January 1944.[13] Congressman William M. Colmer (D-MS) chaired the committee, and Congressman Hamilton Fish (R-NY) was the ranking member.[14] Unlike Senator George, Congressman Colmer had been a congressional ally of Roosevelt and supported the New Deal agenda after his election in 1932. A rising star, Colmer had gotten a spot on the House Committee on Rules in 1939.

In a significant move, Colmer selected Marion Folsom to be the staff director of the House Special Committee on Post-War Economic Policy and Planning. Folsom was an executive of the Eastman Kodak Company who had been involved in drafting the national Social Security Act when he served on the President's Advisory Council to the Committee on Economic Security in 1934. Folsom became a member of the Department of Commerce's Business Advisory Council in 1936. Before becoming staff director, Folsom was instrumental in establishing the Committee for Economic Development (CED) in 1942.[15] Along with Paul G. Hoffman, president of the Studebaker Corporation, and

William Benton, cofounder of the Benton & Bowles advertising firm, Folsom formed the CED as a group of business leaders who recognized a role for government in stabilizing the economy through fiscal and monetary policy. Folsom's view of the proper federal role, however, did not extend to full employment. He reportedly said, "A job for every person willing and able to work is absolutely incompatible with the free enterprise system" (Flamm 1994, p. 72).

As did its Senate counterpart, the House Special Committee on Post-War Economic Policy and Planning held hearings, conducted fact-finding, and issued a series of reports. In addition to testimony from key officials in the administration, such as Bernard M. Baruch of the Office of War Mobilization and Harold Smith of the Bureau of the Budget, the committee heard from a variety of business leaders. These corporate leaders included General Motors' Charles E. Wilson, Dodge Corporation's Thomas S. Holden, First Boston Corporation's Col. Allan M. Pope, Studebaker Corporation's Hoffman (representing the CED), the National Association of Manufacturers' Frederick C. Crawford, and the U.S. Chamber of Commerce's Eric A. Johnson. William Batts from the National Planning Association also was called to testify. William Green, president of the American Federation of Labor, was the only labor union leader who testified (U.S. Congress 1944b).

Although the House Special Committee on Post-War Economic Policy and Planning did not garner the media attention that the George Committee had, its fourth report on the economic problems of reconversion gained sufficient interest that it was reprinted several times that autumn. Among other key issues, the report focused on unemployment and reemployment issues, education and job training, public works and private construction, and tax policy. The committee opposed the use of continued war production or public works as "made work." Similar to the George Committee, the House report maintained that government's role was to stimulate business. The fourth report discussed the reemployment challenges posed by the returning veterans as well as by the 18 million workers directly involved in war production. It estimated that between six and seven million more civilian jobs than existed in 1940 would need to be created after the war (U.S. Congress 1944a). A resumption of high levels of unemployment seemed inevitable.

AN AMERICAN WHITE PAPER

The Keynesian approach to full employment was, nonetheless, gaining support around the world. British prime minister Winston Churchill had already made his countryman, Keynes, an economic adviser in 1940; however, it was the publication of William Beveridge's *Full Employment in a Free Society,* followed closely by the British government's *White Paper on Employment Policy*, in 1944 that demonstrated the dominance of Keynesian economics in Great Britain. Also in 1944, Sweden's ruling Social Democrats adopted full employment as one of that party's three major goals for the postwar period. Canada and Australia followed with similar statements (Furniss and Tilton 1977, pp. 125–126; Garraty 1979, pp. 228–230).

Observers and subsequent scholars assumed that, after the dismantling of the NRPB, the administration's postwar economic planning was fragmented and virtually nonexistent. Accounts of the day as well as historical reviews make no mention of the executive branch's role in developing a full employment policy. Yet a group of people from various executive departments began meeting in mid-1944 to discuss and draft a proposal for postwar employment. Many of the issues they debated and the compromises they made foreshadowed the legislative debate on the full employment bill.

Alvin Hansen, who joined the Federal Reserve Board as a consultant after leaving the NRPB, believed that full employment would become a partisan political issue in the 1944 election. In July 1944, he confided to Gerhard Colm, a German-born economist who worked in the Bureau of the Budget, that he had had a conversation with Federal Reserve chairman Marriner Eccles regarding the importance of preparing an American "White Paper on Employment Policy." This paper primarily was to be used for the Democratic platform and Roosevelt's acceptance speech. Hansen and Eccles both feared that Dewey would follow up the reference to full employment in his presidential nomination acceptance speech with a statement on fiscal policy similar to the British government's Keynesian *White Paper on Employment Policy.* Hansen suggested that Colm begin to draft a paper making a clear declaration that the government should accept the primary responsibility for maintaining full employment.[16]

Colm had led the research division of the Institute of World Economics at the University of Kiel until the Nazi *Gleichschaltung*, or process of bringing the country under totalitarian control, in 1933. He fled Germany and became a founder of the University in Exile at the New School for Social Research in New York. Secretary of Commerce Harry L. Hopkins selected Colm in 1939 for a key role in Commerce's industrial economics division to develop national income estimates for economic planning. Colm then went to the Bureau of the Budget as a principal fiscal analyst.

After Hansen contacted him, Colm immediately discussed the American "White Paper on Employment Policy" with Harold Smith, director of the Bureau of the Budget, and J. Weldon Jones, also at the Bureau of the Budget. Smith thought it was too late to have such a proposal included in the Democratic Party platform. However, Smith said he was very sympathetic to the idea and acknowledged that considerable spade work had been done already. Colm then replied to Hansen that he would begin working on the project while Smith discussed the matter with Marriner Eccles.[17]

Within a few weeks, Hansen, in collaboration with Eccles and Smith, had called together a group of men that included Colm, Richard Gilbert (from the Federal Reserve) and Emile Despres (formerly at the Fed and now in the State Department) to discuss a paper on full employment. Soon the study group added Richard Musgrave and Kenneth Williams (both from the Federal Reserve), Harvard economist Walter Salant, University of Chicago economist Jacob Mosak, University of Wisconsin economist Jim Earley (all from the Office of Price Administration), and Harvard economist Arthur Smithies (from the Bureau of the Budget).[18] This group, hereafter referred to as the postwar employment study group (Table 2.1), formed the core unit of full employment planners within the executive branch. The participants reported to Budget Director Harold Smith and Federal Reserve Chairman Marriner Eccles.

The first major issue of debate was the role of government spending. Gilbert thought the report should begin with the statement, "Government would take all action necessary to assure full employment and a high level of consumption." Colm, Salant, Musgrave, and Williams expressed the view that it was unwise to emphasize government spending, noting that the public mind often perceives it as boondoggling. Colm suggested that there should be two phases of expansion in the

Table 2.1 Postwar Employment Study Group Participants

Bureau of the Budget	Federal Reserve	Office of Price Administration
Gerhard Colm	Alvin Hansen	Walter Salant
J. Weldon Jones	Emile Despres	Jim Earley
Arthur Smithies	(moved to State)	Jacob Mosak
	Richard Gilbert	
	Richard Musgrave	
	Kenneth Williams	

postwar period: first, one of business expansion; and second, one of expansion of consumption. When Smith commented on the minutes of this meeting, he agreed that more attention should be placed on the expansion of business.[19]

Recognizing the postwar employment study group's need for more explicit guidance, Smith and Eccles met with Hansen, Musgrave, Williams, and Colm to provide more direction on the full employment policy paper. Smith emphasized the reasons for a consistent program and planning and thus the development of administrative machinery to handle what he identified as the most critical concern: unemployment when war production ended. Eccles agreed with Smith's ideas for economic planning to avert postwar unemployment, but he elaborated on the political aspects, such as states' rights versus national planning and the relationship between a national policy and an international program. They all acknowledged that the difficulty of defining full employment posed political problems. The meeting resulted in two directives: a draft of a presidential message and a more detailed, technical document for background.[20] Thus, the postwar employment study group was charged with the task of preparing the American white paper.

As the momentum to develop a postwar full-employment policy increased, so too did tension over who should administer such a program. Eccles thought the president should appoint a committee for the development of this economic program, but Smith doubted whether the president would want a formal structure. Rather than that, Smith said he would request an informal assignment from Roosevelt.[21] This disagreement marked the first sign of the struggle within the administration over whether the Bureau of the Budget or a specially designated committee should control the direction of postwar economic planning, an issue that would prove significant later.

Subsequently, J. Weldon Jones sent a confidential memo to Bureau of the Budget colleagues Julius Wendzel, Louis Bean, and Paul David discussing the outline of what was jokingly referred to as an American "pink" paper on a postwar employment program, because critics on the right were likely to label it "socialistic," in disregard of its actual objectives. Jones made clear that the project was being kept "within the family," but that contributions were truly to be a joint effort. He outlined the various sections of the report and indicated who had primary responsibility and oversight. These participants extended beyond the Bureau of the Budget to include other interested parties.[22]

The postwar employment study group, meanwhile, became concerned about the lack of coordination on demobilization legislation that was pending in late August 1944. Specifically, the study group feared that its proposal might not be fully consistent with what President Roosevelt was discussing with congressional leaders regarding the legislation proposed by Senator George, chairman of the Special Committee on Post-War Economic Policy and Planning. Given that George had positioned his committee as the authority on postwar planning and had made recommendations at odds with Roosevelt's Economic Bill of Rights, their concerns were not unfounded. They acknowledged that any document written at that time might be in conflict with agreements other members of the Roosevelt administration might have been making with congressional leaders.[23]

The postwar employment study group continued, though the president did not know of its existence. At the beginning of October 1944, Jones prepared a draft of the white paper along with a proposed cover letter addressed to the president from Smith. The accompanying memo to Smith queried whether it was time to inform Roosevelt of the document. At this point, they assumed that it would not be used until after the election, which was only a month away.[24]

As he appraised the final draft, Jones concluded to Smith that "some will think that the document, as it now stands, is too bold; some will think it is not bold enough. As a product of a high-grade group of graduate students in economics, or of a private organization, it can be criticized as being a timid compromise; as a State Paper it is probably more outspoken than the White House, and if issued by the President would be a landmark."[25]

The confidential document was titled "Postwar Employment" and set forth the following goals (Colm 1944):

- To maintain full and stable national production, income, and employment to the maximum possible extent through encouraging the expansion of private enterprise
- To assure minimum standards of health, education, and personal security for all members of the community
- To promote a steadily rising standard of living for the nation as a whole by developing our economic resources and improving the efficiency with which they are used
- To support a high level of world prosperity and world trade in cooperation with other nations

The report provided a transition from the "Economic Bill of Rights" Roosevelt had championed in January 1944 to a plan of action for postwar full employment.

Several critical factors and assumptions constituted the framework of the report. The economic achievements during the war had demonstrated the United States' capacity to produce, and the country would not have tolerated a return to the prewar production levels and accompanying unemployment. Although it gave primary emphasis to policies that directly encouraged private business investments and consumer demand, the report stated that government fiscal policy, on both the revenue and expenditure sides, must be the ultimate stabilizing factor. Some uses of the federal budget and fiscal policies were indicated. The report, furthermore, discussed the need for sufficient flexibility in the administration of the economic program to allow for adequate legislative supervision and control as well as for coordinated action by federal, state, and local governments (Colm 1944).

The document presented a package of postwar programs to achieve long-term economic stability and full employment. The report encouraged measures to promote competition, risk-taking, capital facilities, and industrial research for both large and small businesses. It recommended income support and the principle of the ever-normal granary for agriculture (i.e., storage of overproduced agricultural yields for sale later in order to stabilize prices). The report outlined a plan for the development of river valleys, agricultural resources, transportation facilities, and the redevelopment of urban areas. It sketched the minimum-standard requirements for programs in health, education, social security, and labor. The document extended its recommendations by stating the importance of handling the American postwar economy within a full international context so that American unemployment was not merely exported abroad (Colm 1944).

"Postwar Employment" addressed three of the four central elements of what soon became the full employment bill. First, it stressed national planning and gave examples of the kinds of planning that should occur. Second, although it did not propose a new federal structure to handle this planning, it was implicit from the report and evident from the discussions that the Bureau of the Budget would have assumed the major responsibility for that under this plan. Third, the report acknowledged the option of federal monetary and fiscal policies—for example, compensatory spending—as a tool to stabilize the economy. On the fourth element—the federal government's guarantee of employment—the report was silent. It offered no right to employment as Roosevelt had in his Economic Bill of Rights.

ASCENDANCY OF FULL EMPLOYMENT

Concern with the possibility of a postwar resumption of unemployment coupled with the growing acceptance of Keynesian economics sparked the drive for America to implement a full employment policy. Lessons from the New Deal as well as war mobilization fueled this effort. The extent to which full employment represented a continuation of the New Deal deserves discussion.

The policy of full employment as the postwar employment study group articulated it was harmonious with the New Deal. The report retained the value that the New Deal placed on the practicality and flexibility of federal economic policy as well as on the importance of having public needs drive public works. It also carried on the spirit of compassion and commitment to improving the health and welfare of the American people.

The proposal for postwar employment, however, went well beyond the New Deal. It offered a set of rather tightly woven policies that were grounded in theoretical principles and economic assumptions. It saw compensatory spending as a tool of the federal government. Its flexibility was bounded by the limits of Keynesian thinking—a kind of restriction uncharacteristic of the prewar period. Full employment necessitated long-term economic planning, which was a practice the New Deal did not implement fully.

The working person, who had made gains during the New Deal, especially in terms of collective bargaining, was a natural beneficiary of this postwar employment program. Maintaining high levels of employment and stimulating job creation were at the crux of the proposal. It appeared that the priorities for economic planning were shifting from the perspective of the businessman to the perspective of the working person—who also happened to be the consumer.

Aggregate demand clearly was to be the driving force of the economy. The emphasis on consumer demand definitely moved beyond the New Deal. With so many people destitute during the Great Depression, it was quite difficult for those New Dealers not ascribing to Keynesian economics to have argued that encouraging consumption of goods might have sparked production and employment. Now members of the administration were offering a serious policy proposal that placed the consumer as the keystone in the national economy.

The government has had a long history of being involved in the economy. The nature of this involvement has been debated since the days of Hamilton and Monroe, between the Federalists and the Anti-Federalists (Cornell 1999). The federal government, for example, during the nineteenth century gave subsidies in the form of land and cash to foster economic expansion. At some times the government intervened to break up monopolies, and at other times it encouraged industrial cartels.

The proposal for full employment in the postwar period concluded that the federal government had the ultimate responsibility for the economy when and if private enterprise and consumer demand fell short. This aspect grew out of lessons from the New Deal and the wartime economy. The federal government was no longer to be the reluctant player. Now, it was the locus of national economic planning and, when necessary, employment stimulation.

Notes

1. Dollars are based on 1958 prices.
2. Steinbeck's landmark novel was made into an Academy Award–winning motion picture in 1940.
3. Fourteen years later Wagner compared this bill to the full employment bill and concluded that public works planning, in and of itself, is not enough to maintain full employment and that federal action must be fully integrated and have widespread support. See Wagner (1945).
4. The immense literature on the Great Depression and the New Deal yields a variety of perspectives on the period, several of which are sharply divergent. Carl Degler (1970, pp. 384–391) once labeled the New Deal as the third American Revolution because it altered the responsibilities of the federal government, signaled the end of laissez-faire, legitimized the role of organized labor, and brought groups that had previously been excluded into participatory politics. Degler's initial view was consistent with the impressionistic interpretation that Richard Hofstadter presented. Hofstadter (1955, pp. 302–316) argues that the New Deal was a "new departure" from previous reform traditions because, among other things, it was pragmatic rather than moralistic and welfare-oriented rather than entrepreneurial. Howard Zinn (1966, pp. 244–259) and Barton Bernstein (1968, pp. 263–282), on the other hand, view the New Deal as conservative, stopping far short of its possibilities and neglecting many Americans. "Though vigorous in its rhetoric and experimental in tone," Bernstein concludes, "the New Deal was narrow in its goals and wary of bold economic reform." Such interpretations point to the situation of blacks and those who were caught in structural poverty and conclude that the New Deal contributed very little to improving their plight. Balanced between these two extremes is William Leuchtenberg (1963, pp. 335–348), who argues that the New Deal was a "halfway revolution." Leuchtenberg details the many social, economic, and political accomplishments of the New Deal and discusses those areas unresolved by the New Deal. Also expressing a moderate view, Eric Goldman (1952, pp. 269–289) concludes it was a synthesis and culmination of previous reform movements in America.
5. This piece was originally published as "Nonmonetary Effects of the Financial Crisis in the Propagation of the Great Depression," *American Economic Review* 73, no. 3 (1983): 257–276.
6. Television and cable news as we know it today did not exist, but newsreels were an integral part of the movie theater experience. Moreover, movie theaters were commonplace and inexpensive. According to the Franklin D. Roosevelt Presidential Library in Hyde Park, N.Y., the major motion picture companies, such as Universal, Paramount, and Fox Movietone News, were invited into the White House to film parts of Roosevelt's speeches, which then appeared in movie theaters for several days afterwards to reinforce the President's most important points (Franklin D. Roosevelt Presidential Library and Museum 2012).

7. Sen. Harry Truman chaired the Special Committee to Investigate the National Defense Program, which issued a report that supported some of the accusations. According to Brinkley (1996, pp. 190–192), even *BusinessWeek* acknowledged the conflict of interest.
8. George won a special election in 1922 to succeed Thomas Watson. George was a Democrat who opposed the New Deal and supported racial segregation. He served in the Senate until 1957. Barkley came to Washington as a congressman from Kentucky in 1913. He was elected to the Senate in 1926 and became majority leader in 1937. Truman chose him as his running mate in 1948. Vandenburg was appointed to the Senate in 1928 and was reelected several times until his death in 1951. He was a leading opponent of the New Deal. Hayden was Arizona's first congressman, winning election in 1911 as Arizona was becoming a state. He was elected to the Senate in 1926 and served until 1969. Only Senator Robert Byrd (D-WV) served longer than Hayden. Austin was first elected in a special election in 1931 and served from Vermont until 1946, when he resigned to become U.S. Ambassador to the United Nations. O'Mahoney served from 1934 to 1953. Although defeated in 1952, he was reelected in 1954 to fill the seat vacated by the death of Senator Lester Hunt. O'Mahoney served until 1961. Taft, the son of the president and Supreme Court justice William Howard Taft, was elected to the Senate in 1938 and served until his death in 1953. His son Robert later represented Ohio in the U.S. Senate, and his grandson Robert served as Ohio's governor. Pepper was elected to the Senate in 1936 as a strong supporter of the New Deal, and he was reelected in 1942. His leftist views led to his being painted with the nickname "Red Pepper" and to his defeat in 1950. In 1962 he was elected to Congress from Miami and served until his death in 1989. Hawkes was president of Congoleum-Nairn vinyl flooring company and served as president of the U.S. Chamber of Commerce in 1941–1942. He was elected to the Senate in 1942 and served one term. Lucas was elected to the U.S. House of Representatives in 1934 and to the Senate in 1938. He was reelected in 1944 and became the Senate majority leader in 1949. Wisconsin senator Joseph McCarthy actively campaigned in Illinois against Lucas in 1950, claiming he was sympathetic to communism, and Lucas lost the race.
9. "Post War Economic Planning—1944" file, Papers of Sen. Robert Taft Sr., Library of Congress, Washington, DC.
10. Taft Papers.
11. Ibid.
12. Ibid.
13. House Resolution 408 created this committee on January 26, 1944.
14. Colmer served from 1933 to 1973. Although he remained a Democrat, Colmer eventually broke with his party on the issue of civil rights in the 1960s. When he retired, he endorsed his administrative assistant, Trent Lott, who ran as a Republican for his old seat. Fish served in Congress from 1920 to 1946. He was part of the Stuyvesant-Fish political dynasty from New York, which could trace its family roots back to Peter

Stuyvesant, the governor of New York when it was New Amsterdam, a Dutch colony, in the seventeenth century. His grandfather, Hamilton Fish, was governor and a senator from New York as well as secretary of state under President Ulysses S. Grant. His father, Hamilton Fish II, was also a congressman, as was his son, Hamilton Fish IV.

15. When Dwight D. Eisenhower became president in 1953, he appointed Folsom as under secretary of the treasury. Eisenhower then selected him to be the secretary of the Department of Health, Education, and Welfare in 1955.
16. Alvin Hansen to Gerhard Colm, 11 July 1944, Gerhard Colm Papers, Harry S. Truman Presidential Library, Independence, MO.
17. Colm to Hansen, 15 July 1944, Colm Papers.
18. Colm to J. Weldon Jones, memoranda, 5 and 11 August 1944, Colm Papers.
19. Ibid.
20. Colm to Jones, memorandum, 15 August 1944, Colm Papers.
21. Ibid.
22. Jones to Wendzel, Bean, and David, 19 August 1944 memorandum, Colm Papers.
23. Jones to Harold Smith, 25 August 1944 memorandum, Colm Papers.
24. Ibid., 4 October 1944.
25. Ibid., 10 October 1944.

3
Press and Public Opinion Diverge

In 1943, while President Roosevelt was meeting with Joseph Stalin and Winston Churchill in Tehran, pollster George Gallup asked a sample of the American people what they thought would be the greatest problem facing the country from 1945 to 1949. The second most common answer was "peace," offered by 13 percent of the respondents. Outdistancing all the other possible answers was "jobs and economic readjustment." In the midst of a fierce world war, 58 percent of Americans stated that employment would be the greatest problem in the immediate future (Gallup 1972, Survey No. 301, p. 410).

Obviously, no one wanted a resumption of the high levels of unemployment experienced during the Great Depression, and many expressed the belief that the government should act to alleviate unemployment. It was apparent that people in the Roosevelt administration were seriously considering a full employment policy. The electoral success of the Democratic Party with its New Deal platform implied that a majority favored a strengthened federal role in the economy. At issue, however, was whether there was popular support to redefine that role to encompass economic planning, compensatory spending, guaranteed employment for everyone who sought it, and the federal structure to accomplish these responsibilities.

In addition to drawing on coverage by the national print media,[1] this chapter uses public opinion polls to explore how the government's role in job creation was perceived and to what extent full employment was supported. Public opinion research was maturing as a social science by the 1940s. The methodologies had become much more rigorous than the mass mailing techniques that had led to the demise of the *Literary Digest* in 1936.[2] The public opinion researchers of the 1940s placed strict demographic controls on their samples to achieve what they hoped were representative microcosms of the nation.[3] There were two noteworthy commercial polling firms, one headed by Elmo Roper and the other by George Gallup. Additionally, there were two major university-based survey research centers by the early 1940s: the Office of Public Opinion Research (OPOR) at Princeton University, and the National Opinion Research Center (NORC) at the University of Chicago (Converse 1987).

Fortune magazine published many of Roper's poll results, presenting the findings as human interest rather than breaking news. Gallup issued press releases on a regular basis, but the poll results were not typically front page news. The research findings of OPOR and NORC were disseminated in the academic community as scholarly articles that were not time-sensitive.[4]

POSTWAR EMPLOYMENT WORRIES

The popular press rarely featured stories on public attitudes toward employment problems in the early 1940s. The news of the day centered on war coverage and the response of the home front. War production was the main theme of articles on the domestic economy. Stories on rationing were the only features that touched on personal economic concerns. Given the economic worries that Gallup found, this lack of news coverage on employment issues is perplexing. Perhaps those within the media who set editorial policy might have thought that stories on employment fears were no longer newsworthy, given the high employment levels of wartime, or that accounts of economic pessimism would have undercut the war effort. Regardless of its reasons, the popular press had decided at this point not to be a forum for discussion on the prospects of employment following the war.

When the war began, most people thought there would be high unemployment after the war, as Figure 3.1 makes clear. According to an opinion survey conducted by Elmo Roper for *Fortune* magazine in December 1941, just over 60 percent responded that there would be "lots of unemployment" after the war. Indeed, only a few (11.3 percent) predicted there would be jobs for everyone after the war ended (Cantril 1951, p. 898). As discussed in the previous chapter, in 1938 the number of unemployed workers surpassed 10 million, which was 18.9 percent of the labor force. Given that American industries had not fully geared up for war production at the time of the survey, this grim assessment seemed credible.

Figure 3.1 Public Opinion in 1941 on Postwar Employment Prospects

After the war, do you think there will be jobs for everybody, some unemployment, or lots of unemployment?

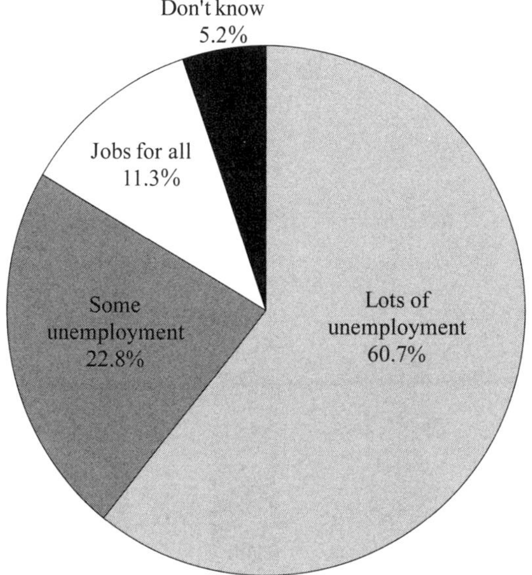

SOURCE: Poll conducted by Elmo Roper for the December 1941 issue of *Fortune* magazine (Cantril 1951, p. 898).

Five months later, in May 1942, George Gallup found that 43 percent of those polled thought the country would experience an economic depression for the first few years after the war. Figure 3.2 provides a breakdown of this Gallup poll by broad occupational groupings and shows that business and professional people were the most optimistic—57 percent predicting prosperity. White-collar workers were the only other occupational group in which at least half thought there would be prosperity in the immediate postwar years. Farmers were the most pessimistic group, with 51 percent predicting a postwar depression (Gallup 1972, Survey No. 268, p. 336).[5]

In July 1944, Gallup asked a sample of the civilian adult population whether they thought they would have a job following the war (Figure 3.3). While 40 percent were "very certain" and 25 percent were

Figure 3.2 Public Opinion in 1942 on Postwar Prosperity

Which do you think the United States will have for the first two or three years after the war—depression or prosperity?

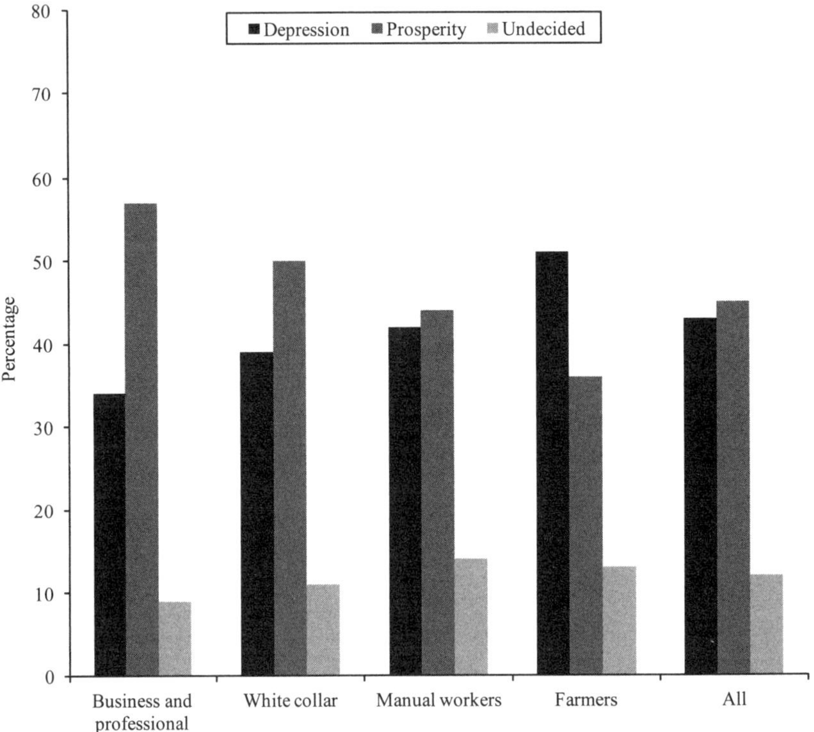

SOURCE: Gallup poll, May 23–28, 1942 (Gallup 1972, p. 336).

"fairly certain" that they would, 35 percent of the respondents reported that they were "not at all certain" they would have a job after the war. Memories of high joblessness before the war, perhaps of their own unemployment experience, limited the hopes of over one-third of adults sampled (Gallup 1972, Survey No. 322, p. 455).

Though a majority of people thought they would have a job, few thought everyone else would, as Figure 3.4 presents. "After the war," asked Gallup during the first week of December 1944, "do you think

Figure 3.3 Public Attitudes in 1944 on Personal Job Prospects

Asked of persons in the civilian adult population who said they planned to work after the war: How certain are you that you will have a job after the war?

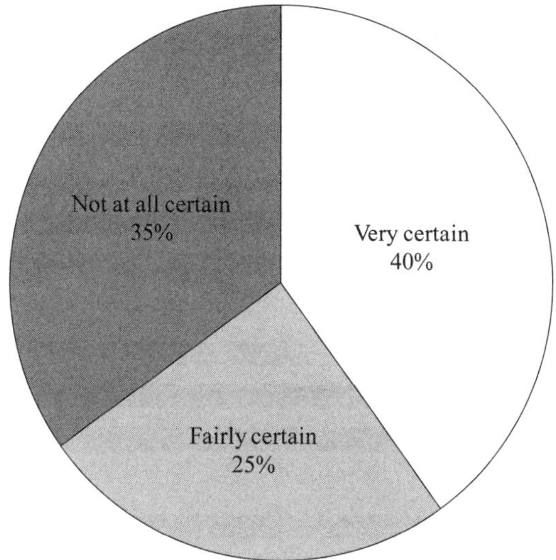

SOURCE: Gallup poll, July 8–13, 1944 (Gallup 1972, p. 455).

that everyone who wants a job will be able to get one?" (Gallup 1972, Survey No. 336, pp. 478–479). Only 25 percent responded with an affirmative answer. Three weeks later, on December 27, the *Washington Post* ran George Gallup's analysis of this poll; the results are detailed over the following three paragraphs (Gallup 1944). These results suggest that while people were confident in 1944 that the nation would achieve a military victory, they were not optimistic that the country would stave off a resumption of unemployment after the war.

Women appeared to be more pessimistic than men, as Figure 3.4 indicates, but more than 70 percent of men also were not confident in the employment outlook. The significant numbers of women workers brought into the labor force during the war who, as evidenced by other Gallup survey data, wanted to continue working in peacetime might

Figure 3.4 Public Opinion in 1944 on Postwar Employment Prospects by Gender, Age, and Occupation

After the war, do you think that everyone who wants a job will be able to get one?

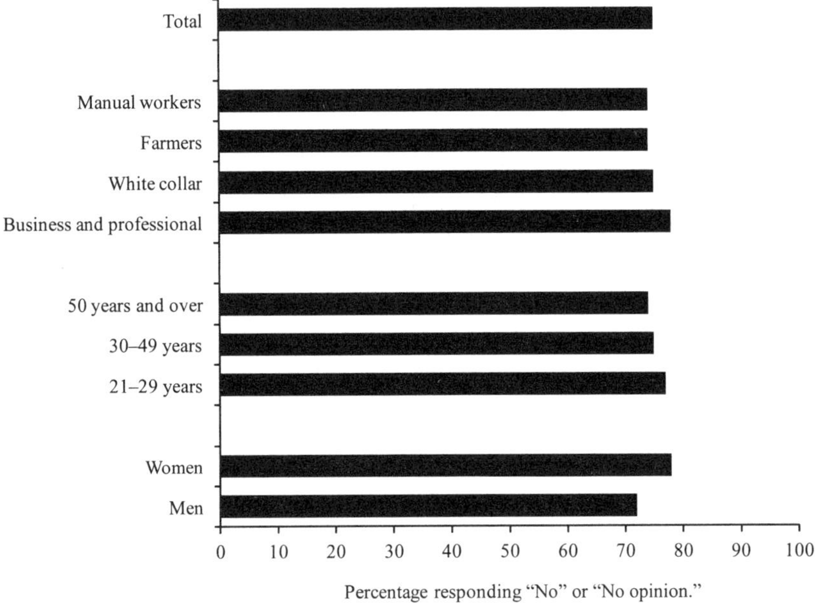

SOURCE: Gallup poll, December 1–6, 1944 (Gallup 1972, pp. 478–479).

have influenced this modest gender difference. Women workers clearly were more vulnerable to dislocation by returning veterans than male workers.

When the question responses were broken down by age groups, those 21 to 29 years old appeared to be the most discouraged, though the differences are small and may not be statistically significant. The oldest age group, 50 years and above, seemed the most optimistic; nonetheless, their replies were a gloomy 26 percent "yes" and 66 percent "no." (Eight percent had no opinion.) That the youngest appeared to be the most discouraged probably stemmed from the fact that the last period of prosperity had occurred when they were children. They had come of age during the Great Depression. That a sense of optimism appeared to increase, albeit slightly, with age could have been due to older people having experienced prosperity as well as hardship and thus having witnessed a wider sweep of fluctuations in the American economy.

Gallup also reported occupational breakdowns in response to the question of whether everyone who wanted a job after the war would find one, with a rather surprising outcome. It is fascinating that the occupational group most affected by the Depression and most likely to have been hurt by postwar unemployment—manual labor—appeared to be the least pessimistic group, though again the differences are small and may not be statistically significant. Conversely, the group arguably the least vulnerable to unemployment—business and professional—was reportedly the most pessimistic. The 1944 data differed from the results Gallup had found in 1942, which are depicted in Figure 3.2. In 1942, those grouped into the business and professional category were the most optimistic. Perhaps because business and professional people were more often in the position of hiring people, they were more likely to answer from the perspective of whether they would have job openings proportionate to the number of job seekers. These results resemble research by Donald Kinder and D. Roderick Kiewiet that differentiate between "personal economic discontents" and "collective economic judgments" and conclude that the two are surprisingly independent (Kinder and Kiewiet 1979).

It is difficult to know whether these data should be interpreted as economic forecasts or as more general worldviews. That is, a person might well have thought it an economic truth that there are always people who want to be employed but cannot find jobs. Conversely, a person might have believed that unemployed people are those unwilling to accept menial jobs or unfit to perform at minimum standards, and thus anyone who sincerely wants a job can obtain one. Gallup, however, phrased the question less as a philosophical issue and more as an economic forecast by beginning it with the phrase, "After the war . . ." Given the skewed results, it is apparent that people were pessimistic regardless of worldview or personal speculation.[6]

MEDIA TREATMENT OF THE POSTWAR ECONOMY

Much of the national media chose to set the context of the postwar economy solely from the point of view of business. The president of the National Association of Manufacturers, Frederick C. Crawford, told the *New York Times* in the summer of 1943 that private industry was up to the task of finding jobs for all returning servicemen after the war. However, Crawford emphasized, cutting the taxes of businesses and restricting the power of organized labor were necessary prerequisites to private-sector job creation. He went on to say that the private sector did not want to compete with government enterprises and called government-"made" work undesirable (*New York Times* 1943).

An editorial in the *Chicago Daily Tribune* asserted that the way to provide jobs after the war was to end the New Deal programs and planning. The *Tribune* piece argued that Roosevelt had prevented private enterprise from creating employment before the war. "The true alternatives are not Rooseveltian fascism or depression," the editorial concluded. "There is a far better way. It is individualism and free government" (*Chicago Daily Tribune* 1943). Some in the business world, however, were not so critical of President Roosevelt; indeed, the business-oriented *Kiplinger Washington Letter* observed that Roosevelt's establishment of the War Productions Board (WPB) in 1942 had preserved private enterprise (Perrett 1985, p. 262).

Optimism was apparently running full throttle at the 150th annual dinner of the Economic Club of New York in December of 1944. The featured speaker, Irving S. Olds, chairman of U.S. Steel, expressed assurance that industry would be able to reconvert quickly to peacetime production. "It would be difficult to conceive of any time in our past when the American people as a whole had been in a better condition to face a temporary reduction in production and employment," Olds opined. "Incomes throughout the nation have been high. Savings are at a peak level." Olds echoed the argument that taxes were impeding business from taking risks on new production (*Wall Street Journal* 1944).

The print media consistently exuded the confidence promoted by business leaders. (*Newsweek*, for example, featured an article under the section heading "Postwar Horizons" carrying the title "Business Planners Concentrate on Free Enterprise and Turn Deaf Ear to Cries for 'Normalcy'" [*Newsweek* 1943].) The stories conveyed an upbeat tone and highlighted the speeches of corporate figures such as Alfred P. Sloan, chairman of General Motors, who would grace the cover of *Time* in the autumn of 1945. "Enlightened management," predicted Sloan, "with cooperative labor, given intelligent government cooperation and freedom from repressive government controls such as stifling free enterprise with unnecessary regulations and confiscatory taxes, can and will bring about a full economy" (*Time* 1943).

Indeed, most articles reported that business was emphasizing free enterprise as the driving force of postwar prosperity. When George Gallup queried a sample of the general public in 1943 on the definition of free enterprise, however, he obtained results that would have surprised the champions of free enterprise. "The great majority of Americans," reported Gallup, "are either without any idea of the term free enterprise or hold an erroneous one" (Gallup 1972, Survey No. 304, p. 416). The pollster did not say whether people, regardless of incorrect definitions, viewed the term positively. It was, most probably, a concept many people valued even if they did not fully understand it.

FORTUNE MAGAZINE'S EXECUTIVE FORECAST

Although newspaper accounts presented business leaders as more optimistic than the average American appeared to be, a sizable majority of business leaders in 1942 predicted that unemployment would be great or fairly large after the war. *Fortune* magazine conducted a series of surveys of business leaders and often focused on their economic prognoses during the war. The magazine invited over 10,000 business leaders to participate in its *Fortune* Forum of Executive Opinion, and the survey results are based upon at least 4,000 responses (Cantril 1951, pp. viii–ix). As Figure 3.5 indicates, *Fortune* found that only one-fifth of the cross section of executives surveyed thought that unemployment would be small following the postwar adjustment and reconversion.

Fortune followed up with those business leaders who had responded that unemployment would be great or fairly large after the war (79.4 percent of the cross section sampled) with two additional questions:

Figure 3.5 Business Leaders' Views in 1942 of Postwar Unemployment Prospects

Asked of a cross section of business executives: After the immediate postwar adjustment and conversion, do you think unemployment in the United States will be small, fairly large, or great?

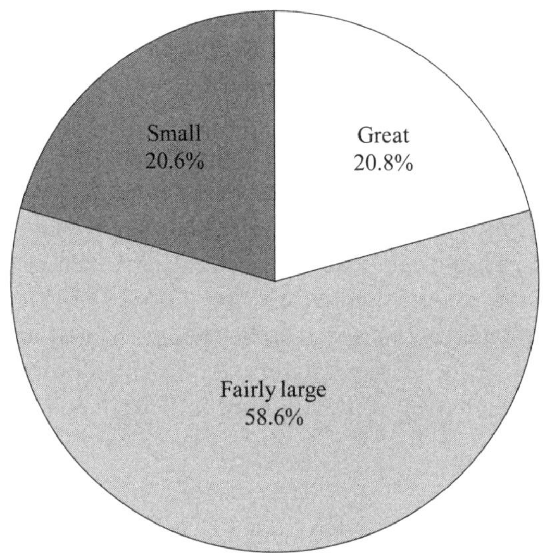

SOURCE: Forum of Executive Opinion, *Fortune*, September 1942 (Cantril 1951, p. 898).

1) Should businesses get together and assume major responsibility for eliminating unemployment, or should business rely on government to do so?
2) What do you think will actually occur?

While 90.5 (Figure 3.6) percent of these business leaders thought that business should coordinate its efforts and assume responsibility for eliminating unemployment, only 15.7 percent actually thought business would assume that responsibility.

The findings depicted in Figure 3.6 raise further questions. Did the 81.2 percent who thought government would assume responsibility for eliminating unemployment after the war reach that conclusion because they thought business would not be willing to coordinate its efforts?

Figure 3.6 Business Leaders' Views in 1942 on Responsibility for Alleviating Unemployment

Asked of the 79.4% of business executives in Figure 3.5 who thought unemployment in the United States would be fairly large or great: Do you think business should get together and assume major responsibility for eliminating unemployment, or should business rely upon the government to do so by large-scale expenditures? Which do you think actually will occur?

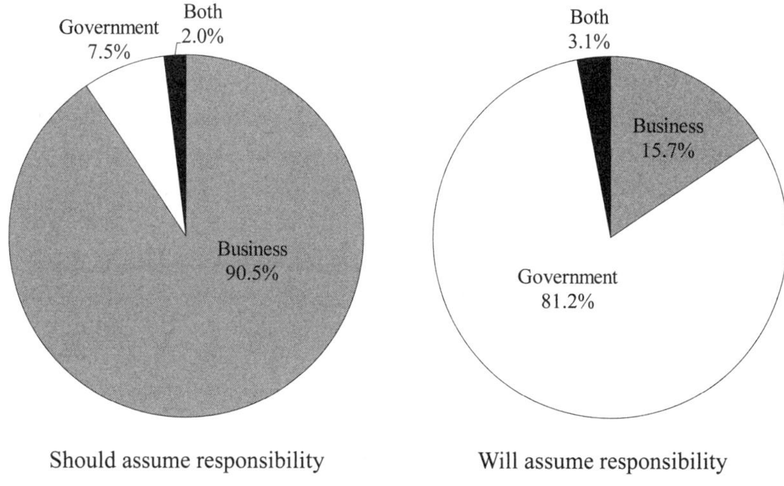

SOURCE: Forum of Executive Opinion, *Fortune*, September 1942 (Cantril 1951, p. 898).

Did they think that government would usurp business's role in job creation? Or, did they think that the levels of unemployment after the war might be too large for business to be able to handle?

Only very small percentages of the business leaders who responded to the survey thought that business and government should jointly assume responsibility (2.0 percent) and actually would work together (3.1 percent) to alleviate unemployment. Given that business and government were ostensibly working together to mobilize war production, this small percentage is intriguing. A closer look at the record of business and government actually working together for war mobilization, however, provides reasons for this cynicism.

The domination by business of the WPB resulted in widespread criticism despite its accomplishments in mobilizing wartime production. Roosevelt had established the WPB in January 1942 after the lack of success by several agencies that had been formed to coordinate war mobilization efforts. The WPB was a federal agency largely staffed with business executives. Some of the business executives became federal employees (with a resulting reduction in pay), some volunteered without taking any salary, and some held official appointments but continued to receive their corporate salaries. By mid-1942, over 10,000 businessmen had reportedly moved into the government's war agencies (Brinkley 1996, pp. 182–192). The *Nation* and the *New Republic* featured exposés on the "dollar-a-year" corporate leaders who were working in the government war agencies and funneling lucrative contracts to their companies (Atleson 1998, pp. 21–22). Allegations of businessmen in the WPB diverting scarce commodities needed for the war effort to their own civilian industries triggered broader press coverage and prompted a congressional investigation led by Missouri senator Harry Truman (Brinkley 1996, p. 191).

As the war was winding down in 1945, *Fortune* again queried business leaders on their postwar employment prognosis—this time asking about their own industrial sector (Figure 3.7). Some leaders appeared more optimistic than in 1942, with 29.1 percent predicting unemployment levels that were "no more than [what would be expected] due to shifts of jobs." However, one-third of those surveyed thought that unemployment in their sector would be worse than during the 1937–1940 period.

FULL EMPLOYMENT ENTERS THE PUBLIC DISCOURSE

The National Resources Planning Board's (NRPB) 1942 report *After the War—Full Employment* received a remarkable amount of public attention for a government report. The *Wall Street Journal* (1942a) article on the NRPB report carried the headline "Heavy Government Spending, Taxes Seen in Post-War Economy." Over one-third of those responding to a Gallup survey in 1943 said they knew about the NRPB report on full employment. (As previously discussed, the report was seminal in the development of the full employment legislation. The author, Hansen [1942], offered policy options aimed at increasing consumption to stimulate full employment.)

Figure 3.7 Business Leaders' Prognosis in 1945 of Employment in Their Sectors

Asked of a national cross section of executives: Do you expect serious unemployment in your industrial community during reconversion?

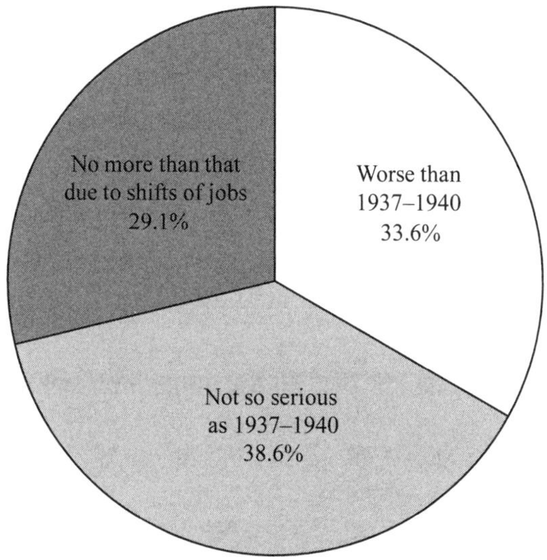

NOTE: Percentages add to more than 100 because some respondents gave more than one answer.
SOURCE: Forum of Executive Opinion, *Fortune*, February 1945 (Cantril 1951, p. 902).

Specifically, when George Gallup (1972, Survey No. 292, p. 380), in a March 1943 poll, queried a sample of Americans regarding the NRPB report, 34 percent indicated they had heard of it, and 13 percent of the sample stated they were familiar with its content. Of those who knew about the report, 69 percent said they viewed it favorably. No one probed further to ascertain whether self-selection drove the results—i.e., whether those who were sympathetic to full employment were more likely to learn about the NRPB report.

An astounding 99 percent of those surveyed in January 1943 by the National Opinion Research Center (NORC) thought that full employment should be a postwar aim. The NORC had become part of the University of Chicago in 1942 and at that time used a hard quota sampling frame based upon gender, age, and four categories of economic class (Berinsky 2006, pp. 499–529). Of the 99 percent who thought that full employment should be a postwar aim, over two-thirds (68.7 percent) stated that full employment could actually be achieved (Figure 3.8).

Some newspapers were critical of the administration's attention to postwar planning, arguing that it should be focusing all of its attention on the war effort. Of those publications in the print media that were opposed to government postwar economic planning, the *Wall Street Journal* was perhaps the most visible (e.g., Moley [1942]; *Wall Street Journal* [1942c]). The *Journal* made clear, however, that it was not opposed to planning per se, but maintained that it was private industry that should do the planning (*Wall Street Journal* 1942b).

As the NORC survey data presented in Figure 3.9 make clear, most Americans (specifically, 72.7 percent of the 99 percent who thought full

Figure 3.8 Public Opinion in 1943 on Feasibility of Full Employment

Do you think that this [full employment] can actually be done?

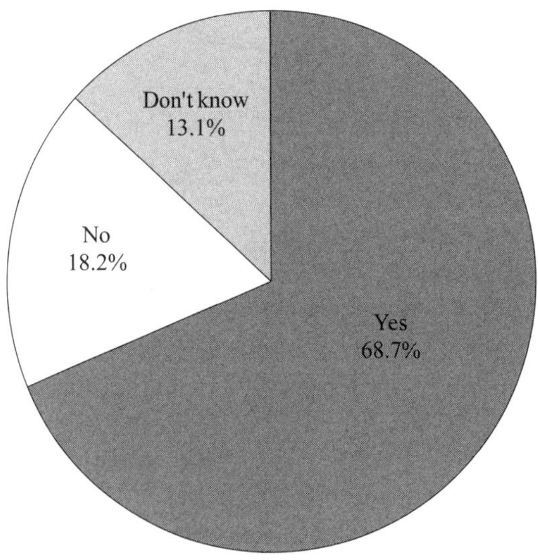

NOTE: This question was asked of the 99 percent of the sample who thought that full employment should be a postwar aim.

SOURCE: National Opinion Research Center, January 11, 1943 (Cantril 1951, p. 898).

employment should be a postwar aim) thought the government should be planning for full employment in 1943. Just under a quarter (23.2 percent) thought the government should wait until later to plan for postwar employment (Cantril 1951, p. 898). As the NORC data shows, the public overwhelmingly preferred that the government begin planning right away to achieve full employment following the war. This was hardly surprising, since other polling data had documented the public's broad-based fears of postwar unemployment. Perhaps full employment had become a concept much like Gallup had found free enterprise to be: that is, an idea held dear by many people, but not clearly understood by most people.

Figure 3.9 Public Opinion in 1943 on Planning for Full Employment

Do you think we should start to make plans for this [full employment] right now, or do you think this ought to wait till later?

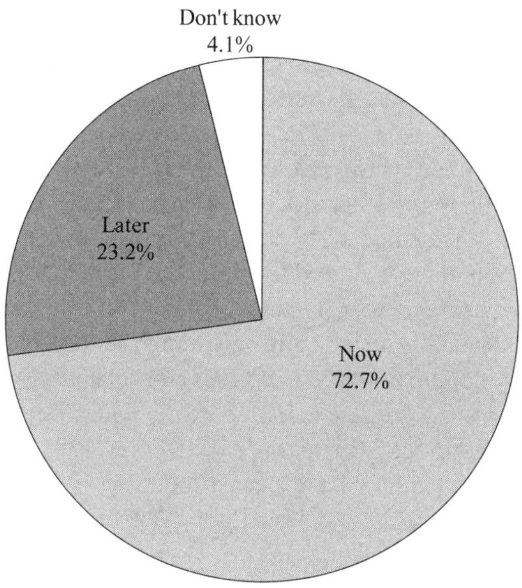

NOTE: This question was asked of the 99 percent of the sample who thought that full employment should be a postwar aim.
SOURCE: National Opinion Research Center, January 11, 1943 (Cantril 1951, p. 898).

Not all corporate executives opposed economic planning, and there was press coverage of the speeches of business leaders who thought planning for the postwar economy was necessary and desirable. The Committee for Economic Development (CED) was formed in 1942 by business leaders as a planning organization, and it gained coverage in the press (Collins 1982). CED Chairman Paul Hoffman, who also was president of the Studebaker Corporation, stressed the importance of business planning in a 1943 speech before the Union League Club of Chicago. "In making these plans we must assume an attitude by the government that is cordial and encouraging to private business," he stated, "a climate favoring business expansion." Hoffman posited that gainful employment would be needed for a labor force of 58 million people after the war (*Los Angeles Times* 1943).[7]

When *Fortune* asked its cross section of business leaders in 1944 whether it was a function of the government to maintain full employment, a somewhat surprising 29.4 percent responded "Yes." The question's wording differed somewhat from that of a question *Fortune* had asked in 1942: "Should business get together and assume major responsibility for eliminating unemployment, or should business rely on government to do so?" In 1942, only 7.5 percent of business leaders thought the government should assume responsibility for alleviating unemployment, compared with 29.4 of business leaders who thought it was a function of the government to maintain full employment in 1944.

The data depicted in Figure 3.10 might have been reflecting a shift in the views of business leaders on the role of government; however, the data also might have captured the idea that full employment policies had a broader base of support than programs to alleviate unemployment. As was discussed more fully in Chapter 1, federal full employment policies encompass tax incentives for business, infrastructure spending that bolsters some business sectors, and other tools aimed at stimulating consumption. Business leaders' views of policies to alleviate unemployment might have been limited to specific government employment programs, such as the Public Works Administration and the Civilian Conservation Corps.

A nationwide public opinion survey conducted in June 1945 found that three-fourths of those surveyed thought the government should do something if workers lost their jobs and could not find work because other jobs were not available (Figure 3.11). The questionnaire did not

Figure 3.10 Business Leaders' Views in 1944 on Government's Role in Full Employment

Asked of a national cross section of executives: Do you think it is a function of government today to see to it that substantially full employment is maintained?

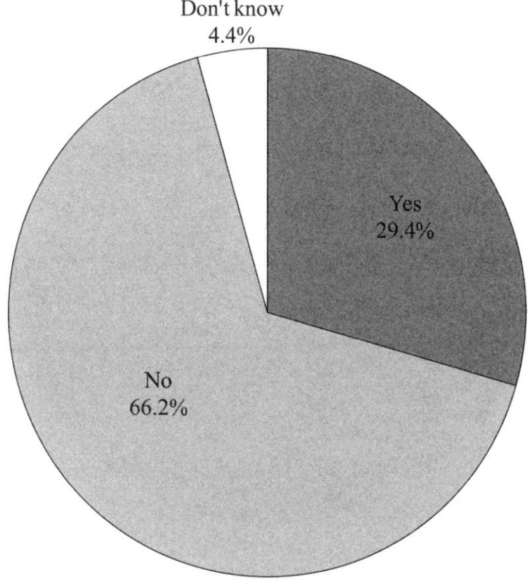

SOURCE: Forum of Executive Opinion, *Fortune*, May 1944 (Cantril 1951, p. 900).

ask those who thought the government should act to elaborate on what programs or policies the government should implement. Although George Gallup's polling results usually garnered attention from the print media, these survey results apparently received little or no newspaper coverage.

A few months later, the *Los Angeles Times* featured an article by Gallup (1945) under the headline "Poll shows public split on employment issue: Half of those with opinions think business can attain high levels without federal aid." The text went on to link these divided opinions with public attitudes on the full employment bill. Analysis of the question's wording indicates, however, that Gallup did not include a policy of full employment as an option in the question asked. Rather,

Figure 3.11 Public Opinion in June 1945 on the Government's Role in Ensuring Employment

Do you think the government should do anything about workers who lose their jobs and are unable to find work because there are not enough jobs?

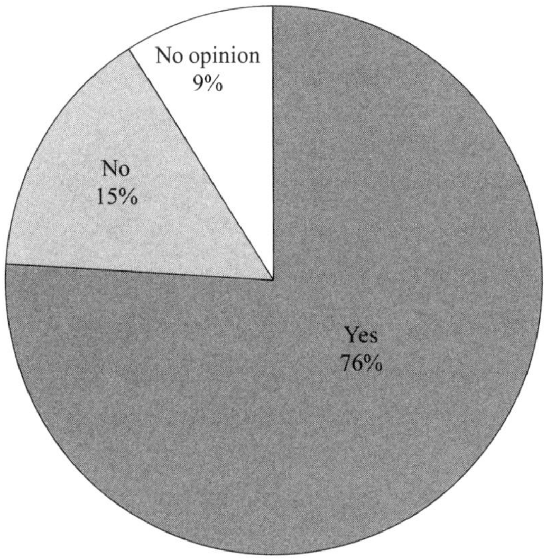

SOURCE: Gallup poll, June 12, 1945 (Gallup 1972).

the question offered as alternatives two New Deal programs: the Works Progress Administration (WPA) or the Public Works Administration (PWA). Figure 3.12 presents the actual wording of the question and the results of the survey cited in that article. The *Los Angeles Times* article was noteworthy, given that Gallup in June had found that 76 percent of the public supported a government role to ensure employment (Figure 3.11).

Notwithstanding the *Los Angeles Times* article, Figure 3.12 reveals a split in public opinion that mirrors the Gallup data depicted in Figure 3.2, from May 1942. In that earlier poll, Gallup had found that 43 percent of those polled thought the country would experience an economic depression for the first few years after the war. Three years later, a comparable portion—42 percent—thought that "the government [would] have to step in and provide work like the W.P.A. or P.W.A.," two of the major

Figure 3.12 Public Opinion in August 1945 on the Capacity of Business to Provide Employment

Do you think that business firms in this country will be able to provide enough jobs for nearly everyone in the next five years, or will the Government have to step in and provide work like the W.P.A. or P.W.A.? Do you think the Government will have to provide work steadily during the next five years, or only part of the time?

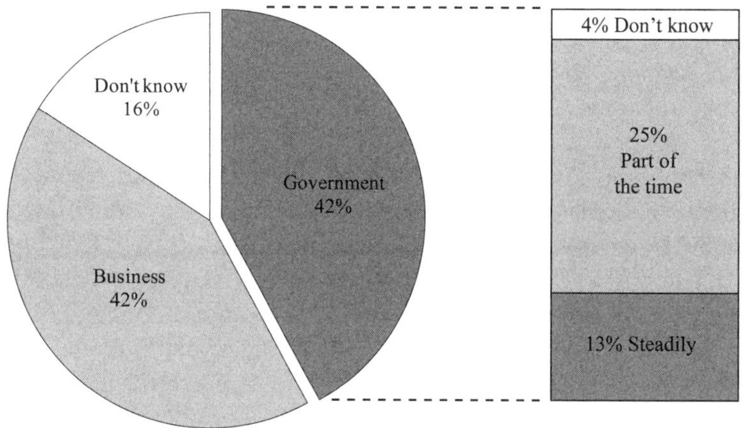

SOURCE: Gallup, August 24–29, 1945 (Gallup 1972, Survey No. 354, p. 526).

programs to combat the Great Depression. A quarter of those interviewed by Gallup thought that the government would have to provide work part of the time, while 13 percent thought the government would have to provide work steadily.

MASS MARKETING OF HAYEK'S *ROAD TO SERFDOM*

An economic treatise written by an Austrian scholar proved fundamental to the debate on full employment. When *New York Times* business writer Henry Hazlitt reviewed *The Road to Serfdom*, by Friedrich August Hayek, in 1944, he described it as "one of the most important books of our generation," and the book soon made it onto the *New York Times* nonfiction best-seller list. One of book's central arguments was that fascism and socialism had common roots in central economic planning as well as the power of the state over the individual. He argued that the abandonment of individualism, liberalism, and freedom inevitably leads to socialist or fascist oppression and the "serfdom" of the individual. Hayek's thesis quickly became the counterargument to Keynesian economics in general and the government's commitment to full employment in particular (Hazlitt 1944, p. BR1).

Soon newspapers across the country were featuring reviews of *The Road to Serfdom,* and references to Hayek's book began appearing on their editorial pages. The *Baltimore Sun* began publishing excerpts from *The Road to Serfdom* as the featured "Thought for Today" on a regular basis in the fall of 1944. Individual liberty and free choice were frequent themes of these excerpts, as exemplified by the following "Thought" from November 9, 1944, which ran on page 16 of the paper: "Our freedom of choice in a competitive society rests on the fact that if one person refuses to satisfy our wishes, we can turn to another. But if we face a monopolist we are at his mercy. And an authority directing the whole economic system would be the most powerful monopolist conceivable."

Hayek had been the director of the Austrian Institute for Economic Research in Vienna until 1931, when he moved to the London School of Economics. He drew on his vantage point in Vienna on the rise of Hitler to assert that fascism or National Socialism resulted from the liberal and progressive traditions and not from conservative roots. Hayek's argument was embraced by American conservatives, who wanted to disassociate themselves from any intellectual links to fascism. Thus Hayek became the intellectual voice for free-market societies and argued against the idea that governments could engineer prosperity (Ebenstein 2001, pp. 128–139).[8]

Hayek's views reached an even wider audience in April 1945, when *Reader's Digest* published a 20-page condensed version of *The Road to Serfdom*. At that time, *Reader's Digest* had an estimated readership of 8.7 million. It was reported that there were an additional one million requests for reprints of the condensed version of *The Road to Serfdom* (Caldwell 2007). In major national newspapers, letters to the editor began citing the *Reader's Digest* condensed version rather than the book itself. One such letter to the *Wall Street Journal* likened postwar economic planning to fascism: "Powerful minorities, which seem to be modeled along lines strikingly similar in many respects to those thriving in Germany, Italy, and Russia, have arisen in this country under the aegis of our so-called 'public servants' in Washington. We are being planned into a lower standard of living which is exactly what happened on the other side of the Atlantic" (Neary 1945).

In making these observations, the author of the letter referenced the *Reader's Digest* condensed version of Hayek's book.

The zenith of the mass marketing of *The Road to Serfdom* was the cartoon version that *Look* magazine published in February 1945. At the time, *Look*'s circulation was estimated at about 2.9 million. The illustrated version made such an impression on executives at General Motors that the company made it into a pamphlet that GM distributed. Three of the 18 cartoon panels from the pamphlet are presented on the next page (Illustration 3.1) and show how Hayek's thesis was simplified to illustrate that "planning" evolves into "fascism." Electronic versions as well as hard copies of the cartoon adaptation of *The Road to Serfdom* remain available today (General Motors 1945).

Buoyed by the popular response, in the spring of 1945 Hayek went on a speaking tour in the eastern as well as midwestern parts of the United States to promote *The Road to Serfdom*. He drew audiences much larger than expected for an academician. Radio stations often broadcast his talks. In May 1945, the *Saturday Review of Literature* observed, "Seldom have an economist and a nonfiction book reached such popularity in so short a time" (Ebenstein 2001, pp. 128–139).

REACTION TO THE FULL EMPLOYMENT LEGISLATION

One week after the Full Employment Act of 1945 was introduced on January 22, 1945, the *New Republic* featured an editorial written by one of the country's leading advocates of full employment—former vice president and soon-to-be-named secretary of commerce Henry Wallace. Wallace emphasized the international importance of full employment and stated that "Jobs for all!" should be the battle cry for all the peoples of the world for the next few decades. He praised the ideas on federal

Illustration 3.1 Panels from the Cartoon Version of *The Road to Serfdom*, Published in *Look* Magazine

NOTE: Electronic versions as well as hard copies of the cartoon adaptation of *The Road to Serfdom* remain available today. Here are three sample panels chosen from among the 18 pictured in the original booklet.

SOURCE: Originally published in the February 1945 issue of *Look* magazine and subsequently reproduced in a booklet by General Motors as No. 118 in its Thought Starter Series (General Motors 1945).

spending expressed by James Patton of the National Farmers Union, the legislative proposal of Sen. James Murray (D-MT), and the report of Lord William Beveridge (1944) in Great Britain. He asserted that "in the economy of the future, the only true national deficit will be labor unemployed." In summary, he concluded that "the essential idea is that the federal government is ultimately responsible for full employment" (Wallace 1945, p. 140).

Vice President Harry Truman emphasized full employment a few days later in a radio program that was broadcast nationwide by the National Broadcasting Company. "As long as we Americans work together and utilize wisely our great wealth of manpower, technical skills, and natural resources," Truman stated, "we can expect full employment in our peacetime economy in a reasonably short time after hostilities end." Truman was joined on the radio broadcast by American Federation of Labor president William Green, U.S. Chamber of Commerce president Eric Johnson, and National Farmers Union president James Patton. During that broadcast, both Green and Patton endorsed the full employment legislation that had been introduced in the Senate (*Washington Post* 1945).

An indication of the importance that Truman gave to full employment is that in his first speech after Japan surrendered in August 1945, a nationwide radio broadcast, he labeled full employment "must-pass" legislation. The Senate had held extensive hearings on the full employment bill over the summer of 1945 and began its floor debate shortly after Labor Day 1945. Political scientist Stephen Bailey reviewed a sample of local newspapers across the United States during that time and reported that an overwhelming majority of these local papers ran editorials against full employment legislation while Congress was debating it. Bailey also noted many editorials against the full employment bill in the major metropolitan papers and from a number of syndicated columnists, such as Paul Mallon and Raymond Moley, who wrote columns hostile to the full employment bill (Bailey 1964, pp. 96–97, 186–187).

Illustrative of the intensity of the media critics of the full employment bill was *Newsweek's* Ralph Robey. Robey devoted four columns from July through September of 1945 to expressing his opposition to the legislation. In one column, he labeled the Senate bill as a costly gamble and attacked the economic forecasting component. Robey asserted that every error of 1 percent that economists made in calculating the gross national product would cost the average American family $600 (a figure he later retracted). In another column, he equated federal spending to head off predicted unemployment with having your appendix removed because a "bureaucrat thinks you're likely to have appendicitis some time next year." Full employment was, concluded Robey, "one of the most outlandish proposals ever offered to the American public" (Robey 1945b).

Publications such as the *Chicago Sun*, the *New York Post*, the *Nation*, and *The New Republic* were notable for being rare voices among the media that spoke favorably of full employment legislation (Bailey 1964, pp. 96–97, 186–187). The circulations of the *Nation* and the *New Republic* reportedly averaged 100,000 each during the 1940s. The *New Republic* went so far as to champion full employment. Hardly a week went by in 1945 that this magazine did not have an article on economic planning, reconversion, or full employment.

When Elmo Roper surveyed a cross section of the American public in August 1945, he found that only 6.6 percent thought that full employment was a bad idea. Less than one-fifth (18.9 percent) thought it was a good idea only if handled by industry. As Figure 3.13 shows, 55.3 percent of those Roper interviewed thought that "full employment is something we should try to get, and it will require government action as well as planning by industry to get it." Only 10.4 percent agreed that it was "something we have got to have, even if it means government ownership of business" (Cantril 1951, p. 903).

Full employment was supported by a majority of Americans across the broad income categories that Roper used, as shown in Table 3.1 (Cantril 1951, p. 903). There was little difference across income levels among those who thought it was a bad idea, with percentages ranging from 5.8 to 6.8. The opinion that full employment was "something we have got to have, even if it means government ownership of business" was inversely related to economic status, as the percentage of those expressing it decreased as their economic status increased. A striking difference was that the proportion of those whom Roper grouped as "poor" choosing this option totaled 17.7 percent, compared with 0.8 percent of those whom Roper labeled "prosperous," 5.6 percent of those labeled "upper middle class," and 9.3 percent of those labeled "lower middle class."

Figure 3.13 Public Opinion in August 1945 on the Concept of Full Employment

Full employment is . . .

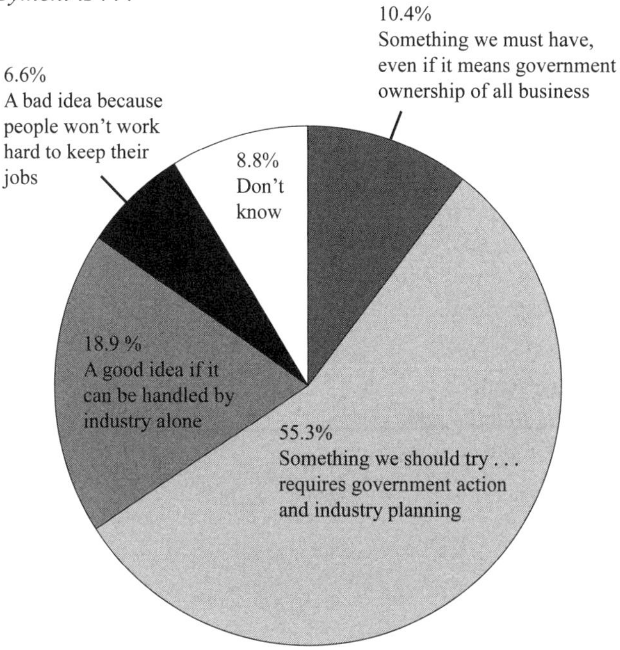

SOURCE: Elmo Roper, *Fortune*, August 1945 (from Cantril 1951, p. 903).

There was an 11-point difference between those who were grouped as "prosperous" and those who were grouped as "poor" on the concept that full employment was "a good idea if it can be handled by industry alone, but it's not government's job to try to bring it about." Support for this choice increased with economic status. Among those whom Roper labeled "prosperous," 26.7 percent identified with this view. The percentage of those responding "don't know" decreased as income levels rose, but among those grouped as "poor" this category constituted 17.2 percent.

Roper found that college-educated respondents most frequently agreed with the statement that "full employment is something we should try to get, and it will require government action as well as plan-

Table 3.1 Public Opinion in August 1945 on the Concept of Full Employment, by Economic Status

	Economic status				
Full employment . . .	Prosperous	Upper-middle	Lower-middle	Poor	Total
is something we have got to have, even if it means government ownership of all business.	0.8	5.6	9.3	17.7	10.4
is something we should try to get, and it will require government action as well as planning by industry to get it.	64.1	61.3	59.0	43.0	55.3
is a good idea if it can be handled by industry alone, but it's not government's job to try to bring it about.	26.7	23.1	19.8	15.3	18.9
may sound good, but it is actually a bad situation, because people then won't work hard in order to keep their jobs.	6.4	6.8	5.8	6.8	6.6
Don't know.	2.0	3.2	6.1	17.2	8.8

SOURCE: Elmo Roper, *Fortune*, August 1945 (from Cantril 1951, p. 903).

ning by industry to get it." As Table 3.2 shows, 69.5 percent of the college-educated people expressed that opinion (Cantril 1951, p. 903).[9] Support for the position that full employment was "something we have got to have, even if it means government ownership of business" was inversely related to education levels. Those with grade-school educations reported opinions on this question in a pattern quite similar to those whom Roper grouped as "poor."

In September 1945, NORC found overwhelming support—79 percent—for the view that it should be the "government's job to see to it that there are enough jobs in this country for everybody who wants to work." The survey was taken at the same time the Senate was debating full employment legislation on the floor and was the last public opin-

Table 3.2 Public Opinion in August 1945 on the Concept of Full Employment, by Education

	Education			
Full employment . . .	Grade school	High school	College	Total
is something we have got to have, even if it means government ownership of all business.	14.7	10.1	2.9	10.4
is something we should try to get, and it will require government action as well as planning by industry to get it.	43.4	59.0	69.5	55.3
is a good idea if it can be handled by industry alone, but it's not government's job to try to bring it about.	17.4	19.5	20.6	18.9
may sound good, but it is actually a bad situation, because people then won't work hard in order to keep their jobs.	5.7	7.9	5.5	6.6
Don't know.	18.8	3.5	1.5	8.8

SOURCE: Elmo Roper, *Fortune*, August 1945 (from Cantril 1951, p. 903).

ion data available on the topic in 1945. These data exhibited comparable levels of support for the federal role as Gallup had found in June 1945 (Figure 3.11): NORC at 79.0 percent and Gallup at 76.0 percent. A review of the major newspapers found no coverage of these NORC results, which are depicted in Figure 3.14.

NORC further probed those who expressed the view that the government should not ensure employment and found that 5.4 percent volunteered that it "kills initiative of individuals" or "makes people lazy." Another 4.5 percent expressed the belief that the government "had enough to do" or "should stick to politics." Those who stated that "business can provide more jobs" or "it kills efforts of business" totaled 3.6 percent. Despite the mass marketing of *The Road to Serfdom*, only 1.8 percent expressed concerns that government should not ensure employ-

Figure 3.14 Public Opinion in September 1945 on the Government's Role in Ensuring Employment

Do you think it should or should not be up to the government to see to it that there are enough jobs in this country for everybody who wants to work? If not, why do you think that it should not be up to the government?

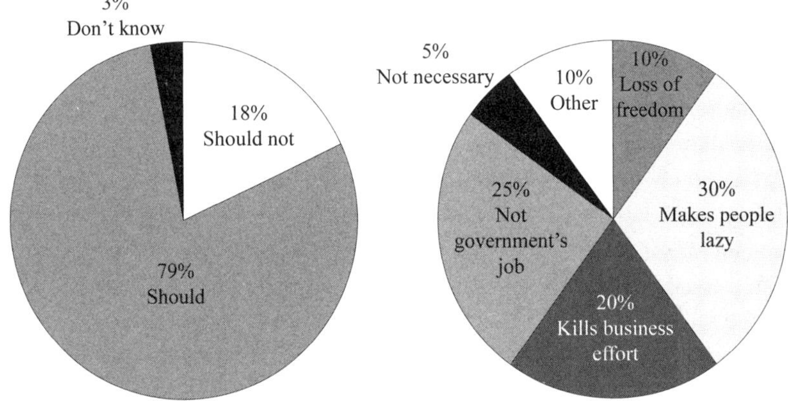

SOURCE: National Opinion Research Center, September 1945 (Cantril 1951, p. 904).

ment because it would lead to "loss of freedom," "too much dictatorship," or "communism."

RELEVANCE OF RADIO NEWS

Unlike the print media, whose publications remain for historians to study, much of the radio news was broadcast live and did not become part of the historical record. Program schedules were regularly published in local newspapers, but recordings of most broadcasts elude those who wish to research their content. For that reason, this chapter does not provide a systematic analysis of radio coverage of the debate on job creation and employment policies. Nonetheless, radio news was quite relevant in this era. According to data collected in the 1940 census, 82.8 percent of American households had radio receivers. By 1945, the National Association of Broadcasters estimated that 90 percent of households had radios. Radio broadcasts were largely for the purpose of entertainment in the 1940s, with 70 to 75 percent of the programming hours allocated to music, drama, comedy, sports, and variety shows. For a week in October 1943, the National Broadcasting Company reported that 19.6 percent of its program time was spent on news and another 3.2 percent on "talks and discussion"; the other 77.2 percent fell into one entertainment category or another (Ackerman 1945, pp. 1–18).

The foreign correspondents who brought live coverage of the war into homes and workplaces across America played a major role in radio broadcasts surpassing newspapers as the leading medium for news. By 1945, an estimated 61 percent of Americans reported that radio was their primary source of daily news. Most Americans expressed the opinion that radio stations were fair in their coverage of controversial issues, especially in contrast to newspapers. Noted social scientists Paul Lazarsfeld and Patricia Kendall asked a sample of Americans in 1945 how "fair" they thought radio broadcasts and newspapers were. They found that 81 percent of those interviewed thought radio stations were generally fair in giving both sides of the issue; only 39 percent of those interviewed thought newspapers were fair in their coverage (Lazarsfeld and Kendall 1948, pp. 18–58).

CLOSING COMMENTS

The stage was set for the legislative debate on the full employment bill. The limited polling data from the period indicated that a substantial majority of the American public wanted the federal government to strive to ensure that everyone looking for work would be able to find a job after the war. The views of many business leaders, as well as the views expressed in the press, however, evidenced that the opposition to such a federal policy was quite strong, despite being the minority opinion.

As we turn our focus to Congress and the White House in the following chapters, it is important to note that elected officials of the 1940s were not enamored of, nor beholden to, public opinion polls.[10] Indeed, many of them expressed distrust of public opinion polls as unreliable and as a challenge to, in the words of Martin Kriesberg (1945, p. 337), "their prerogative of interpreting the public will." Most elected officials maintained that they knew their constituents well and did not need public opinion polls—or the press for that matter—to tell them what was in the best interests of their constituents.

Notes

1. Daily newspapers accessed for this chapter include the following: the *Atlanta Constitution, Baltimore Sun, Chicago Daily Tribune, Christian Science Monitor, Los Angeles Times, New York Times, Wall Street Journal,* and *Washington Post.*
2. On October 31, 1936, the *Literary Digest* predicted that Republican presidential nominee Alfred Landon would win 57 percent of the popular vote and 370 electoral votes. President Roosevelt, however, won 60.8 percent of the popular vote and 523 electoral votes. The *Literary Digest* had sent a mass mailing to 10 million people, who were mostly made up of the magazine's subscribers, people who owned cars, and people who had telephones. The resulting projection was based upon 2.3 million people who returned the postcards.
3. This quota-controlled approach distinguishes these polls from contemporary public opinion research based upon random samples (Berinsky 2006, pp. 499–529).
4. This muted coverage contrasts sharply to the coverage of the contemporary media, which treats polling data as political news.
5. Gallup reports that prior to 1950, his polling firm used a sampling approach that combined two methods: a purposive design for the selection of cities, towns, and rural areas; and a quota method for the selection of individuals within chosen areas. First, a national sample was drawn of places—i.e., cities, towns, and rural areas. These places were then distributed by strata according to region and city size. Additional places were selected within each region to ensure that, within each state, the vote cast by these places in the last three elections matched the percentage distributions of the actual statewide vote. Finally, within each place sampled, the interviewers were given considerable latitude in selecting the respondents so long as they fit the age, sex, and socioeconomic quotas established by Gallup (Berinsky 2006, pp. 499–529).
6. There are several caveats to bear in mind when interpreting these Gallup data. Foremost, the statistical significance of the differences noted above are not available. Since the subgroup differences are rather small, one should not assume they are significant. It is reasonable to assume that the total distributions of those answering "Yes" and "No," however, are significant because of the sheer size of the differences.
7. As a basis of comparison, the actual U.S. labor force was 57 million in 1950.
8. Hayek would go on to win the Nobel Prize for Economics in 1974.
9. Roper did not indicate whether these differences were statistically significant.
10. President Roosevelt, however, did utilize public opinion polls and relied on Hadley Cantril of Princeton University to analyze attitudes on a range of topics for him. Roosevelt may well have been the first U.S. leader to tap into public opinion on a systematic basis (Converse 1987).

4
Senate Passes Full Employment

The U.S. Senate took the lead on full employment legislation during the 79th Congress. The full employment bill that was introduced as Senate Bill 380 had its genesis not in the Special Committee on Post-War Economic Policy and Planning, but rather in a subcommittee of the Military Affairs Committee. Senate Bill 380 embodied for the first time the four elements of full employment identified in the introduction: 1) national planning, 2) employment stimulation tools (e.g., compensatory spending), 3) guarantee of employment, and 4) a federal structure to implement it.

The executive branch contributed significantly to the arguments in support of S. 380, despite some internal disagreements within the administration. Liberal and labor groups embarked on a national campaign advocating for the legislation. While many in the print media continued to criticize the bill, the political and business interests opposed to the legislation were unprepared to stem the tide of support for full employment in the Senate.

THE EMERGENCE OF A FULL EMPLOYMENT BILL

The most logical center of legislative activity on full employment should have been the Senate Special Committee on Post-War Economic Policy and Planning. This committee, however, had as its chair Senator Walter F. George (D-GA), who clearly had different ideas about post-war economic planning. As Chapter 1 discussed, the George Committee did not embrace Keynesian economics. Suffice it to say that legislation for full employment did not emerge from Senator George's committee.

The antecedents to the full employment bill in the Senate can be traced to bills that originated in the House of Representatives. In 1943, Rep. John Dingell Sr. (D-MI) sponsored a comprehensive bill that would have established a United States Employment Service, compulsory national health insurance, extensive national unemployment insurance, expansion of old-age and survivors insurance, and a new program of temporary and permanent disability benefits. This sweeping legislation, which Senators James E. Murray (D-MT) and Robert Wagner (D-NY) introduced in the Senate, expanded upon New Deal ideas and offered an American version of Britain's Beveridge Plan (Hamby 1973, p. 8).[1] It carried a largely symbolic value, as it did not capture many supporters in Congress.

During the summer of 1944, the Senate considered several legislative proposals regarding postwar economic planning. One originated with Sen. Harley Kilgore (D-WV) and had Senator Truman (D-MO) as the chief cosponsor in the Senate.[2] The Kilgore-Truman bill was broad in scope and innovative in approach. The other proposal, sponsored by Senator George, was rather modest in scope and traditional in approach. Murray was quite active in the legislative maneuvering on both the George and the Kilgore-Truman bills.

In the Kilgore-Truman bill, full employment was explicitly stated as a goal, though it was nestled in the preamble. The bill contained a section that would have entitled returning veterans "to placement in suitable employment," a limited but patriotic precursor to the right-to-employment idea. It also included a provision for a National Production-Employment Board with a Bureau of Programs that would have been responsible for permanent economic planning.[3]

National Farmers Union (NFU) president James Patton and NFU legislative secretary Russell Smith advocated the concept of a Bureau of Programs when they proposed a plan for full employment during testimony before the War Contracts Subcommittee of the Senate Military Affairs Committee in April 1944.[4] Patton also argued before this subcommittee (which included both Murray and Truman) that the government should guarantee a $40 billion level of capital investment every year. The assumptions were that this level of capital investment would provide for a full employment economy and that the federal government should intervene when investment by private enterprise fell short of that level (Bailey 1964, pp. 22–23).

The George bill reflected the recommendations of the Senate Special Committee on Post-War Economic Policy and Planning. Foremost, the bill would have created an Office of Demobilization to coordinate postwar economic activities. It emphasized postwar contract settlement to hasten reconversion as well as the prompt disposal of surplus government property. It did not advocate full employment.[5] George redrafted his bill to incorporate compromises with conservatives but lost Murray's sponsorship in the process.

The senator from Montana instead shifted his support to a compromise Kilgore-Truman-Murray bill. Murray added to that bill the elements of the NFU proposal that required public investment if private investment fell short of the amount needed to maintain full employment levels. In a complex series of moves that offered a rewritten George-Murray demobilization bill and the Kilgore-Truman-Murray bill as amendments and secondary amendments, the Senate passed the War Mobilization and Reconversion Act of 1944 without any of the provisions for economic planning and full employment (Bailey 1964, pp. 33–35; Flamm 1994, pp. 74–75).[6]

Despite the failure of the Kilgore-Truman-Murray bill, Murray had framed the debate so that he had one advantage remaining: he had successfully recast the question of postwar economic planning in terms of military contracts and conversion. Partly as a result of his maneuvering and partly because the George Committee had expired, the subcommittee Murray chaired on war contracts was now positioned to set the agenda for postwar economic planning.

The War Contracts Subcommittee circulated the proposal that Patton of the NFU had made for postwar planning to other members of Congress and to various executive agencies and departments. Murray tasked Bertram Gross, staff director of the subcommittee, with adapting the NFU proposal that Patton had presented into legislative language. Gross proved to be the key congressional staff person involved in the development of the full employment bill. Gross met with Gerhard Colm, V.O. Key, Louis Bean, Walter Salant, and several others involved in the executive branch's study group on postwar employment as he drafted the senator's proposal. The War Contracts Subcommittee presented this legislative proposal for reconversion and full employment as part of its *Year-End Report*. Senator Truman joined Murray in signing the subcommittee document.[7]

The centerpiece of the *Year-End Report* was the legislative proposal confidently titled the Full Employment Act of 1945. The assumptions and goals of the *Year-End Report* and the executive branch's confidential *Postwar Employment* report (Colm 1944) were very similar. Both acknowledged that government spending had transformed the economy from one of depression to one of unprecedented production. Both conveyed a sincere fear that high levels of unemployment would resume when the economy reconverted from wartime to peacetime. Both reaffirmed that the government should maintain national policies to stimulate private enterprise, but that if the private sector could not achieve full employment it was the responsibility of the federal government to assure that a postwar economic depression would not occur (U.S. Congress 1944c).

The perspective, nevertheless, had shifted in the second report, for now the economic role of the working person was merged even more tightly with the implicit concept of aggregate demand. Domestic programs that addressed needs of constituents, rather than fiscal machinations, were the primary devices that would achieve the desired results, according to the congressional architects. This difference in the points of view of the two reports is conveyed aptly by this excerpt from the subcommittee's *Year-End Report*: "Statisticians may debate among themselves as to whether the precise goal should be a little more or a little less than the President's 60,000,000 figure. But no thoughtful American—no matter what his creed or station in life—would deny that every man or woman in the country who is willing to work and capable of working has the right to a job" (U.S. Congress 1944c, p. 11).

Indeed, the proposal asserted the right of all Americans able and seeking work, who had finished school and did not have full-time housekeeping responsibilities, to useful, remunerative, regular and full-time employment. The right-to-employment concept now was formally incorporated into a full employment proposal as a feature on a parity with national planning, compensatory spending, and a responsible federal apparatus.

After some modifications and revisions, the full employment bill was introduced as S. 380 by Senators Murray, Wagner, Joseph O'Mahoney (D-WY), and Elbert Thomas (D-UT) during the first session of the 79th Congress.[8] Many other liberal legislators joined in sponsoring this innovative bill, which stated as its purpose "to establish a national policy and program for assuring continuing full employment in a free competitive economy, through the concerted efforts of industry, agriculture, labor, state and local governments and the federal government" (*Congressional Record* 1945a, p. 377).

The declaration of policy promised that the bill would accomplish nine things: 1) promote the general welfare of the nation; 2) foster and protect the American home and family as the American way of life; 3) raise the standard of living; 4) provide employment for veterans; 5) contribute to the full utilization of national resources; 6) develop commerce among states and with foreign nations; 7) preserve and strengthen competitive private enterprise, particularly small businesses; 8) strengthen national defense and security; and, 9) contribute to the establishment and maintenance of lasting peace (*Congressional Record* 1945a, p. 377).

The National Production and Employment Budget was the centerpiece of the legislation. At the beginning of each session of Congress, the president was to submit a detailed budget for the fiscal year or longer. The budget was to perform several important functions. It would estimate the size of the labor force and estimate the aggregate volume of prospective investment and expenditure by private enterprise, consumers, and all levels of government necessary to achieve full employment of the labor force—i.e., the volume of the gross national product (GNP) that would accomplish full employment. The budget would estimate whether the aggregate volume of prospective investment and expenditure was sufficient to assure full employment. In the case of a prospective deficiency, the bill required the president to propose a general program for nonfederal investment by private enterprise to prevent the deficiency. If full employment otherwise could not be achieved, it was the responsibility of the federal government to provide the necessary volume of investment and expenditure (*Congressional Record* 1945a, pp. 377–378).

The original bill also proposed a Joint Committee on the National Budget, composed of ranking members of the Senate committees on Appropriations, Banking and Currency, Education and Labor, and Finance as well as seven additional members of the Senate. The House designees on this committee included the ranking members of the House committees on Appropriations, Banking and Currency, Labor, Ways and Means, and seven additional members of the House of Representatives. The responsibilities of the Joint Committee included an annual study of the proposed national budget and a report to both chambers setting forth a general policy to serve as a guide for committees dealing with legislation relevant to the national budget (*Congressional Record* 1945a, pp. 379–380).

The bill posed a dramatic departure from existing policy, for several reasons. Foremost, it marked the first legislative embodiment of comprehensive economic planning and the use of Keynesian economics to achieve a full employment economy. It was more sweeping in scope than the Kilgore-Truman-Murray bill and more grounded in Keynesian theory than the Dingell bill. It asserted, moreover, the federal responsibility to stabilize the economy and maintain full employment levels and recognized compensatory spending as a tool to do so. The principle of a "right to employment"—i.e., guaranteeing the right to employment for all those seeking work—emerged as the most controversial factor in the postwar economic policy debates. The proposed legislation offered a fundamental change in economic policy because its reference point was the working person rather than the business community.

DEBATE WITHIN THE EXECUTIVE BRANCH

Although previous studies have assumed that the administration was not particularly involved in the progress of the full employment bill, it is evident that some senators made a point of including the administration. When senators sought the judgments of economists in the executive branch, the discussions on full employment broadened well beyond the ad hoc study group. Almost every department and agency speculated on how S. 380 might affect their operations, and they frequently engaged in lively debates on how best to implement S. 380.

One of the most important of these debates occurred when Murray asked about the possibility of developing a comprehensive system of estimating future expenditures. This particular debate within the executive branch boiled down to two themes. The official position was expressed in the Bureau of the Budget memorandum sent to Murray, but it was the unofficial response that proved to be more influential. The debate surrounding this memorandum uncovered a fundamental difference of opinion within the administration over the feasibility of economic forecasting.

The Bureau of the Budget responded to Murray with a 16-page staff memorandum titled "The Problem of Estimating Future Expenditures by Consumers, Business, and State and Local Governments." This document reviewed all of the available sources of economic data that were necessitated by the full employment bill. The report was matter-of-fact and concluded, "In spite of the sparsity of direct forecasts of individual expenditure items of consumers, business, and government, projections of the totals by major groupings are being made on the basis of current trends and past relationships. These projections are useful as approximations of general orders of magnitude. But a considerable improvement of statistical information is needed if these projections are to become reliable with regard to the details" (Colm 1945). The report did not advocate the proposed legislation, nor did it present economic forecasting as a panacea.

The interpretation that countered the official response of the executive branch was one of optimism toward economic forecasting and advocacy of full employment. Walter Salant, head economist at the Research Division of the Office of Price Administration, as well as a study group participant, most succinctly articulated this position. While a graduate student in economics, Salant had spent a year at Harvard studying with Hansen and became a sophisticated exponent of Keynesian economics. Salant confided to Bertram Gross, the Senate staff person responsible for drafting S. 380, that the Bureau of the Budget response was too cautious because it emphasized the limitations rather than the possibilities of economic forecasting. Salant pointed out that economists had made great strides in statistics in the previous decade and had discovered certain stable relationships and theoretic principles that increased the understanding of economic relationships.[9]

As one might expect, Gross preferred Salant's approach and indicated to Gerhard Colm that he wanted a memorandum from Salant's perspective that addressed possible objections to the feasibility of economic forecasting. Colm and J. Weldon Jones knew that Bureau of the Budget director Harold Smith would never sign a memo such as Salant had written. Instead, they suggested that Gross incorporate Salant's ideas into a memorandum written under the auspices of the Senate committee and use the Bureau of the Budget report as background material.[10]

Senator Wagner, chairman of the Committee on Currency and Banking and of the Subcommittee on Full Employment, expanded the discussants well beyond the postwar employment study group when he sent a letter to approximately 40 federal agencies and offices requesting preliminary comments on four questions. To each agency, he asked what the effect of full employment after the war would be on the sectors of the economy with which that agency was concerned. He queried each agency about the role it would play if S. 380 were enacted. Wagner also wanted to know what assumptions, if any, the agency had made about postwar levels of the GNP, the national income, and employment. Finally, the senator solicited any improvements in S. 380 that the agency might have to offer.[11]

The Bureau of the Budget, no doubt, wished to avoid responding to Wagner with divided opinions like those that had reached Sen. Murray just a few weeks earlier. Thus, the Bureau of the Budget informally called a meeting of interested parties from all of the pertinent agencies of the federal government. Those persons that attended represented the following: the departments of Agriculture, Commerce, Interior, Labor, Treasury, and State, as well as the Office of Economic Stabilization, Federal Loan Agency, Federal Reserve Board, Federal Security Agency, Federal Works Agency, National Housing Agency, Office of Price Administration, War Department, War Manpower Commission, Office of War Mobilization and Reconversion, and War Productions Board.[12]

At the outset of this meeting, it became clear that many important people within the administration were poorly informed about the progress that had been made by the executive branch's postwar employment study group on formulating a full employment policy. Many of the issues that the postwar employment study group had addressed months before were being rehashed again by this larger set of interested parties. The participants discussed such topics as the problems with statistics and what agency would be the focal point for administering the full employment proposal. Wilbur Cohen questioned whether the Roosevelt administration supported this bill or whether it recommended an alternative approach. Jones and Colm both assured Cohen that the administration had given clear indications of support.

Several people present questioned the idea that the replies to Senator Wagner should be coordinated. They maintained that the Senate wanted as much information as it could get from these agencies and that the usefulness of the information would depend on its diversity. Others feared that a plethora of different responses would create the worst possible impression and provide ammunition for those opposed to the bill.

The participants were also undecided as to whether their responses should discuss programs the agencies were already administering that would relate to full employment or whether they should discuss potential programs of their agencies that would result from passage of the bill. Colm emphasized that no one had suggested that a "canned" letter be used for the reply, but that the agencies could write better responses if they had an idea of how the other agencies were responding. Meeting chairman Jones closed the session by offering the bureau's assistance to any agency that might need it.

Of all the questions that S. 380 raised, the organizational control issue provoked the sharpest difference of opinion. When George Graham, a staff member under Bureau of the Budget Director Smith, circulated a memorandum on the mechanics of administering the policy laid out in S. 380, he discovered that there was not even a consensus within the Bureau of the Budget. Graham questioned what the functions of the central administering agency would be and what mechanisms could be used to meet the objectives of the full employment bill.[13] In answering Graham's questions, a division of opinion emerged.

Should full employment policy be administered by the Bureau of the Budget or by a specially designated agency? V.O. Key argued that the bureau would have to be radically strengthened and reorganized if it assumed responsibility for full employment.[14] Key also observed that "the administration of a new function can often be best undertaken by the creation of a new organization . . . (otherwise) we would run the danger of molding the job to fit our past habits and the program might turn out to be just about what we have been doing all along." Colm highlighted the advantages of a new agency, specifically that its creation would dramatize the importance of full employment and that it might obtain the authority which the bureau lacked to iron out cabinet-level differences. Colm pointed out that the bureau was an unpopular agency with a conservative reputation, largely because it acted as a watchdog to keep down expenditures.[15]

This difference of opinion stayed within the administration, and all who participated in Graham's circular, including Colm, ultimately went on record that the bureau should be vested with the responsibility of full employment policy. Arthur Smithies summarized their views, saying that the fiscal policy entailed by the full employment bill probably would not bring major additional tasks to the bureau because it was already involved in this same kind of estimation and planning.[16] It was becoming clear, nonetheless, that the Bureau of the Budget, as it was then configured, was not well-suited to manage a national program for full employment.

Senate staff did not appear to have concerns regarding the Bureau of the Budget's ability to implement S. 380. Samuel Thompson, a staff member for the Banking and Currency Committee, expressed a definite preference for the bureau to act as the hub of the administration's preparation. When Gross and Thompson began to pull materials together for the hearings, they met with Jones, Bean, Colm, and William Leonard, all of the Bureau of the Budget. They formed teams of two—one from the committee, one from the bureau—to draft letters requesting information from the appropriate government agencies.[17] The committee consequently published a summary of the responses of the various agencies. This collaborative effort allowed the bureau to play a pivotal role in the legislative development of S. 380.

The death of President Franklin Delano Roosevelt in April of 1945 leveled both a psychological and a strategic blow to the efforts for a full employment policy. Roosevelt's eloquent emphasis of the right to employment during his Economic Bill of Rights speech in 1944 had set the bar high for the federal role in employment stimulation. Roosevelt, however, had not endorsed full employment legislation, nor had he been particularly engaged in the development of the policy. Consequently, his death had little effect on the day-to-day work the administration did in developing the full employment bill.

In contrast to Roosevelt, his former vice president, Henry Wallace, had played a much more visible role as a champion of full employment. Wallace often made it a central theme of his wartime speeches and was the first prominent member of the cabinet to endorse full employment legislation (Markowitz 1973, pp. 135–146). Many advocates of full employment were disappointed that Senator Truman had replaced Wallace as Roosevelt's vice president and was assuming the presidency upon Roosevelt's death.

Regardless of liberals' qualms about President Truman's convictions and abilities, he brought a promising record on full employment to the presidency. Truman had served as federal reemployment director for Missouri during the early years of the Depression. He established himself in the field of planning, organizing the Regional Planning Association of Greater Kansas City, and eventually became a director of the National Conference of City Planning (Hamby 1973, pp. 41–43). As a senator he consistently supported New Deal legislation and cosponsored bills for postwar economic planning and full employment. Just before leaving the Senate, he had signed onto the 1944 *Year-End Report* of the War Contracts Subcommittee that unveiled the original proposal for the full employment bill.[18]

Some were concerned that confusion might create discord on full employment during the presidential transition. Staff from the bureau and from the Office of War Mobilization and Reconversion expressed a desire to brief Truman on the background work done regarding full employment so he could issue presidential guidance. These staffers were particularly worried about coordinating the testimonies of the various administration officials invited to participate in the Senate hearings.[19]

As a result, Bureau of the Budget Director Smith had a long talk with Commerce Secretary Wallace. Though Wallace was a champion of full employment and Smith was more cautious in his embrace of the concept, they shared the view that a "confusion of tongues" would result if there was not some degree of coordination. Wallace agreed to take the lead in talking to the president and said he would recommend that Truman appoint a cabinet-level committee to handle the situation.

LIBERAL GROUPS MOBILIZE FOR FULL EMPLOYMENT

Many in the print media were presenting a critical view of full employment to the American public, and to counteract this, liberal interest groups began a large-scale information campaign advocating full employment. Several liberal interest groups loosely coalesced around a strategy to mobilize support by explaining full employment in terms that were simple, straightforward, and consistent with a free economy. These interest groups represented rather diverse sets of people, including small-scale farmers, blue-collar workers, middle-class intellectuals, racial minorities, and women.

The National Farmers Union had a seminal role in the development of legislation for full employment. Of the major liberal organizations of the day, the NFU was the oldest, having been founded in Point, Texas, in 1902. Unlike its conservative counterparts in the agricultural community, the National Grange and the American Farm Bureau Federation, the NFU was grounded in a neopopulist ideology that celebrated the small family farmer and found most of its membership in the Rocky Mountain and Plains states. Its energetic president, James G. Patton, articulated the thinking that rural prosperity was dependent on a healthy urban economy because urban workers would pass on the benefits of their wages through increased consumption of agricultural products. A farm worker as a youth, Patton had worked his way through college and was only 38 years old when he was elected president of the NFU in 1940. Working closely with the American Federation of Labor (AFL) as well as the Congress of Industrial Organizations (CIO), he articulated a vision of a union of the producing classes (Flamm 1994; Hamby 1973, pp. 33–34; *Time* 1942).

Patton, along with his NFU colleague Russell Smith, was an early advocate of some kind of a full employment policy, notably the Kilgore-Truman-Murray bill for postwar economic planning proposed in 1944. They were involved from the outset in the nuts and bolts of drafting legislation for full employment, and they followed through, both by lobbying congressional leaders and by mobilizing their members to support full employment (Bailey 1964, pp. 21–25, 37–60).

In addition to their pragmatic efforts, they bore a significant symbolic role. They were, in many ways, the contemporary manifestation of Jefferson's agrarian vision as well as the spirit of liberal populism. Their merger of rural and urban working people under the banner of a full employment economy created potent imagery that was distinctively American. This basis of support for full employment was an effective shield against subsequent charges of socialism and communism.

Although not involved in drafting the policy, the Union for Democratic Action (UDA) almost immediately seized upon the issue of full employment and became a lead group in mobilizing support. In 1944, the UDA was the smallest and weakest of the major liberal organizations.[20] Despite its prestigious leaders, James Loeb and Reinhold Niebuhr, and having Eleanor Roosevelt on its membership rolls, the UDA had a difficult time making ends meet. Its strong anticommunist stance and its frequent contributions to the *New Republic* kept it at the liberal fore; however, it was the full employment debate that breathed life into the UDA (Hamby 1973, pp. 36–37).

The UDA constructed an impressive effort for that time to mobilize support for full employment. Foremost, it mounted a public information campaign to counter the opposition of most local newspapers to full employment. It disseminated material—largely written by Paul Sifton, who was on loan from the NFU—by means of a mailing list of an estimated 10,000 to 15,000 "public opinion formers"—groups that Stephen Bailey identified as union locals, liberal associations, farm groups, business groups, professional societies, and newspaper columnists (Bailey 1964, pp. 83–84).

In March of 1945, the UDA compiled an official "Full Employment Kit" which encouraged people to write their senators and congressmen and talk to their friends. The reoccurring emphasis of the kit was to stimulate informed discussions of full employment. The readers were advised to talk about the bill at every opportunity, both informally and within the context of organizations to which they belonged. The UDA even offered to help arrange panels of senators and congressmen to come to meetings on full employment and to provide other kinds of follow-up support to local groups interested in full employment. The kit was mailed to all individuals and groups on the UDA's mailing list, a list two to three times the organization's estimated membership of 4,000 people (Bailey 1964, pp. 83–85).

Most of the major labor unions also engaged in educating their membership on full employment and in advocating its enactment into public policy. In general, organized labor did not see full employment as a panacea nor a single solution, but as an integral part of a comprehensive legislative program. While the various unions differed on many components of such a comprehensive program, they did agree on full employment.

The CIO was the dominant group representing organized labor that was pushing for full employment. The CIO leadership recommended that each of its affiliates review the problems of unemployment so that their analyses could be incorporated into statements supporting full employment. In the summer of 1945, the *C.I.O. News* featured articles demonstrating the need for a full employment program. The CIO Political Action Committee, moreover, printed a pamphlet, "The Answer is FULL EMPLOYMENT," that it disseminated during August of that year, the month the House held hearings on full employment. Within weeks after the war against Japan had ended, the CIO organized marches in Washington, D.C. Hundreds of workers carrying signs saying "Full Employment," "Fair Employment," and "Jobs for All" demonstrated during the period in which the Senate was debating and voting on the full employment bill (Bailey 1964, pp. 93–94; *Time* 1945c).

AFL President William Green came out in favor of a federal program for full employment and promised to mobilize AFL membership across the country on behalf of legislation. The AFL's *American Federationist* printed editorials advocating full employment legislation as the Senate and House were considering the bill in the summer of 1945. The AFL was not as engaged in the advocacy for full employment in Congress as some of the other labor groups, reportedly because of tensions with the CIO on the legislative agenda. Nevertheless, the AFL played a very important function because it distributed educational information on full employment legislation to all of its members—a number the organization estimated at six million (Bailey 1964, pp. 85–87).[21]

The importance of the full employment bill to organized labor was illustrated by a letter that Milo Lathrop, educational director of the United Electrical, Radio, and Machine Workers of America, wrote to Senator Wagner. Lathrop stated that the union was gearing up the entire educational program to inform its members and the community about the legislation. At least some of the fruits of Lathrop's work were not missed by Wagner, who received numerous letters supporting the bill from local affiliates of the Electrical, Radio, and Machine Workers of America.[22]

Many other unions busily supported a program for full employment, including the United Mine Workers, the United Auto Workers, the National Women's Trade Union League, and the Railroad Brotherhoods. Since the unions had existing structures, regular meetings, and newsletters, their potential to arouse public support for full employment was considerable. Victor Riesel might have been speculating when he wrote that labor publications reached 15 million American families in 1945, but he was sound in emphasizing the important function of these labor papers (Riesel 1946).[23] Union locals, furthermore, had among their members individuals who were talented in the arts of persuasion and organization.

National women's organizations were involved in the public education campaign for full employment as well. For example, both the Young Women's Christian Association (YWCA) and the National

Council of Jewish Women actively disseminated information to their members and featured full employment in their publications. The Association of American University Women embarked on a letter-writing campaign. The National Council of Negro Women, particularly their leader Mary McLeod Bethune, voiced support for a strong full employment policy (Bailey 1964, p. 87).[24]

In addition to the National Council of Negro Women, other African American organizations engaged in the public education campaign for full employment. Many African American groups had long been engaged in the struggle against employment discrimination, so they were already mobilized around employment issues.[25] The National Association for the Advancement of Colored People (NAACP) mailed reports on full employment to its 700 chapters and distributed information to an estimated 500,000 people on its mailing list. The National Urban League also spoke out on behalf of a federal program for full employment (Bailey 1964, p. 87).[26]

THE SENATE COMMITTEE ON BANKING AND CURRENCY MOVES ON S. 380

The Full Employment Subcommittee of the Senate Committee on Banking and Currency had intended to consider full employment at a rather leisurely pace, with hearings beginning at the end of July and resuming after the scheduled August-to-October adjournment. However, the dramatic end of the war with Japan on August 14, 1945, altered plans. In a radio address two days later, President Truman labeled full employment "must" legislation and put pressure on Congress to act expeditiously (Truman 1961a). As a result of Truman's intervention, the subcommittee accelerated its schedule on full employment. The longstanding tradition of the August recess gave way to the goal of completing the Senate hearings on the full employment bill by Labor Day.

Concurrently with Truman's speech and the hearings on S. 380, the letter-writing campaign that the liberal and labor groups had organized reached its zenith. Senator Wagner, for example, received dozens of letters during this period, from New York to Alaska. These letters urging his leadership in enacting the full employment bill came mostly from local unions but also from chapters of the Parent-Teacher Association (PTA) and various religious and neighborhood organizations.

A few days before the hearings on S. 380 began, four Republican senators joined their liberal colleagues in endorsing the proposal. The four senators were George Aiken of Vermont, William Langer of North Dakota, Wayne Morse of Oregon, and Charles Tobey of New Hampshire.[27] Although the Republican standard-bearer in 1944, New York governor Thomas Dewey, had advocated the principle of full employment, he never supported the right-to-employment idea. The Republican platform did not include a full employment proposal. Since Keynesian economic policy was incongruous with the fiscally conservative ideology of the Republican Party, the action of these four senators was noteworthy and served as a harbinger of subsequent Senate action on the bill.

The Full Employment Subcommittee conducted extensive hearings from July 30 to September 1, 1945, with Wagner as chair. Other members consisted of Senators George Radcliffe (D-MD), Abe Murdock (D-UT), Glen Taylor (D-ID), J. William Fulbright (D-AR), Hugh Mitchell (D-WA), Charles Tobey (R-NH), Robert Taft (R-OH), C. Douglass Buck (R-DE), and Bourke Hickenlooper (R-IA).[28] Almost 70 individuals representing a diversity of organizations testified, and just as many groups or persons submitted statements for the record.

Mark Sullivan, a columnist with the *Washington Post*, commented on the unusual length of the hearings on the full employment bill and pointedly added that the need for a thorough discussion was apparent. Sullivan was among those print journalists who questioned the bill, not because he opposed the concepts (so he said), but because he doubted whether it could possibly achieve its objectives (Sullivan 1945). Sullivan was somewhat unique among journalists in that he was not openly hostile to the bill.

In contrast, Ralph Robey, chief economist at the National Association of Manufacturers, wrote a four-part series for *Newsweek* criticizing the full employment bill as the hearings began. Robey conceded that the government spending for welfare relief during the Great Depression was a proper use of taxpayers' money because there was no alternative relief for the unemployed; however, he argued that the full employment bill embodied government spending gone awry because it would trigger spending whenever bureaucrats anticipate a rise in unemployment, regardless of whether that unemployment ever were to occur. Robey was convinced that the spending would rise unnecessarily and summarized the full employment bill as "a clever trick designed just to fool you" (Robey 1945a, p. 66). In essence Robey argued that a federally funded dole was an acceptable response to unemployment, but that federally stimulated jobs were not.

Views such as Robey's did not prevail during the series of hearings. Spokespersons from veterans groups, civil rights groups, unions, social welfare agencies, religious organizations, educational associations, and academia voiced support of the principles embodied in S. 380. Two major farm groups paired off, with the National Farmers Union advocating for and the National Grange opposing the bill. Representatives from the business community reflected mixed attitudes toward full employment: a few were strong adversaries; some acknowledged positive features; most favored S. 380. The 10 spokespersons from the Truman administration presented a rather solid front in support of the bill and an air of optimism that they were ready to handle the job of carrying it out (U.S. Congress 1945b).

Several themes emerged from the varied perspectives that the supporters brought to the hearings. One was a fear that unemployment would resume after the war if the legislation was not enacted. This need for S. 380 was backed up by statements of overwhelming public support. Advocates asserted that S. 380 would help workers, farmers, and businessmen, especially small businessmen. Social workers, religious leaders and educators professed that many of society's problems would be alleviated if America were fully employed. Finally, they argued that it was the responsibility of the federal government to institute an economic program of full employment (U.S. Congress 1945b).

During these hearings it was rare to hear voices of opposition to S. 380, and usually these voices offered a simplistic reaction to the bill. The New York Chamber of Commerce opined, "Depressions are the price we pay for freedom."[29] Such a statement, although sincerely offered by opponents to the bill, inspired few to join the ranks of the opposition.

A more sophisticated argument against the full employment bill did appear in a letter that Rufus Tucker, chief economist at General Motors, sent Wagner. Tucker feared that if the government promised to provide work for all citizens, the taxpayers might end up paying money irrespective of the value of the work performed. He reasoned as follows: "The taxpayers collectively may have a moral obligation to keep any citizen from starvation or excessive suffering, but it may frequently happen that the obligation can more adequately and cheaply be fulfilled in other ways than by providing jobs."[30] Tucker, much like Robey, was among those who thought it more cost-effective to provide public welfare assistance than to provide jobs.

That few people formally testified against S. 380 was somewhat surprising because opponents had been invited to speak. Senator Taft, the ranking Republican, had secured several opposition witnesses, but their voices seemed faint in contrast to the bill's supporters. Its sponsors speculated that this reluctance of their adversaries to come forward was a result of their strategy to paint the opposition as a small and selfish minority who did not want a stable, growing economy. Senator Murray spoke of the critics of full employment as wanting a floating pool of unemployed to keep wages down and maintain discipline over labor. Anyone who had reservations about S. 380 presumably risked being portrayed as favoring unemployment (Bailey 1964, pp. 105–107; U.S. Congress 1945b, pp. 16–17). Such concerns, however, hardly had stopped others from expressing opposition to full employment in the media. More likely, opponents of the legislation were not taking the hearings seriously. Indeed, it was August, a time when few people who had a choice stayed in Washington.

Later, *Newsweek* called the hearings of the Senate Banking and Currency Committee "Selling FE" and credited Wagner and Murray, among others, with maneuvering "one of the neatest jobs of legislative stage setting in more than a decade." The magazine also observed that the opposition to the full employment bill was disorganized and ineffective. It seemed, according to *Newsweek's* sources, that the opponents of the full employment bill expected the conservative Democrats aligned with Sen. Harry Byrd of Virginia to join forces with the Republicans to stop the bill (*Newsweek* 1945a).[31]

Cosponsors of the bill only acquiesced on one point during the hearings: the exclusion of full-time housekeepers. When Senator Murray presented his case for S. 380, Senator Murdock questioned him about the exemption from the law for persons with full-time housekeeping responsibilities. Essentially, Murdock argued that everyone should have the same opportunities. Murray hedged slightly, saying he did not want to force housewives out of the home. Over the course of the exchange, however, Murray agreed that women should have the same employment opportunities as men. Subsequently, the committee concurred and eliminated this exemption from the bill (*Time* 1945a; U.S. Congress 1945b, pp. 16–17).

When the subcommittee met to act on the legislation following the hearings, Taft, Radcliffe, Buck, Hickenlooper, and Fulbright offered amendments to dilute the provisions of the bill. These senators agreed that some sort of economic planning was good, but objected to the term "full employment," to the guarantee of a "right to employment," and to the ultimate reliance on federal expenditure and investment. Wagner, Taylor, Mitchell, Murdock, and Tobey held the line, and the resulting tie vote insured that the original language was reported from the subcommittee (Bailey 1964, p. 113; *Congressional Quarterly* 1945).

The minority continued to press its case when the Senate Committee on Banking and Currency met to consider S. 380. Taft, Radcliffe, Buck, and Hickenlooper were joined by John Thomas (R-ID), Hugh Butler (R-NE), and Arthur Capper (R-KS) in pushing for substantial amendments. Carter Glass (D-VA), Alben Barkley (D-KY), Ernest McFarland (D-AZ), and Sheridan Downey (D-CA) lined up with the subcommittee members who wanted the legislation approved without changes. Nine amendments were decided in close, critical votes: 9-9, 8-10, 8-11, 7-12, 9-10, 10-9, 8-11, 9-10, and 8-11. Two Democrats, William Fulbright and E. P. Carville (NV), played the pivotal roles (Bailey 1964, p. 113; *Congressional Quarterly* 1945).

The only amendment that passed sought to soften the right-to-employment clause by replacing the phrase "*the right to* useful, remunerative, regular and full-time employment." The new phrase, offered by Fulbright, became "*entitled to an opportunity for* useful, remunerative, regular and full-time employment." The committee then defeated a motion by Radcliffe to report the bill without a favorable recommendation by an 8-11 vote. Murdock's motion to favorably report out S. 380 passed by a vote of 13-7. The bill emerged with only its right-to-employment clause weakened (Bailey 1964, pp. 115–116; *Congressional Quarterly* 1945).

Meanwhile, celebrations of Labor Day across the United States featured signs labeled "Full Employment" and "Jobs for All." Workers and their families paraded in the streets during the Labor Day festivities, which were then commonplace in cities and towns across America. At least one national publication speculated that the fear of a resumption of unemployment when veterans returned home clouded the parades (*Time* 1945c).

DEBATE ON THE SENATE FLOOR

On September 24, 1945, the Senate began floor debate on the full employment bill. Wagner opened the debate in support of the bill by providing an overview of the bill's main elements. Wagner also addressed what he identified as the three main arguments against the legislation. First, to those who maintained that full employment cannot be achieved in a free enterprise system, Wagner asserted, "No hostile foreign agent could do more to wreck the fabric of our society than to tell our people that unemployment is the price we pay for freedom." Second, Wagner spoke of those who feared that full employment would stimulate inflation, giving too much power to organized labor and undermining individual work initiative. To them, Wagner countered, "Fear of unemployment and depression is one of the fundamental causes of inflation." He further argued, "The desire for betterment is the driving force in our free enterprise system. Nothing can stultify initiative more than a lack of opportunity." Finally, Wagner challenged the view that government-provided relief (i.e., public assistance) was cheaper than full employment, saying that critics holding such a view "take depression[s] for granted. They have no faith in the vitality of our free-enterprise system" (*Congressional Record* 1945b, p. 8957).

Murray followed with an address that highlighted how the bill would foster business, particularly small businesses. Referring to his years as the chairman of the Committee on Small Business, Murray said, "I have found that, above all, the one thing that small business needs in America is customers" (p. 8963). He maintained that the full employment bill would increase the purchasing power of consumers, which in turn would fuel the high-volume market that benefits business. Joseph O'Mahoney presented the economic overview, using graphs and charts to advocate S. 380. The leading Republican sponsor, Wayne Morse, concluded this quartet of speeches that formally endorsed the bill on the final day of the Senate debate. Amidst these orchestrated presentations, a lively and sometimes bitter debate ensued over four days (*Congressional Record* 1945b, pp. 8954–9146).

Despite the Committee on Banking and Currency's acceptance of the Fulbright amendment that replaced the "right to employment" language with the phrase "entitled to an opportunity for useful, remunerative, regular and full-time employment," some senators warned of workers abandoning less desirable jobs to demand better positions. Burton K. Wheeler (D-MT) spoke of workers leaving the farm because "the Government . . . owes us a job at a remuneration such as we think we ought to get." He also spoke of "the housewife . . . who ought to be at home taking care of her children" as among those who should not be guaranteed employment (p. 9060). In contrast to those who feared that people would demand better jobs, Sen. Kenneth Wherry (R-NE) expressed the view that some people, presumably striking union workers, did not want to work. "Is there any way to avert unemployment," Wherry asked, "if we cannot get labor back to work?" (p. 9053).[32]

Although the proponents of the legislation argued as if all of their opponents considered economic depressions natural fluctuations in the business cycle that should be endured, and as if their opponents also considered a certain number of unemployed workers necessary to keep wages from rising, these were not the most meaningful critiques of the bill. The critical points of contention centered on issues of deficit spending for public works and taxation to balance the budget (*Congressional Record* 1945b, p. 8958). Senator Taft, for example, asserted,

> I suggest that public spending outside of public works is not helpful in curing a depression. There are many better methods which can be used. There is no panacea to which we may resort . . . If there should be any increase in employment the increase would be merely temporary in character. The spending of public money for public works is one remedy, but to say that it is the final solution of our difficulties is only to lay down for this country a policy which will lead to destruction. (p. 9029)

Hickenlooper echoed Taft's concern about resorting to public funding when he remonstrated that "the proponents of the bill are now proposing to embark on a program of unlimited financing, without giving one single thought, in the provisions of this bill, to where the money is coming from" (p. 9036). Colorado senator Eugene Millikin[33] warned,

> We would destroy our economy by relying on the printing presses as the source of our wealth and the panacea of our troubles. That is what the Senator would have us do, because he has resisted every effort to bring the objective of his bill into relation with a balanced budget or into relation with the other essentials to good, sound government . . . This country now has a debt of $300,000,000,000 and an annual deficit of $50,000,000,000. Let us govern ourselves accordingly, and at the same time remember where the wealth of the country is. (*Congressional Record* 1945b, p. 9033)

It was O'Mahoney who responded to these critiques, largely by relying on his familiarity with economic statistical analysis (pp. 9048–9062). In regards to taxation, the senator from Wyoming cited tax revenue data and presented graphic depictions of federal receipts by tax bracket to illustrate that full employment would increase tax revenues. There would be no need to raise taxes to pay down the deficit if people were gainfully employed. When he emphasized that "in order to support our economy we must raise the standard of living of those at the bottom of the scale," the *Congressional Record* (1945b, p. 9062) noted that there was applause from the galleries.

O'Mahoney additionally offered a rather nuanced analysis of the role federal government might play in job creation and the promotion of small business through tax policy:

> It goes to the creation of an atmosphere in which the investment of private capital may be encouraged. I believe it is based primarily upon a system of incentive taxation, taxation that will stimulate the owner of private capital to put his money into new enterprises. That is lacking now because of many factors of our taxation system which I do not desire to go into now. But the second method of preserving and stimulating free enterprise would be to develop such a policy toward monopoly or concentrated power as to stake out a region in which little business would be free from suppression by the powers of concentrated economy. (p. 9051)

While O'Mahoney was willing to reduce the highest tax brackets, he advocated tax policies aimed at curbing monopolies and benefiting small businesses. Most importantly, he appreciated the role that federal tax policy might have in job creation (pp. 9053–9054).[34]

O'Mahoney was also the bill sponsor who addressed the concerns of deficit spending on public works. He used Hoover Dam—then known as Boulder Dam—at that time the nation's largest producer of hydroelectric power as well as one of the largest man-made structures in the world, to illustrate the value of federal construction projects (*Congressional Record* 1945b, p. 9056):

> I think of the building of Boulder Dam, authorized by the Congress under the Hoover administration. I think of the billions of dollars which were expended from the Federal Treasury in the construction of that dam. Every penny of that expenditure has been justified, because it produced business. It created income, not only for the people who were employed upon the project, but for those who supplied materials and commodities in connection with its construction. It provided income for cities and States. It was in every sense of the word an expenditure which produced revenue.

The Senate floor debate prompted five major proposed amendments and six minor voice votes. Radcliffe and Taft offered an amendment to provide that there would be no government investment except as consistent with other obligations and except for accelerated public works. Carl Hatch (D-NM) substituted, in place of the Radcliffe-Taft amendment, a provision that government investment and expenditure must be consistent with other obligations and considerations of national policy to achieve full employment. Most sponsors of S. 380 agreed with the compromise, and it passed by a voice vote. The Senate also adopted by division an amendment by Eugene Millikin (R-CO) that inserted the language of the Hatch amendment uniformly throughout the bill (*Congressional Record* 1945b, p. 9125).

Senator Taft offered an amendment that strove to prevent an increase in the national debt by requiring that a taxation program over a period of years must accompany the program of investment and expenditure. He won the approval of the bill's sponsors when he added the phrase "without interfering with the goal of full employment." The Taft amendment passed unanimously, 82-0 (*Congressional Record* 1945b, p. 9144).

Hickenlooper continued the struggles he had waged in the subcommittee and committee meetings. He proposed two amendments to rectify what conservatives deemed the major problem with S. 380: that it interfered with and inhibited the free enterprise system. His amendment that would have prohibited government competition with free enterprise lost 30-49. The Senate also rejected (by a vote of 35-44) his amendment that government avoid unnecessary restrictions on industry. In opposing the amendments, Senator O'Mahoney stated, "Great care has been exercised in drafting the bill, to make it clear that its primary purpose is to make the free enterprise system work" (p. 9146). Those who spoke against the Hickenlooper amendments rejected the premise that S. 380 restricted free enterprise and stated that the amendments confused and diluted the bill (*Congressional Record* 1945b, pp. 9145–9151).

The final vote on the full employment bill was a surprising 71-10 (p. 9153). Given the close margins in the Full Employment Subcommittee and the Banking and Currency Committee, this outcome was impressive. The amendment that provided for increased taxes over a period of years to recoup any excess federal investment and expenditure necessary to maintain full employment levels was key to the broad support for final passage. That revision gave some reassurance to fiscal conservatives who feared there would be negative repercussions from the bill—namely deficit spending.

Gaining the support of prominent conservative Republicans like Taft was particularly noteworthy. Earlier, Taft had called the NRPB report on full employment "nonsense" and cited Henry Wallace's advocacy of full employment as the chief reason he opposed the confirmation of Wallace as secretary of commerce. Taft also had been critical of the full employment language in the Kilgore-Murray-Truman bill.[35] Taft biographer James T. Patterson acknowledged, "Taft upset right-wing businessmen by agreeing that the federal government must play an important role in stabilizing business cycles and by admitting the need for compensatory spending under certain adverse conditions" (Patterson 1972, pp. 303–304).

As passed by the Senate, S. 380 addressed each of the four key elements identified at the start of this book. First and foremost, it would have given the federal government the responsibility to ensure full employment when the private sector falls short, primarily through compensatory spending and other Keynesian tools. Second, to implement the responsibility, the president would have been required to submit a National Production and Employment Budget (shortened to National Budget) annually, and the Congress would have been required to establish a Joint Committee on the National Budget. Thus, the third element would have come about—the concept of national economic planning would have been integrated with the proposed administrative and legislative structures to ensure full employment. The right to employment, the fourth key element, became an opportunity for useful, remunerative employment. Most of the original Senate sponsors stated that the bill remained strong, but they maintained that they had compromised as much as possible without undermining the objectives of the bill. It was clear they wanted to preempt any further tampering with the bill by the House (Bailey 1964, pp. 125–127; *Congressional Record* 1945b, pp. 9114–9153).

Notes

1. Murray was a staunch ally of Roosevelt and maintained a liberal record for his entire Senate career, 1934 to 1960. Wagner was a leading New Deal liberal, serving in the Senate from 1927 to 1949.
2. Kilgore represented West Virginia from 1941 to 1956.
3. Robert A. Taft Sr., "Folder on Senate Select Committee on Postwar Economic Policy," Robert A. Taft Sr. Papers, Library of Congress, Washington, DC.
4. Russell Smith had worked at the Bureau of Agricultural Economics in the Department of Agriculture with Louis Bean. The source for the $40 billion estimate was reportedly Bean, who was at the Bureau of the Budget and soon to be working on the administration's policy paper on "Postwar Employment" (Flamm 1994, p. 74–75).
5. Folder on Senate Select Committee on Postwar Economic Policy, Taft Papers.
6. Ibid.
7. Leon Keyserling, formerly with Senator Wagner, worked with Gross at the U.S. Housing Authority and helped arrange for Gross (on loan from the Department of the Navy) to go to work for Senator Murray in 1942 (Spritzer 1985).
8. O'Mahoney served from 1934 to 1953. Although defeated in 1952, he was reelected in 1954 to fill the seat vacated by the death of Sen. Lester Hunt. O'Mahoney served until 1961. Thomas represented Utah from 1933 to 1950.
9. Walter Salant to Bertram Gross, 27 February 1945, Gerhard Colm Papers, Harry S. Truman Library and Museum, Independence, MO.
10. Gerhard Colm to J. Weldon Jones, 7 March 1945, Colm Papers.
11. Robert Wagner to Harold Smith, 3 March 1945, Colm Papers.
12. "Minutes on Full Employment Meeting," 19 March 1945, Colm Papers. The material covered in the next three paragraphs also comes from these minutes.
13. George Graham, "Summary of Views of Staff Members on Problems in Central Coordination Raised by Murray-Patman Bill," 10 April 1945, Colm Papers. The material in the next two paragraphs also comes from this memorandum.
14. Valdimer Orlando Key had already published his classic textbook, *Politics, Parties, and Pressure Groups,* in 1942. He was then a political science professor at Johns Hopkins University, and later had a distinguished career at Yale and Harvard.
15. Graham, "Summary of Views," 1–6.

16. Ibid., 4.
17. Colm to J. Weldon Jones, 16 July 1945, Colm Papers.
18. A comment from President Truman during a May 2, 1945, press conference in which he indicated that he was not familiar with the Murray bill has often been cited as evidence that Truman was not engaged on the issue. Here is the actual text: "Q: Mr. President, can you say anything on your attitude toward the full employment bill of Senator Murray? TRUMAN: I would—I am not familiar with Senator Murray's full employment bill, but I am for full employment, and shall do everything in my power to create full employment as soon as hostilities end and we start back on the civil program" (Truman 1961b).
19. Colm to Herman Loeffler, 29 May 1945 memorandum, Colm Papers; Loeffler to Harold Smith, 29 May 1945 memorandum, Colm Papers; J. Weldon Jones to Colm, 8 June 1945, Colm Papers. The material in the next paragraph also comes from these memoranda.
20. The UDA was cofounded by theologian Reinhold Niebuhr, political organizer James Isaac Loeb, labor leader Murray Gross, and actor Melvyn Douglas, among others, on May 10, 1941. It was the precursor to Americans for Democratic Action (ADA), which was established in 1947.
21. This citation is supplemented by a letter from James Loeb Jr. to Harry Truman, 8 February 1946, Harry S. Truman Papers, Harry S. Truman Library and Museum, Independence, MO.
22. Milo Lathrop to Robert Wagner, 7 August 1945, Series B124, Robert Wagner Papers, Georgetown University Library, Washington, DC.
23. This citation is supplemented by Loeb, letter, 8 February 1946, Truman Papers.
24. Citation supplemented by Loeb, letter, 8 February 1946; and by Series B124, Wagner Papers.
25. A few years earlier, A. Philip Randolph, founding president of the Brotherhood of Sleeping Car Porters, had prompted Roosevelt to issue Executive Orders 8802 and 9346, which established the Fair Employment Practices Commission (FEPC) and barred discrimination based upon "race, creed, color, or national origin" in defense and government employment and in all government contracts (Roosevelt 1941b, 1943). Racial discrimination in employment was a major issue, intensifying when African American servicemen faced violent attacks as they returned home from the war. The authority of the FEPC expired with the end of the war. Congress defunded the FEPC even as Truman sought to extend it. Truman subsequently pushed for legislation to make the FEPC permanent, but congressional filibustering stopped the bill.
26. Citation supplemented by Loeb, letter; and by Series B124.
27. Aiken served in the Senate from 1941 to 1975. Langer was a prominent isolationist as well as an advocate for universal health care. He represented North Dakota in the Senate from 1940 to 1959. Morse was elected as a progressive Republican in 1944 but became an Independent in 1952. He became a Democrat in 1955. He is perhaps best known for his opposition to U.S. involvement in Vietnam. He was defeated for reelection in 1968. Tobey won election to the Senate in 1938. He was

an early opponent of Sen. Joseph McCarthy's sensationalist tactics. He died in office in 1953.

28. Radcliffe went on to lose the primary in 1946. He had been elected to the Senate in 1934. Orrice Abram "Abe" Murdock Jr. represented Utah in the Senate from January 3, 1941, to January 3, 1947. He was defeated for reelection in 1946 and went on to serve on the National Labor Relations Board from 1947 to 1957. Taylor was elected in 1944. He was the vice presidential nominee of the Progressive Party in 1948, running on a ticket with Henry Wallace. Fulbright served from 1945 to 1975 and was the longest-serving chair of the Senate Foreign Relations Committee. Among his accomplishments, the Fulbright Program for International Exchange may be his most lasting legacy. Mitchell was appointed to fill a vacancy in the Senate in January 1945 and served until the end of 1946. Taft was the preeminent conservative Republican leader of his day and narrowly lost in his bids to be the presidential nominee in 1940, 1948, and 1952. Buck served one term as senator. Hickenlooper was elected in 1944 and served until 1969.
29. Series B124 Folder, July 1945, Wagner Papers.
30. Rufus Tucker to Robert Wagner, undated, Series B124 Folder, Wagner Papers.
31. Byrd was a powerful force in Virginia politics and served in the Senate from 1933 to 1965. He was best known for his opposition to the *Brown v. Topeka Board of Education* Supreme Court decision, as he called for "massive resistance" against desegregation of public schools, which led to many Virginia schools closing rather than be forced to integrate.
32. Wheeler was first elected to the Senate from Montana as Democrat in 1922. The Progressive Party selected him as that party's vice presidential candidate in 1924. Initially a supporter of the New Deal, Wheeler broke with Roosevelt in 1937 and became active in the "America First" movement. He also became an adversary of fellow Montanan James Murray. Wheeler lost in the Democratic primary in 1946. Wherry was the Republican whip at that time. He was elected from Nebraska in 1942 and served until his death in 1951.
33. Millikin was president of Kinney-Coastal Oil Company when he was appointed to the Senate as a Republican in December 1940 upon the death of Colorado senator Alva Adams. He was elected in 1942 and went on to serve until 1957.
34. O'Mahoney chaired the Temporary National Economic Committee, which was a congressional investigation into monopolistic business practices from 1938 to 1941.
35. Robert A. Taft Sr., "Personal Legislative Folder, 1943–45," Taft Papers.

5
Opponents Take Aim in the House

Observers of Congress frequently conclude that it is easier to obstruct bills than it is to enact legislation. Those opposed to a bill—even when they hold a minority opinion—can draw on an assortment of maneuvers that may potentially block action on a bill. When those opposed to a bill happen to include the chair and ranking minority member of the committee that has jurisdiction over the bill, the chances that the committee will favorably report the bill are remote. Only when supporters are able to exert considerable force can a bill be dislodged from stubborn committee leadership.

Such was the case of the full employment bill in the House, and it took the intervention of the president to resolve the stalemate. The groups against the full employment bill emerged forcefully when the House considered the issue. The House action on the full employment bill exemplifies the struggle that occurs when strong forces for change collide with the unswerving power of the status quo.

COMMITTEE ASSIGNMENT ALTERS THE BILL'S COURSE

From the outset in the House, H.R. 2202, a bill almost identical to the original Senate bill, faced an uphill battle because the House parliamentarian assigned it and a similar bill (H.R. 4181) to a committee with conservative leadership. The House Committee on Banking and Currency was chaired by Brent Spence (D-KY), a loyal supporter of the New Deal, and had among its members H.R. 2202 cosponsors Wright Patman (D-TX) and George Outland (D-CA).[1] Banking and Currency would have seemed a more appropriate committee to handle such a major economic policy measure. However, the Committee on Expenditures in the Executive Department (hereafter referred to as the Executive Expenditures Committee) had jurisdiction over all matters concerning the Bureau of the Budget. Parliamentarian Lewis Deschler referred it to the Executive Expenditures Committee because he concluded that the budget process was the central thrust of the proposal.[2] Although there had been internal discussion within the administration over whether the Bureau of the Budget or a newly created agency should set full employment policy, the administration as well as the bill's congressional sponsors had apparently not weighed the committee jurisdictional consequences of designating the bureau as the lead agency.

The conservative reputations of Executive Expenditures Committee Chairman Carter Manasco (D-AL) and ranking minority member Clare Hoffman (R-MI) signaled that the bill would not receive a warm reception.[3] During the 1930s, Manasco had been the secretary to Representative William B. Bankhead when Bankhead was Speaker of the House. After Bankhead's death in 1940, Manasco won that seat in the House in 1941. Although Bankhead had been a strong supporter of the New Deal, Manasco did not share his mentor's liberalism. Hoffman, the ranking member of the Executive Expenditures Committee, was a vociferous critic of organized labor and the New Deal. His staunch isolationist stand and his popularity with anti-Semitic groups and other extreme elements on the right led to accusations that Hoffman had fascist sympathies.[4] Hoffman was much more strident and controversial than the ranking member of the Banking and Currency Committee, Jesse Wolcott, who was also from Michigan.[5]

Although H.R. 2202 and S. 380 were introduced simultaneously, the House proceeded more slowly on the legislation. The Senate was in the midst of the final floor debate and vote on S. 380 before the House Executive Expenditures Committee even began hearings on H.R. 2202 and H.R. 4181. The slow start, however, did not prevent the Executive Expenditures Committee from devoting most of its attention during this session of the 79th Congress to the full employment bill.

The character of the Executive Expenditures Committee's deliberations differed markedly from the tone of the deliberations in the Senate Committee on Banking and Currency. Unlike the Senate Banking and Currency Committee, the House Executive Expenditures Committee did not solicit the views of people within the administration who would have been responsible for implementing the full employment bill. Although the Executive Expenditures Committee did invite administration representatives and proponents of the full employment bill to testify, they gave free reign to those opposed to the proposal. As the House hearings proceeded during the autumn of 1945, the arguments against the full employment bill were diverse—sometimes sophisticated, sometimes strident, and always strongly held.

The vagueness of the term "full employment" was the object of much criticism by those testifying against H.R. 2202. Walter Spahr, professor of economics at New York University and spokesman for the National Association of State Chambers of Commerce, questioned not only whether full employment could be defined but also what constituted regular and full-time employment.[6] Spahr wondered further whether the term full employment applied to seasonal and migratory workers and those in between jobs (U.S. Congress 1945c, p. 468).

This criticism of vagueness, as the proponents realized, was difficult to respond to because the term "full employment" was conceptual rather than tangible. Economists offered theoretical definitions and formulae for full employment that were too sophisticated for a general audience to comprehend. While someone educated in Keynesian economics was able to answer Spahr's questions satisfactorily, most people were confounded by such questions.

In addition to the charges that the terms were nebulous, opponents raised doubts about the validity of economic forecasting, a necessary ingredient in the bill. The California State Chamber of Commerce characterized the bill as requiring "the President and Congress to take immediate action to fill some unknown gap between this obviously unreliable forecast of spending and employment and a vaguely defined condition of full employment." The opposition was quick to point out that the federal government had often erred in its economic forecasts. A spokesman for the Illinois Manufacturers Association remarked that estimates of federal expenditures had been off target by 14 percent in 1935, by 30 percent in 1937, and by 27 percent in 1939. One speaker feared that if the bill was approved a small group of statisticians would control the entire economy. This distrust of forecasts and econometricians pervaded the remarks of those who testified in opposition to the bill (U.S. Congress 1945c, pp. 473, 495, 707).

Opponents of H.R. 2202 also maintained that the government was incapable of achieving full employment. The West Virginia Chamber of Commerce held that since the bill's provisions could not be enforced nor its objectives attained, the measure would lead to frustration and discord. The New York Chamber of Commerce asserted that "only a totalitarian government could assume and possibly fulfill the responsibility of directing all economic activities and providing jobs for everybody" (U.S. Congress 1945c, pp. 451, 455).

The extent to which some committee members agreed with the criticisms that the bill was nebulous, ill-defined, and unfeasible was revealed in the members' reactions to Walter Spahr's statement that the bill was a series of assertions cut loose from realities. Clare Hoffman and Robert Rich (R-PA) both echoed Spahr's remarks and used them as springboards for their own observations. When Charles La Follette (R-IN) objected to Hoffman and Rich's unsolicited testimonies, which he called "stump speeches," a feisty exchange ensued. The acrimony peaked as John Cochran (D-MO), a liberal who had cosponsored the bill, asked Spahr rather challenging questions, and Hoffman interjected his own remarks to disrupt the discussion.[7] It was apparent that House members opposed to the legislation were much less restrained than their counterparts in the Senate and went on the offensive with zest (U.S. Congress 1945c, p. 470).

The provision that aroused the greatest concern among opponents of H.R. 2202 was that of right to employment. They surmised that H.R. 2202 would disrupt the free market by guaranteeing jobs to all workers. They expressed particular objection to the implication that the government would be the employer of last resort. They maintained that business would have to compete with government for workers and that inflated wages would result. A few opponents also speculated that the bill would establish legal grounds for unemployed workers to sue the government for employment (U.S. Congress 1945c, pp. 606, 658).

The right-to-employment provision was caught up in a sometimes subtle, sometimes overt hostility toward organized labor on the part of those testifying against the bill. James Donnelly, executive vice president of the Illinois Manufacturers' Association (IMA), asserted that workers should be free to work where they pleased without paying tribute to persons or organizations for the right to employment, an obvious reference to the open-versus-closed shop debate (U.S. Congress 1945c, pp. 47, 638, 666–667, 708).[8]

Personal disgust over the United Auto Workers strike occurring in his home state of Michigan prompted Hoffman to interrupt the testimony of fellow congressman Patman to declare his own views regarding idle workers: "Now wait a minute," he challenged. "You were speaking about these men who can't get jobs. In Michigan today there are many employers who can't get workers." Hoffman went on with his veiled criticism of labor unions: "And while we are talking about full employment, have you any plan whereby those who apparently don't want to work now can be persuaded, peacefully I mean, of course, by inducement, to go to work?" (U.S. Congress 1945c, pp. 47, 638, 666–667, 708). The fear that the enactment of this legislation would increase the power of organized labor was implied by various other opponents of the bill and foreshadowed the sentiments that led to the passage of the Taft-Hartley Act the following year.[9]

The opponents of H.R. 2202 also stated that a right-to-employment clause would destroy incentive. Indeed, they argued that the entire bill undermined the work ethic. They maintained that the legislation would create a secondary labor force that would be continuously dependent on government funds and whose numbers would escalate. Workers, they contended, would simply lose the motivation to find jobs in the private sector if the government pledged to find jobs for them (U.S. Congress 1945c, p. 1123).

Several of those who testified against the bill voiced the fear that the legislation would induce individuals to sacrifice their personal freedom for the promise of full employment. The Merchants and Manufacturers Association went so far as to say, "Full employment is closely akin to slavery." Millard Brown of the Philadelphia Textile Manufacturers Association concluded that full employment legislation was the first step toward Nazism and communism.[10] This charge of totalitarianism was not uncommon among those who testified against the bill. Echoes of Hayek's *The Road to Serfdom* were heard throughout the hearings (U.S. Congress 1945c, pp. 803, 1161).

Several of the arguments against the full employment bill derived from ideological controversies within the field of macroeconomics, specifically regarding Keynesian theory. As one would have expected, those who rejected Keynesian economic theory also opposed full employment legislation. The New York Chamber of Commerce called the theories of Lord Keynes fallacious. The *New York Times* economics writer Henry Hazlitt, who was testifying on behalf of the American Enterprise Association, quipped regarding Keynesian theory, "It is to economics what chiropractic is to medicine."[11] More evenhandedly, Spahr indicated that there were intellectual disputes among economists regarding Keynesian economics (U.S. Congress 1945c, pp. 196, 451).

Hazlitt also warned against the dangers of deficit spending. Most of those testifying against the bill compared the federal budget to an individual's personal finances, concluding that debts were bad, regardless of who incurs them. Chairman Manasco joined James Donnelly of the IMA in speculating that deficit spending by the federal government would lead to totalitarianism (U.S. Congress 1945c, pp. 197, 711).

A few opponents expanded the arguments, stating that deficit spending would stimulate inflation. Willford I. King, economist and chairman of the Committee for Constitutional Government, maintained that providing full-time, remunerative employment for anyone not employed by private industry would require approximately $68.5 billion annually, and that this amount pumped into circulation each year would result in inflation.[12] This inflation would wipe out profits and thus would stymie industrial expansion. Hazlitt concurred with King and warned that the bill's lack of antideficit provisions came at the very time a balanced federal budget was essential (U.S. Congress 1945c, pp. 133, 197, 203).

The opponents of H.R. 2202 emphasized that it would harm private enterprise during the critical postwar period. Donnelly stressed that the bill would retard production and decrease job opportunities, particularly in small businesses. "This bill, if enacted," the Connecticut Chamber of Commerce stated, "will prove another link in a chain to fetter free competitive enterprise, thus discouraging the investment of private capital in trade and commerce, retarding development of our natural resources, and creating unemployment rather than full employment." This reasoning argued that incentives to private enterprise, rather than a full employment program, would foster a strong postwar economy (U.S. Congress 1945c, pp. 446, 706).

Critics suggested that forecasting unemployment and recessions would prove to be self-fulfilling prophesies. The Committee for Economic Development's Ralph Flanders used a folksy analogy of the Joneses deciding not to buy kitchen linoleum because the newspapers had predicted a depression.[13] Donnelly and Manasco concurred that pessimistic economic predictions would accelerate a depression because manufacturers would reduce inventories and consumers would curtail purchases (U.S. Congress 1945c, pp. 593, 711).

Witnesses speaking in opposition to H.R. 2202 described depressions as natural fluctuations in the business cycle. Donnelly advanced the view that depressions were not typical of the U.S. economy, stating that there were only three instances prior to the 1930s when more than three million people were unemployed. Several of those opposed to H.R. 2202 implied that the personal hardships precipitated by depressions had been exaggerated. Speaking from his own experiences and observations of depressions in both the 1890s and 1930s, Hoffman asserted that people "had enough to eat, a good place to sleep, and enough to wear." He challenged one witness to cite evidence of local communities that did not take care of people in need. Hoffman, however, cut off the response when the witness proceeded to cite specific instances of hardships that went unmet by local communities (U.S. Congress 1945c, pp. 81, 713).

Chairman Manasco struck a chord that harmonized with those testifying against H.R. 2202 when he rhetorically asked, "I am just wondering if our people are sufficiently alarmed with the essential dangers of a planned economy." To many of those opposed, the planning embodied in the legislation connoted something more than elite statisticians determining policies through forecasts, more than strong unions setting high wages, more than unemployed workers suing for jobs, more than unbridled deficit financing (U.S. Congress 1945c, pp. 802, 997).

Economic planning, for those who shared Manasco's view, was something that violated the essence of the free enterprise system. No one captured this sentiment better than Albert S. Goss, master of the National Grange. "The government's chief role in a free enterprise system," he asserted, "is to see that it is free . . . Under such a system America has developed a standard of living so much higher than any other nation in history, that we can see no sound reason for abandoning it" (U.S. Congress 1945c, pp. 802, 997).

Manasco and Hoffman represented constituencies that were overwhelmingly rural, as did Goss. It was this rural base of many opponents to full employment legislation that led Stephen Bailey to conclude that the legislation the House passed was the product of the provincial perspective of many House members. Chairman Manasco, from the rural coal-mining region of Alabama, however, had a very different background from that of Clare Hoffman, who hailed from an agricultural area along Lake Michigan, or that of Goss, who came from the eastern part of Washington State. Observers at that time were oversimplifying matters when they assumed that rural Americans held uniform views.

A more nuanced view from the nonurbanized portion of America emerged in the testimony of Republican businessman James S. Schramm of Burlington, Iowa.[14] Schramm provided a midwestern assessment of the legislation, referring to Iowa farmers as rugged individualists who do not like bureaucracy and unnecessary controls. He acknowledged that they had learned there were some things they could not do for themselves: Iowans agreed, he said, that there were "some things the city and county governments must do for them, some the State must do, and some things only the Federal Government can do . . . And I don't think we can trust to luck for economic stability and full employment in peacetime any more than we could trust American war production to luck" (U.S. Congress 1945c, p. 206).

Despite the various arguments voiced against full employment, and despite the interjections of Manasco and Hoffman, most of the opinions expressed during the hearings reflected the sentiments of James Schramm. Spokespersons for a variety of religious and social welfare organizations, such as the YWCA, the National Council of Jewish Women, the American Association of Social Workers, and the Congregational Christian Churches, endorsed the legislation. The American Federation of Labor, the United Mine Workers, and the Congress of Industrial Organizations delivered the support of organized labor. Representatives of the agricultural community were split, as the American Farm Bureau and the National Grange opposed the bill and the National Farmers Union and the Agricultural Workers Union advocated it. African American groups represented by the National Association for the Advancement of Colored People and the National Urban League offered unified support for the bill.

The Truman administration sent Secretary of Commerce Henry Wallace, Secretary of Agriculture Clinton Anderson, Secretary of Labor Lewis Schwellenbach, and Secretary of the Treasury Fred Vinson to Congress to stress the importance of this legislation. Harold Smith, director of the Bureau of the Budget, John Snyder, director of War Mobilization and Reconversion, and General Omar Bradley, administrator of Veterans Affairs, also testified in favor of the measure.

Perhaps Mrs. Henry Ingram of the YWCA best captured the essence of the support for full employment legislation in her testimony. She declared the following:

> This bill is championed by numerous organizations, covering the social work field, religious leaders, small business and labor. But the demand, however inarticulate, for full employment is far wider and far stronger than any organization can indicate. It is the one thing that American workers, be they white collar or industrial, have on their minds. They may not know about legislative proposals but they know they want jobs for all. Everyone remembers and dreads another depression. Everyone has seen what America can produce when it has to. Workers will not forget these lessons . . . The American people will not tolerate more depressions. (U.S. Congress 1945c, p. 1142)

TRUMAN PRESSES FOR ACTION

Many liberal leaders of the day, as well as subsequent scholars of the period, have criticized President Truman for not acting with sufficient conviction and speed on the full employment bill. The thrust of this criticism is that Truman did not push for the passage of S. 380/H.R. 2202 until the autumn of 1945 and that he was too willing to sacrifice major features of the bill in order to have some kind of employment legislation enacted. The critics characterized Truman's stance as drifting and indecisive (Bernstein and Matusow 1966, pp. 11–13; Donovan 1977, pp. 122–124; Hamby 1973, p. 63).

Several factors, however, point to the need for a reappraisal of these judgments. Most important is the fact that since the bill had passed the Senate with bipartisan support and few changes, there had been little need for Truman to engage in active lobbying for the bill's passage. Second, within weeks of the victory in World War II in August, Truman had turned his attention to the domestic front and had begun to push for passage of the full employment legislation. Truman thus entered the fray at the earliest appropriate time.

Truman made it clear that full employment was a top priority of his domestic agenda. He emphasized full employment legislation as a major objective in his September 6 radio message. *Time* magazine, though critical of the full employment bill, reported that the public response to Truman's speech was positive. *Time* also pointed out that, immediately following the speech, the stock market jumped to its highest point in eight years, and the magazine implied that Truman's postwar economic plan was the stimulus (*Time* 1945f).

Truman followed his public pronouncements by assigning to specific agencies of the executive branch the tasks of supporting various aspects of this legislation and giving the Office of War Mobilization and Reconversion the job of overall coordination. By October he had established a special cabinet-level committee (hereafter referred to as the cabinet committee) to work exclusively with Congress to ensure quick passage of the full employment bill.[15]

The cabinet committee consisted of Secretary of the Treasury Vinson, Secretary of Commerce Wallace, Secretary of Agriculture Anderson, and Secretary of Labor Schwellenbach. At its first meeting on October 16, the cabinet committee decided that it could operate most effectively if its existence were not revealed, because the members wanted to avoid the impression of an organized campaign.[16] The effect of this covert strategy was difficult to assess, but it no doubt contributed to scholars' underestimating the administration's role in the process.

It was abundantly clear to the members of the cabinet committee that their task of lobbying the House on the full employment bill was going to be a tough assignment. Chairman Manasco had just been quoted in a national publication as saying he was "leery" of the bill. The Alabaman went on to say that he thought the only jobs that the full employment bill would create would be jobs for bureaucratic planners (*Newsweek* 1945b).

In addition to Manasco, the cabinet committee identified William Whittington (D-MS) and Joseph Mansfield (D-TX) as key congressmen who were hostile to the bill.[17] They recommended that Truman talk to each of these congressmen personally to underscore how important this bill was to the administration. They were especially emphatic that the president see the members individually so that the three would not be able to present a united front.[18]

Within a few days of the receipt of the cabinet committee's recommendation, Truman met separately with Manasco, Whittington, and Mansfield. To the cabinet committee in a meeting to outline lobbying strategy, the president appraised the men's responses in these discussions. Manasco had remained fundamentally opposed to any legislation for full employment but was noncommittal regarding a completely emasculated employment bill. Mansfield had remained unconvinced but indicated he would support some employment measure. Whittington had said that he might go along if his own ideas on employment policy were incorporated into the measure. By the end of October, it was clear to the administration that Whittington would play the pivotal role in determining the fate of the full employment legislation.[19]

Truman wrote House Speaker John McCormack on October 29 to express his concern that the House act on the legislation. "I am most anxious," Truman began, "that the House Committee on Expenditures of Executive Departments report out the full employment legislation. Such legislation is of the utmost urgency and importance to the future of our nation." Truman went on to say that it would be reckless to "wait and see" if mass unemployment reoccurred before enacting the legislation and that it was not enough to have a transition to temporary prosperity. Truman indicated that he was not referring to any specific bill, but to the general purposes and principles of full employment legislation.[20] This remark probably referenced the fact that Truman was aware that the Executive Expenditures Committee was rewriting S. 380 and that he was willing to approve any bill reported out as long as it adhered to the basic tenets of full employment.

Replying to a letter from Eleanor Roosevelt urging him to do all he could to ensure that Congress enacted full employment legislation, Truman affirmed that he was most anxious to have the full employment program enacted. The new president also conveyed the frustration of a reformer. "As you probably learned long ago," he related to Mrs. Roosevelt, "it is not easy to get the right kind of people with the correct social point of view who have influence with those Congressmen who are blocking the program."[21]

HOUSE MEMBERS NEGOTIATE A COMPROMISE

The oft-repeated version of the House action on the full employment bill maintains that the Executive Expenditures Committee overwhelmingly voted down the original proposal and subsequently wrote a substitute bill. Hoffman asserted during the floor debate in December that the committee had voted down H.R. 2202 by a resounding vote of 17 "nays" to 3 "yeas" at a November 7, 1945, committee meeting. Apparently Hoffman was trying to minimize support for full employment (Bailey 1964, p. 164–166).

Although the minutes of the Executive Expenditures Committee are terse, they provide sufficient detail to contradict the Hoffman account and to reveal a series of close votes and compromises. During the first meeting after the hearings on November 7, Edward Gossett (D-TX) moved to appoint a subcommittee to study a substitute measure that would not be reported before January 1946.[22] To stymie this delaying tactic, Cochran, a sponsor of H.R. 2202, offered a substitute motion to appoint a subcommittee to study and draw up a substitute bill to be submitted to the whole committee but with no set date. The Cochran substitute passed in the committee with an 8-7 vote. Both liberals and conservatives voted for the Cochran plan. The subcommittee they formed consisted of Manasco, Whittington, Cochran, Hoffman, and George Bender (R-OH).[23] In setting no date for the committee to report, Cochran no doubt assumed that public, presidential, and congressional pressure would compel the subcommittee to offer a bill before the session ended.[24]

By this time, the Truman administration had already mapped out a strategy to ensure that the Expenditures Committee reported out H.R. 2202 before the session ended. When Secretary Vinson had confidentially conferred with Whittington early in November, he realized that the Mississippi congressman would drive a hard bargain before acquiescing on full employment legislation. Truman and the cabinet committee agreed to a set of compromise points on the bill as "an approach that will work."[25]

Although some have written that Truman consented to Vinson's suggestion that the term "full employment" be dropped from the bill in order to appease the conservatives, Truman instructed Vinson that the compromise terms should preserve the full-employment language as well as the right-to-employment clause. The Truman administration offered to change the title to the "Full Production and Full Employment Policy Act" and to add the words, "full production" wherever the bill mentions full employment, thereby broadening and diffusing the purpose of the measure. They also agreed to emphasize that "action by the Federal Government shall be consistent with our system of free, competitive private enterprise." They further offered that no benefits under the act would be extended to persons able but unwilling to work (Donovan 1977, p. 122).[26]

As it turned out, the major point of controversy and negotiation between the administration and the subcommittee was the machinery for administering the policy. Whittington was adamant that a board of experts appointed by the president and approved by the Senate should administer the legislation. Although this idea had not received much attention during the Senate and House hearings, questions over administrative structure had been raised in various quarters.

Whittington's idea for a board of experts might well have been influenced by the Committee for Economic Development (CED). The CED had been formed in 1942 and was considered one of the most progressive business groups of the day, particularly because it endorsed economic planning (Graham 1976, pp. 10–15). The CED's Ralph Flanders had testified before the Executive Expenditures Committee's hearings on the full employment bill and had just unveiled the CED plan for full employment. This plan called for a "small working body of the ablest men" to serve as a presidential commission on full employment (*Time* 1945g).

Such an idea was not a new concept. In 1944, Leon Keyserling had proposed a "joint congressional executive structure" to prepare national budgets and engage in economic planning.[27] Since the previous year, economists in the executive branch had been debating whether full employment was best administered by the Bureau of the Budget or by a newly created agency. For example, V.O. Key had suggested a "Division of Economic Policy" within the Executive Office. Both Key and Colm had expressed the view that a new agency would be focused on full employment and that it would not have the competing responsibilities that the Bureau of the Budget had.[28]

The Truman administration responded to Whittington's proposal by agreeing to six of its conditions: 1) that the president would direct and supervise the preparation of the national budget as stipulated in S. 380; 2) that the bill would establish a National Budget Council composed of the secretaries of Treasury (who would serve as council chairman), Agriculture, Commerce, and Labor; 3) that this council would advise and assist the president in the preparation of the national budget and would consult other agencies of government, business, and labor; 4) that the council would coordinate and direct the statistical planning and research and work with the Bureau of the Budget to obtain necessary data; 5) that this council would cooperate with the Joint Committee on the National Budget, furnish it with copies of reports, and provide technical personnel when requested; and 6) that the council would appoint an executive director and such staff as necessary to discharge its functions.[29]

Meanwhile, the subcommittee had drawn up a confidential substitute proposal. This recommendation struck out all of the original bill after the enacting clause and replaced it with what was basically a new bill.[30] Although some of the language changes retained ideas consistent with the original bill, other provisions of the new bill were at odds with the fundamental principles of full employment.

One of the most ardently argued provisions of the full employment bill, the right-to-employment clause, did not survive. The subcommittee even rejected Senator Fulbright's compromise language stating that "all Americans able to work and seeking work are entitled to an opportunity for useful, remunerative, regular and full-time employment." The subcommittee's substitute bill offered instead only an occasional reference to "aiding and assisting the employables."[31]

The original HR. 2202 and the Senate-passed bill provided for a carefully planned economic program and specified a wide variety of tools to be utilized and areas to be targeted in planning for a full employment economy. The subcommittee proposal did not mention any specific policy areas. Rather, it made more general references to "planning and adopting a program of sound public works, consistent with a financially sound fiscal policy."

The subcommittee substitute stripped the bill of its provision of countercyclical, compensatory spending by the federal government. H.R. 2202 and S. 380 designated the government to provide "such volume of Federal investment and expenditure as may be needed, in addition to the investment and expenditure by private enterprises, consumers, and State and local government, to achieve the objective of continuing full employment." The revised version no longer mandated such Keynesian economic policies.

Both the original and the subcommittee substitute provided for the creation of a joint congressional committee, the former bill calling it the Joint Committee on the National Budget and the latter bill designating it the Joint Committee on the Economic Report. The size of the committee was altered in the revision, but in each proposal it was made up of an equal number of Senate and House members and required that the partisan composition should reflect the relative membership of the majority and minority parties in each chamber.

The "Economic Report of the President" replaced the "National Production and Employment Budget" in the subcommittee substitute. The latter required the president to transmit a budget detailing estimates for the number of employment opportunities needed for full employment, the production of goods and services at full employment, and the volume of investment and expenditure needed for such; current trends in employment opportunities, production, investment, and expenditures; a general program to ensure full employment, including measures to prevent inflation or deflation; and a review of the performance of the previous year's economic program. The president was to submit this budget annually as well as transmit quarterly economic reports to Congress.

The Economic Report of the President was to be submitted at the beginning of each session of Congress. Although the language of the substitute provision was entirely new, the basic thrust was the same. The economic report was not a budget per se, but it served to review and forecast economic conditions and to offer specific programs to attain high levels of employment, production, and purchasing power and to alleviate inflationary conditions. The significant element in this new language emerged when viewed alongside the Budget and Accounting Act of 1921. The latter gave the president sole responsibility for the national budget and created the position of director of the budget to carry out this responsibility under the direction of the president. The new language retained presidential responsibility but assigned the task to a newly created entity, not the Bureau of the Budget.

This new entity was the Council of Economic Advisers, Whittington's board of experts. Although Whittington had not agreed to the Truman administration's compromise offer of a "cabinet committee/executive director" structure, he dropped the stipulation that council members be confirmed by Congress, and he went along with reducing the area in which they could make independent investigations and limiting the authority of Congress to obtain reports from the council. Now the president was to appoint to this three-member council individuals whose training, experience, and attainments made them "exceptionally qualified to analyze and interpret economic developments, to appraise programs and activities of the government . . . and to formulate and recommend national economic policy to promote employment and production under the American system of free competitive enterprise."[32] As a result, this consolidation of the planning authority created a flexible, and possibly powerful, apparatus for national economic planning.

Whittington sought the views of Secretary of the Treasury Vinson regarding the subcommittee substitute. Treasury Department economists who had reviewed the draft had called it "a stinker." Vinson's formal comments to Whittington were less colorful but quite critical. Beginning his reply by stating that the Senate bill was superior, Vinson acknowledged that the subcommittee had made a sincere effort and conceded that they had spotted two weaknesses in the bill: its insufficient emphasis on full production and purchasing power and its inadequate machinery for the preparation of the national budget. Vinson advanced justifications for full employment and the need for the bill to specify those objectives to achieve full employment. He also contended that the Council of Economic Advisers undermined presidential authority in the budget process. Vinson recounted that Congress had decided not to have the Senate confirm the director of the Bureau of the Budget because the Budget and Accounting Act of 1921 gave the president sole responsibility and freedom in the preparation of the federal budget. Vinson opposed the council as a staff agency of the president that would be the "handyman for Congress."[33]

Following the receipt of Vinson's letter, Whittington advised the secretary that he was willing to yield to some degree to the administration, but not on the establishment of the council. The final subcommittee bill reduced the extent to which Congress would have had authority over the council and the extent to which Congress could make requests of the council. Most importantly, Whittington assured Vinson that he would be "reasonable" when the conference committee considered the bill.[34]

THE HOUSE MOVES ON THE LEGISLATION

When the Executive Expenditures Committee met on November 27, 1945, to consider the subcommittee substitute for S. 380, which Whittington presented, various committee members offered minor amendments that would have weakened the compromise bill even further. These amendments failed by close votes that reflected the ideological alignment of the committee. Gossett again moved to postpone consideration of the bill until January 15, 1946, but this delaying action failed by a 10-10 split.[35]

The first committee vote on the bill became entangled in a series of amendments, in part because of the refusal of some sponsors to compromise. While other sponsors were willing to support the substitute, some joined the opponents in voting against the compromise. Bender first moved to strike all of the bill's language after the enacting clause of S. 380 and insert the text of H.R. 2202, the original House version. Bender was one of four committee members who sponsored the initial legislation and was the only Republican committee member to have done so. The other sponsors on the committee were Alexander Resa (D-IL), William Dawson (D-IL), who later chaired the Executive Expenditures Committee, and Cochran.[36] It was Cochran who interceded, offering a substitute amendment to strike out all of the bill's language after the enacting clause of S. 380 and insert the text of the subcommittee version. The Cochran motion failed by a vote of 13 "nays" to 7 "yeas," with several advocates of full employment voting against the amendment. When the initial Bender motion finally came to a vote, three people voted for it.[37]

The subcommittee met the following day to resume consideration of the subcommittee substitute. After making some semantic changes, the committee once again voted down a motion to postpone consideration of the bill until January 15, 1946. The split was a narrow vote of 7 "nays" to 6 "yeas." The committee then ironed out details such as the composition of the Joint Committee and the salaries of the council.[38]

When the committee convened on November 29, Rep. Ralph Church (R-IL) yet again moved to withhold action until after recess—i.e., until January 15, 1946. This time more members were present, and the margin was 11 opposed versus 9 in favor. At last, on December 5, 1945, the

Executive Expenditures Committee met and voted to delete everything after the enacting clause and insert the substitute, now known as Committee Substitute 380, Print No. 3. The vote was 13 "yeas," 5 "nays," and 1 "present." The members asked Whittington to write the committee report.[39]

Both at the time and subsequently, observers criticized the assignment of the bill to the Executive Expenditures Committee, maintaining that the committee's conservative reputation doomed the bill. Wright Patman speculated that a different committee might have reported out the original bill he had sponsored. Stephen Bailey puts the referral of the bill to the conservative Executive Expenditures Committee first on his list of factors that determined the fate of the full employment bill (Bailey 1964, p. 178; *Congressional Record* 1945c, p. 12024).

The construction of an ideology score based upon 10 roll call votes that the Union for Democratic Action (UDA) highlighted as key liberal votes in a *New Republic* article enables us to further explore this question of the conservative bias of the Executive Expenditures Committee.[40] The members of the Executive Expenditures Committee as a whole averaged an ideology score of +0.05, in the middle of the spectrum. When one compares the committee score to the average ideology score for the entire House of Representatives, which was +0.02, one can hardly maintain that the Executive Expenditures Committee was uniquely conservative. However, the House Banking and Currency Committee, a logical alternative, averaged an ideology score of +0.10, had a liberal chairman in Brent Spence, and arguably might have been more likely to report out a version more akin to the Senate-passed bill.[41]

In mid-December, Congressman Whittington submitted the majority report of Executive Expenditures Committee to Congress. He contrasted the substitute version with the Senate bill and asserted that government assurance of full employment would destroy the free enterprise system. Whittington emphasized that it was definitely not a federal responsibility to guarantee the right to employment. He also contended that experience demonstrated that government spending did not promote high levels of employment or prosperity. He did, however, make a strong case for economic planning. He maintained that the substitute bill would provide for sound coordination of public works programs and stimulation of private industry. He concluded that the Council of Economic Advisers would give the best available economic advice and, thus, enhance the quality and efficiency of handling the national economy (U.S. Congress 1945a).

Hoffman, Church, Gibson, and Rich submitted a minority report that stated, "At its best, the bill can only be construed as a planning measure, a new version of the discarded National Resources Planning Board." They argued that public support for H.R. 2202 was the result of fraudulent propaganda, and conjectured that the only jobs created by the bill would be the three positions on the council (U.S. Congress 1945a, pp. 16–18).

La Follette, Dawson, Hart, and Resa filed separate views with the Executive Expenditures Committee report. They echoed the principles of the original bill, particularly regarding the federal responsibility. Although they did not agree with all aspects of the committee report, they voted to report out the legislation so that the entire membership of the House could vote on the subject (U.S. Congress 1945a, pp. 18–20).

S. 380 COMES TO THE HOUSE FLOOR

The two-day debate in the House, which began on December 13, 1945, differed markedly from the Senate debate a few months earlier. The members of the House of Representatives spent little time discussing the matters of public finance and federal budgets that the Senators had debated for several days in September. Issues such as public works, inflation, taxes, and compensatory spending were not among the major themes when the House considered S. 380. Rather, much of the House debate was between two streams of American populism—one that warned against unfettered big business and one that warned against unfettered big government.

Opponents of H.R. 2202 gained a critical procedural advantage when Manasco obtained the order of the rule regarding the debate and floor action just as he had requested it. The committee substitute to S. 380 was to be the legislative vehicle. The Democratic leadership of the House Committee on the Rules had broken with Speaker of the House John McCormack over New Deal legislation. At this point in time, Speaker McCormack held no sway to structure the debate over legislation he strongly supported. The control of the debate would be equally divided between Manasco and Hoffman. Such a division of the debate between the ranking committee members of each party was not uncommon, but in this case it resulted in two members controlling the debate who were hostile to both H.R. 2202 as introduced and S. 380 as passed by the Senate.[42] More importantly, the Rules Committee had consented to a five-minute rule that permitted the exclusion of the original and the Senate-passed versions from consideration and forced the choice to be between the substitute or a vote to recommit (*Congressional Record* 1945c, p. 11972).

Manasco opened the debate with his arguments against H.R. 2202 as introduced and S. 380 as passed by the Senate. "Of course, you can give full employment by tax dollars or by borrowing money," he said (*Congressional Record* 1945c, p. 11973), "but when the Federal Government borrows money or when it taxes people you are taking money that would ordinarily be used by private investors to give jobs to our people." Manasco speculated that the federal government would have had to pay the prevailing wage to employ a man to "count trees" to maintain full employment. As he concluded his opening statement, the congressman from Alabama became passionate, populist, and personal:

> I have heard a lot of these people beating their chest for the under dog and the under privileged . . . I think I know as much about the under dog and the under privileged as any man in this House. I was born the son of a tenant farmer who had pellagra, and anybody knows that a man who has pellagra has it because of deficiency in his diet. My father lay flat on his back and my mother was keeping boarders to feed five hungry mouths, and yet I am accused of being a tool of Wall Street when I get up and protect a system that made it possible for a son of a tenant farmer to be a Member of Congress. (*Congressional Record* 1945c, p. 11976)

Manasco subsequently turned much of the time he controlled over to Whittington, who presented the case for the substitute measure. Whittington proceeded to take the middle course. "I assert that the sound policy of government is to promote rather than guarantee employment." he said (p. 11980). He devoted much of his time to describing the economic planning features and procedural elements of the legislation. When queried by Hoffman, Whittington acknowledged that he objected to H.R. 2202 because he was convinced it would lead to socialism. He maintained that the committee substitute was a "constructive approach to the problem of unemployment" (*Congressional Record* 1945c, p. 11982).

Along with Whittington, Cochran spoke on behalf of the committee substitute. He stated that the employment planning envisioned in the bill would create beneficial public works, rather than jobs to "rake leaves." Cochran also pointed out, "Do not forget that when you talk about private industry, that private industry did not hesitate in 1933 to appeal to the President and the Congress to save it from destruction. It was willing then to have the Government come to its rescue" (*Congressional Record* 1945c, p. 11978).

The states' rights issue—perennially a hot-button topic—prompted an extended exchange between Congressmen Benton Jensen (R-IA) and Charles La Follette (R-IN) that echoed the Anti-Federalist populism of earlier times in American history.[43] As he spoke on the floor for full employment, La Follette asserted that his fellow Republicans "ought to abandon the idea of States' rights, because, actually, there is no State sovereignty." He continued, "The man who speaks of State sovereignty speaks the language of totalitarianism" (p. 11979). Jensen challenged La Follette by stating that certain rights had been left to the states and that state governments were closer to the people. "Because a government close to the people is more effective is why I think we should preserve States' rights," Jensen said. He concluded, "I still contend there are such things as States' rights" (*Congressional Record* 1945c, p. 11980).

La Follette did not relent to Jensen or to a subsequent challenge by Congressman George Bates (R-MA).[44] Instead, he grew more emphatic in his argument countering the Anti-Federalist tradition:

> Let me repeat, there are no States' rights. There are rights of the people who live in the State of Iowa, but they themselves can delegate to the government of the State of Iowa those things which they think the State of Iowa will do better for them . . . Of course, there was an argument about States' rights in the Continental Congress and the Convention which created the Constitution, because it is always true that people who have power to govern other people—government—hate to give it up, but the people of the State of Massachusetts determined that in order to have a full government—a government which could serve them better—they would delegate a part of their sovereignty to a new Federal Government so that they might be better served. (*Congressional Record* 1945c, p. 11980)

Congressman Fritz Lanham (D-TX) offered his view on the role of the federal government in opposition to La Follette and to the other supporters of the employment legislation:[45]

> I think it is high time that we get back to our organic law, which in my judgment has been disrupted in a great many respects, and adhere to the principles upon which this Government was established. Give free enterprise a fair chance to go into operation, and remove these restrictions that are preventing it from operating and from giving employment. There is a lot of employment in this country available today that people will not accept. (*Congressional Record* 1945c, p. 12008)

The preceding rhetoric over states' rights and the role of the federal government, however, seemed tame in retrospect after Congressman John Gibson (D-GA) asked, "Do you people actually believe we are doing anything but destroying this country when we set the Government up in business throughout the length and breadth of this land?"[46] Gibson grew more agitated. "Talk about this do-good business, helping the poor. I get so sick of that, I get so sick and tired of hearing it until I become nauseated" (p. 11986). It was Gibson, along with Church, who led much of the floor fight against the passage of any employment bill, including the committee substitute to S. 380. Frequent innuendos, and sometimes accusations, of socialism, communism, or fascism peppered the remarks of some who opposed the employment bills (*Congressional Record* 1945c, pp. 11966–12028).

In the meantime, it appeared that a sufficient number of members who had sponsored H.R. 2202 were ready to vote "no" on the committee substitute to S. 380, which Emanuel Celler (D-NY) quipped had been "written by the best minds of the eighteenth century" (*Congressional Record* 1945c, p. 12071).[47] Along with the opponents to any employment bill, these discontented proponents of full employment seemed prepared to stop passage of the committee substitute to S. 380. As Walter Granger (D-UT) stated, "It is like the choice that is sometimes given to a criminal when he has been convicted. They ask him whether he would rather be shot or hanged" (p. 12085).[48]

H.R. 2202 sponsors Wright Patman and George Outland continued to argue for the strongest bill possible. Patman began on December 13 by charging that his bill had been misunderstood as well as misrepresented. He made clear that he was "opposed to all of these 'isms,' like fascism, communism, and socialism." He also quoted Thomas Dewey, the Republican presidential nominee in 1944, who reportedly had said, "If at any time there are not sufficient jobs in private employment to go around, the Government can, and must, create job opportunities, because there must be jobs for all in this country of ours . . . That is everybody's business. Therefore, it is the business of government" (p. 12088).[49] Patman concluded on December 14 by advocating for a "real full employment bill" to prevent the boom and bust of postwar conversion. In direct response to House members who had labeled the Senate-passed version of S. 380 socialistic and communistic, Outland asked that the Senate roll call on S. 380 be read into the House record, noting the names of the senators who had voted for the bill (*Congressional Record* 1945c, pp. 11986–11990, 12084).

On December 14, Outland offered his own observation about states' rights and the role of the federal government: "You will recall . . . during the last depression how every mayor, every Governor of every State in this Union came to Washington asking for relief," he said. "We did not hear anything about communism then. We did not hear anything about socialism then. All we heard was the cry for help, because that help had to come from the Government as a whole." Outland spoke about the urgency "to fulfill our responsibilities to the American people" and "to take constructive action" to prevent depressions (*Congressional Record* 1945c, p. 12084).

Other proponents of H.R. 2202 rose in support of the original bill. To those who argued that full employment was the antithesis of free enterprise, Congressman Andrew John Biemiller (D-WI) asserted, "There is just one way the American free enterprise system will fall. That is if we continue to have recurring depressions, with large numbers of unemployed and nothing being done about it" (p. 12086). Congressman Jerry Voorhis (D-CA) expanded on this theme: "There are duties of government today which, if performed wisely and well, can increase the true freedom of not only our people but also our industry and agriculture" (*Congressional Record* 1945c, p. 12064).[50]

The floor action on December 14 intensified as the advocates for full employment legislation sought to circumvent the Rules Committee, which had prevented a vote on H.R. 2202 and the Senate-passed version of the bill. House Speaker John McCormack shared the objective of the Truman administration that at least some employment bill be passed by the House. The strategy assumed that the conference committee then would pattern the final legislation after the Senate-passed version. Supporters of the original legislation succeeded in bringing H.R. 2202 to a vote while the House was operating in the Committee of the Whole. The teller vote (roll call votes are not taken during proceedings of the Committee of the Whole) of 185 "nays" to 95 "yeas" signaled the failure of the full employment bill. A voice vote adopted the committee substitute (*Congressional Record* 1945c, pp. 12094–12095).

When the House came out of the Committee of the Whole, Hoffman moved to recommit the substitute bill. This tactic was defeated by a roll call vote of 243 "nays" to 136 "yeas." Finally, the House voted to enact the committee substitute with a roll call vote of 255 "yeas" to 126 "nays" (*Congressional Record* 1945c, pp. 12094–12095).

The House had yielded a very different version of S. 380 than the Senate had passed a few months earlier. The House-passed version had stripped S. 380 of its provisions on countercyclical, compensatory spending by the federal government. Instead, it made general references to planning and public works that were meant to be consistent with a financially sound fiscal policy. The provision that all Americans were entitled to useful remunerative work, which had been present in S. 380 as passed by the Senate, was replaced by language on aiding and assisting the "employables." The House-passed S. 380, however, had strengthened the structures responsible for economic planning by proposing a Council of Economic Advisers in the executive branch as well as a Joint Committee on the Economic Report in Congress. It now remained for the House-Senate Conference Committee to resolve the differences between the two bills.

Notes

1. Spence was elected in 1930 and served until 1963. He became chairman of the Banking and Currency Committee in 1943. Patman served in the House from 1926 to 1976. He advocated liberal social programs from the New Deal through the Great Society and chaired the Banking and Currency Committee from 1963 to 1975. Outland served from 1943 to 1947. He was defeated for reelection.
2. Deschler was appointed parliamentarian by Speaker Nicholas Longworth (R-OH) in 1927 and served to 1974. He is best known as the author of *Rules of Order* (1976, posthumously).

3. In 1948, liberal Carl Elliot defeated Manasco in the Democratic primary. From 1949 to 1985, Manasco served as the legislative counsel for the National Coal Association. Hoffman was elected from western Michigan in 1934 and served until his retirement at the end of 1962.
4. Although Hoffman remained a Republican throughout his congressional career, he reportedly flirted with the America First Party in 1944. Not to be confused with the America First Party formed in 2002, this party ran Gerald L. K. Smith for president in 1944 and later became the Christian Nationalist Crusade. For more on Hoffman and his alleged ties to fascist groups, see Walker (1982).
5. Wolcott generally opposed the New Deal. He served in Congress from 1931 to 1957. President Eisenhower appointed him to be a director of the Federal Deposit Insurance Corporation in 1958, where he served until 1964.
6. In 1933, Spahr was a founder of the Economists' National Committee on Monetary Policy, which lobbied for a return to the gold standard and opposed the monetary policies of the New Deal.
7. Rich was the general manager (and later president) of Woolrich Woolen Mills when he was elected to Congress in 1930. He served in Congress through 1950, with a break in 1943–1944. La Follette served from 1943 to 1947. He was a distant cousin of the Progressive congressman Robert La Follette, as well as a great-grandson of Congressman William Heilman. Cochran had served as staff for various congressmen from Missouri and was first elected to the House in 1926 to succeed the member for whom he had worked. In 1934 he ran unsuccessfully in the Democratic primary against Sen. Harry Truman. He retired at the end of 1946.
8. Donnelly later became a prominent attorney in Illinois, where he served as state finance chairman for Ronald Reagan's presidential campaigns.
9. The Taft-Hartley Act, which rolled back some of the worker rights that the National Labor Relations Act of 1935 had provided, proved to be one of the most controversial laws passed by the 80th Congress. It was enacted over President Truman's veto and became a rallying cry in his 1948 reelection campaign.
10. Brown had gained national attention during the 1934 strike of the textile workers in Pennsylvania (Salmond 2002).
11. The American Enterprise Association is now known as the American Enterprise Institute.
12. The Committee for Constitutional Government was interconnected with the National Committee to Uphold Constitutional Government, which had formed in opposition to Roosevelt's plan to increase the size of the U.S. Supreme Court. It evolved into an advocacy group with a broader conservative agenda.
13. Flanders was a successful businessman and president of the Federal Reserve Bank of Boston. He was appointed to the Senate in 1946 by Vermont governor Mortimer Proctor and represented Vermont until 1959.
14. Schramm managed the family business, Schramm's Department Store, from 1934 to 1962. He was active in the Iowa Republican Party, including a stint as chairman of the State Committee in the 1950s.
15. Harry S. Truman to Fred Vinson, 16 October 1945, Truman official file, Harry S. Truman Library and Museum, Independence, Missouri; Vinson to Truman, 22 October 1945, Truman official file.

16. Ibid.
17. Whittington represented the delta region of Mississippi from 1925 to 1950. He distanced himself from his fellow Mississippian, Sen. Theodore Bilbo, who was known for his adherence to the views of white supremacy and who was under Senate investigation for corruption when he died in 1947. Mansfield was elected in 1916 and served until his death in 1947.
18. Vinson to Truman, 22 October 1945, Truman official file.
19. Memorandum from the secretary of the treasury, "The Cabinet Committee Formula and the Full Employment Legislation," n.d., Truman official file (hereafter cited as Memorandum, "Cabinet Committee Formula").
20. Truman to John McCormack, 29 October 1945, Truman official file.
21. Eleanor Roosevelt to Truman, 1 November 1945, Truman official file; Truman to Eleanor Roosevelt, 6 November 1945, Truman official file.
22. Gossett was a conservative Democrat who served from 1939 to 1951.
23. Bender was first elected to Congress in 1938 and was a close ally of Ohio senator Robert Taft. Bender was appointed to serve out Taft's Senate term when Taft died in 1953.
24. Minutes of the Committee on Expenditures in the Executive Departments, U.S. Congress, House of Representatives, 79th Cong., 1st sess., 7 November 1945, National Archives and Records Service, Washington, DC (hereafter cited as Minutes, Expenditures Committee).
25. Secretary of the treasury, "Basis for a Compromise on Full Employment Legislation," November 1945, Truman official file.
26. Ibid.
27. Keyserling had been a top legislative staffer of Sen. Robert Wagner from 1933 to 1937 and is credited with drafting significant portions of Wagner's New Deal legislation. He served as counsel for several housing agencies in the Roosevelt administration. Truman appointed him vice chairman of the Council of Economic Advisers in 1946.
28. Keyserling, oral history interview by Gerhard Colm, Harry S. Truman Library and Museum, Independence, MO; memorandum, V.O. Key to George Graham, 31 July 1945, Gerhard Colm Papers, Truman Library, Independence, MO.
29. Memorandum from the secretary of the treasury to Truman, "Basis for Compromise on Full Employment Legislation," November 1945, Truman official file.
30. Confidential subcommittee print, "Proposed Substitute For S. 380 Recommended by the Subcommittee," 21 November 1945, National Archives and Records Service, Washington, DC (hereafter cited as Subcommittee Substitute).
31. Subcommittee Substitute, 21 November 1945. This source covers the material in the next five paragraphs.
32. Memorandum, "Cabinet Committee Formula"; Subcommittee Substitute.
33. Vinson to William Whittington, 24 November 1945, Colm Papers; memorandum, Gerhard Colm to J. Weldon Jones, 26 November 1945, Colm Papers.
34. Memorandum, "Cabinet Committee Formula."
35. Minutes, Expenditures Committee, 27 November 1945.
36. Resa served only one term in Congress, representing Chicago. Dawson was elected to Congress from Chicago in 1942. He is perhaps best known as the first

African American to chair a standing committee of the House of Representatives, becoming chairman of the Executive Expenditures Committee (later the Government Operations Committee) in 1949 and serving until his death in 1970.

37. Minutes, Expenditures Committee, 27 November 1945.
38. Minutes, Expenditures Committee, 28 November 1945.
39. Minutes, Expenditures Committee, 29 November and 5 December 1945.
40. To test the interpretation that that committee was conservative, an ideology score from 10 roll calls identified as critical by the UDA was calculated. The ideology score could range from +1.0 at the liberal end to −1.0 at the conservative end. For a more detailed discussion of this ideology score, see Appendix B.
41. Manasco scored a −0.3, and the ranking Republican, Clare Hoffman, scored a perfect −1.0. Whittington had an ideology score of +0.4, which was one of the most liberal scores of any Southern member of Congress. The average ideology score of the Democratic members of the Executive Expenditures Committee was 0.4, and the average for the Republican members was −0.5. The House Banking and Currency Committee Democrats scored more liberally (+0.6) and the Republican members more conservatively (−0.7) than their counterparts on the Executive Expenditures Committee.
42. By 1937, the House Committee on the Rules was controlled by an alliance of conservative Southern Democrats and Republicans, even though it was chaired by liberal Chicago Democrat Adolph Sabath. The conservative domination endured into the 1960s (Davis 2003).
43. Benton Jensen represented Iowa in Congress from 1935 to 1965.
44. George Bates represented Salem, Massachusetts, from 1937 until he died in a plane crash in 1949.
45. Son of a former Texas congressman and governor, Frederick Garland (Fritz) Lanham was elected to Congress in a special election in 1919 and served until 1947.
46. John Gibson represented Georgia from 1941 to 1947, when he lost in the primary election.
47. Celler represented New York City from 1923 until he was defeated in the 1972 Democratic primary by Elizabeth Holtzman. As chairman of the House Judiciary Committee, Celler led the passage of the Civil Rights Acts of 1964 and 1968, the Voting Rights Act of 1965, and the Immigration Act of 1965, which ended the national origins quota system.
48. Granger was elected to represent Utah in 1940 and served until he ran for the Senate unsuccessfully in 1952.
49. The Dewey quote has been frequently cited as an excerpt from a campaign speech he gave in Seattle, Washington, on September 21, 1944.
50. Labor and civil rights activist Biemiller was elected from Wisconsin in 1944, defeated in 1946, and reelected in 1948. He served as the director of the AFL-CIO's Department of Legislation from 1956 to 1978. Horace Jeremiah "Jerry" Voorhis represented Los Angeles County from 1937 until he was defeated by future president Richard Nixon in 1948.

6
Socioeconomic and Political Forces

The issues that defined the debate on the full employment bill are clear. The positions of most key leaders are also apparent. Indeed, the outcome of the legislative action on the full employment bill is now well known. The question that remains is whether legislators who favored a redefinition of the government's role and responsibility for maintaining economic well-being differed, in systematic and meaningful ways, from their colleagues who did not.

We know that why a member of Congress votes a certain way extends beyond how he or she assesses the merits of the issue. Members are influenced by the needs of their constituents, the priorities of their party, and their sense of what may be in the best interests of the nation. The field of legislative behavior has a rich literature on the factors that relate to congressional decision making.[1] This chapter builds on this scholarly research to explore a subset of socioeconomic and political factors that are measurable and analyzes the degree to which these variables are linked to support for full employment. The resulting statistical analysis sheds further light on the dynamics that shaped the enactment of the Employment Act of 1946.

MEASURING SUPPORT FOR FULL EMPLOYMENT

At the heart of this analysis is crafting an unambiguous measure of support for full employment. In this instance, there is a very limited set of observed behaviors on which to operationalize support for the full employment bill, and these behaviors form the basis of the full employment score. It is interesting to compare the House's distribution on the full employment score with the Senate's distribution, as Figure 6.1 presents. In contrast to the Senate, where 55 percent of the members consistently supported the bill, only 21 percent of the House members had perfect support scores.

Figure 6.1 Legislative Support for Full Employment: Comparison of Senate and House Scores

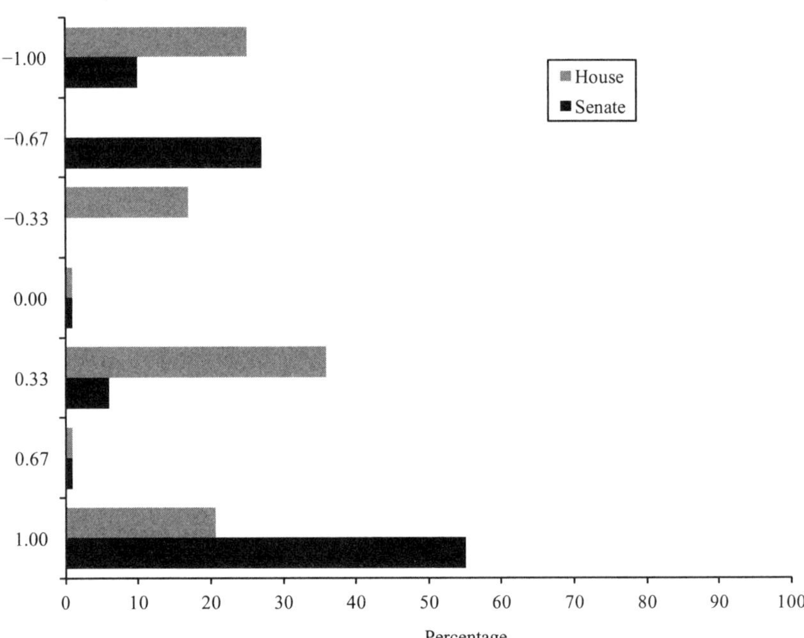

NOTE: There were zero members of the House at the −0.67 level of support for full employment and zero members of the Senate at the −0.33 level of support for full employment.

The full employment score is actually two different measures—a score for the Senate and a score for the House.[2] In the Senate, the score comprises three roll call votes on S. 380, two that amended it and one that passed it. In the House, the three components consist of sponsorship of H.R. 2202, a roll call to recommit the compromise bill, and a roll call on its final passage. That a member had to be a sponsor of H.R. 2202 in the House to obtain a perfect score, while sponsorship of S. 380 in the Senate was not used in the score, may account for the lower percentage of perfect scores in the House. Conversely, the Senate score is based on votes that were taken on legislation much closer to the original full employment proposal than the version of H.R. 2202 that came to the House floor.

CORRELATES OF SUPPORT FOR THE FULL EMPLOYMENT BILL

The full employment bill was preceded by more than a decade of economic upheaval, social change, and political realignment. The existing research leads us to expect that the forces of constituency, economics, electoral security, ideology, and party all were potentially influential in the legislative action on the full employment bill. The challenge is in drawing on data from the 1940s to measure these concepts of constituency, economics, electoral security, ideology, and party in order to clarify our understanding of the dynamics that led to the passage of the compromise version of the full employment bill. Despite the various problems inherent in operationalizing these concepts, the variables do offer a basis for exploring statistical models of legislative action on full employment.[3]

The Senate

Descriptive analysis of the senators' rankings on the full employment score by party shows clear differences. For the 55 Democratic senators, the average of 0.71 on the full employment score is almost twice the overall mean of 0.36. The average score for the 40 Republican senators (−0.15), however, falls well below the total average score. Senators from the regions of New England and the Pacific coast have the most consistently high scores, regardless of party identification. Democratic supporters of full employment represent states that experienced somewhat greater average unemployment than those Democrats who had negative scores on full employment. Those favoring the bill came from states that had lower average per capita personal income in 1943 as well as in 1933 than those opposing the bill, but these differences fade when party is taken into account.[4]

The paucity of cases and the constrained statistical variation of this state-level data limit the use of more powerful statistical techniques for the Senate. A limited multivariate analysis of Senate support for full employment, however, does reveal a bit about how these measures work in concert. In this instance, simple correlation and regression techniques are used.[5]

Being a member of the Democratic Party clearly correlates most strongly with support for full employment, as Table 6.1 shows. Senators from high unemployment states were only somewhat more likely to have supported full employment. This analysis hints that support for full employment increases somewhat with the candidate's electoral percentage. As a state's per capita income rises slightly, support for full employment appears to decrease.

When a regression equation is used to measure the multivariate effects of party, employment, urban change, working class, and per capita income upon the full employment scale, it is apparent that party is the dominating variable. State unemployment rates and per capita income both have modest effects on the full employment scale; however, the multiple correlation coefficient of the regression of 0.45 is modest (Table 6.2).

The importance of this analysis lies not in the strength or weakness of its findings, but rather in its identifying the vulnerable elements of what appeared to be overwhelming support for full employment in the Senate.[6] When one examines the distinguishing characteristics of the senators and the states they represent, one sees subtle differences between supporters and opponents that sketch the dynamics of support for the full employment bill. Moreover, the importance of party—and to a lesser extent per capita personal income and state unemployment levels—foreshadow the forces that the full employment bill encountered subsequently in the House of Representatives.

The House of Representatives

The number of representatives in the House and the diversity of their districts provide a richer source of data for analysis. Such data enable us to speculate on how these measures of constituency, economics, electoral security, ideology, and party may relate to support for the full employment bill. The 79th House of Representatives consisted of 242 Democrats, 193 Republicans, and 1 Progressive. In general, the eastern and midwestern sections of the country were dominated by the Republicans, while the southern and western parts were controlled by the Democrats.

New England, the Pacific coast, and the east and west North-Central regions were the wealthiest according to the adjusted living

Table 6.1 Senators' Support for Full Employment and Selected Measures: Simple Correlation Coefficients

	Full employment score
Party (1 = Democrat)	0.65
Unemployment rate	0.27
Most recent percentage of vote	0.20
Per capita personal income, 1943	−0.16
Percentage working class	0.13
Percentage urban change	0.02

level, in contrast to the South, Border, and Mountain regions. The unemployment rates tended to differ in a pattern across regions that show the Mid-Atlantic and Border districts with the highest averages and the Pacific and North-Central districts with the lowest. New England and the Mid-Atlantic had the largest average proportions of working-class people.[7]

The typical sponsor of full employment in the House was a liberal Democrat elected during the New Deal realignment from a district that was more working class, had experienced urbanization and an influx of immigrants, and had been hardest hit by the Great Depression. The members who voted for the final measure were generally nondescript in contrast to the sponsors, but they still were characterized as Democrats (and some Republicans) who represented districts that had more foreign-born, more African Americans, and more working-class people—all groups who were more likely to have been unemployed in 1937.[8]

Table 6.2 Senate Full Employment Score Regressed on Selected Variables

	Partial *R*
Party	0.59
Per capita personal income, 1943	−0.13
Unemployment rate	0.12
Most recent percentage of vote	−0.09
Percentage change in urban population	−0.05
Percentage working class	0.01
Multiple correlation coefficient	0.45

NOTE: Partial *R* is the correlation between two variables after removing the effects of other variables.

Simple correlation coefficients measuring the extent to which the full employment scale varies along with the constituency, economics, electoral security, ideology, and party measures are presented in Table 6.3. Political party (recoded in this analysis as "1" for Democrats and "0" for all others) has the highest correlation with support for full employment, 0.65. The percentage working class has the second-highest correlation coefficient, followed by percentage foreign-born, percentage African American, and percentage unemployed. Those characteristics that have noteworthy negative relationships with full employment are biographical status, tenure in office, and age of the member.

These findings are consistent with the analysis presented earlier because they indicate that Democrats were much more likely to have supported full employment. To a lesser extent, several of the constituency and economic characteristics are correlated with full employment; districts with larger proportions of African Americans and unemployed persons, as well as those with a lower level of living standards, all are somewhat more likely to support full employment.

Table 6.3 House Full Employment Score upon Party, Electoral, and District Traits: Simple Correlation Coefficients

	Full employment score
Political party	0.65
Percentage working class	0.27
Percentage foreign-born	0.26
Percentage unemployed, 1937	0.22
Biographical status	−0.13
Percentage African American	0.11
Age	−0.11
Tenure in Congress	−0.09
Percentage urban change	0.06
New Deal realignment	0.06
Median education	0.06
Living-level index	−0.05
Margin of victory	0.02

NOTE: For definitions of terms in this table, see Appendices A and B.

The next logical question becomes, "What is the effect of each of these variables on full-employment support when all of the other independent variables are held constant?" Multiple regression equations enable us to address this question, because such equations aid us conceptually in differentiating the direct relationships from the indirect relationships. Table 6.4 presents these results.

The political party of the member again dominates the support for full employment. Percentage foreign-born and percentage unemployed lose strength as predictors of support for full employment when the other variables are taken into account, but they remain statistically significant.

The analyses thus far reveal that there are several independent variables that are at least partially related to support for full employment. However, it is also apparent that the partisan identification of the member overwhelms all other variables in terms of explaining support. This finding logically follows from the simple analysis presented above, which suggest that Democrats were more likely to support the legislation regardless of the other measures.

Table 6.4 Multiple Regression: House Full Employment Score on Party, Electoral, and District Traits

	Partial *R*
Political party**	0.62
Percentage unemployed, 1937**	0.11
Percentage foreign-born**	0.11
Percentage working class	0.08
Median education	0.08
Tenure in Congress	0.05
Living-level index	0.05
Margin of victory	−0.05
Age	−0.04
Percentage urban change	0.03
Percentage African American	−0.03
Biographical status	−0.03
Multiple correlation coefficient	0.72

NOTE: **significant at the 0.05 level.

The dominance of party is not surprising given previous research on the importance of party in legislative behavior. It is furthermore consistent with the qualitative research on the debate over full employment. This legislation was a top priority of the Democratic president and was supported in Congress by key leaders in the party. It grew out of economic, constituent, and electoral forces that had shaped the Democratic realignment of the previous decade and reflected the next generation of policy perspectives that had created the New Deal. That partisan identification overwhelms other measures bearing on the members' support for full employment may, in part, tap the degree to which all Democrats advocated this major change in the federal role regardless of the economic, constituency, electoral, and personal influences upon them.

It is intuitively clear that the forces of constituency, economic factors, personal ideology, party, and electoral security all did not converge simultaneously in 1945 to influence the outcome of the full employment bill. The economic traits of the district and the constituency characteristics already had affected the type of person elected to Congress, particularly whether the representative was a Democrat or Republican. These district characteristics may also have had a further effect on the likelihood that the representative supported the full employment bill, an effect that is distinct from the party of the member, as the earlier analysis of those who deviated from their party's position suggests.

An additional explanation for the dominance of party in the regression equation is that party is colinear with many of a given district's socioeconomic characteristics.[9] The case of party being colinear with constituent and economic traits is not an issue of multiple measures of the same basic concept. The concepts are distinct, but the actual measures available have patterns so similar that it is difficult to discern the differences, as Table 6.5 illustrates.

When support for full employment is approached as a sequential process, political party again dominates. Being a member of the Democratic Party yields a 0.70 direct effect on support for full employment in the House of Representatives. Percentage working class, which has one of the highest simple correlation coefficients with full employment, appears to have more of an indirect effect through party than a direct effect on the House full employment scale. Most of the effect of urban change is felt through party, as are the effects of race and ethnicity. The unemployment rate, on the other hand, has some direct effect on

Table 6.5 Multiple Regression: Democratic Party on District Traits of the House

	Partial *R*
Living-level index**	−0.32
Percentage African American**	0.28
Percentage foreign-born**	0.24
Percentage urban change**	0.20
Percentage working class**	0.16
Median education	0.06
Percentage unemployed, 1937	0.03
Multiple correlation coefficient	0.63

NOTE: **significant at the 0.05 level.

support for full employment over and above its effect on party. When regional groupings are taken into account, party remains the leading predictor, and the percentage of urban change decreases to the point where its effect becomes trivial. The South, as one might expect, has a noteworthy positive effect on electing a Democrat and a negative effect on support for full employment.[10] Overall, the structural equation models presented in Appendix E yield multiple correlation coefficients of 0.71 to 0.74 and explain about half of the variance in the House full employment score.

It is difficult to assess whether a model explaining 50 percent of the variance is a cup half empty or a cup half full. Given that several of the measures lack the precision one might wish and that the exogenous variables are "muted" for the metropolitan congressional districts (see Appendix A), one might speculate that better data would have produced stronger results. It is best, nonetheless, to say the cup is half full and only half full.

Still, the other half of the cup poses unanswered questions that are not explained by the statistical models. The crudeness of the variables makes it plausible to attribute much to measurement imperfections. At least a portion of the unexplained variance is due to aspects of legislative behavior that defy measurement in this study: the judgment of the member, the influence of interest-group lobbying, the power of the press, the role of political brokering, and the power of the status quo.

The matter of a member's judgment and worldview may have played out in several different scenarios. The debates in the House offered many forceful arguments concerning full employment that spoke to national concerns and ideological beliefs. A member could have represented a district that was "vulnerable" to unemployment as characterized by the exogenous variables, but that member might have concluded that the full employment bill would have assigned too much power to the federal government. Such a member might have viewed a small group of economic planners directing a national employment policy as a potentially tyrannical bureaucracy that would have been far worse than cyclical problems of unemployment. On the other hand, a member from a district that was not especially vulnerable to unemployment might have concluded, regardless, that it was in the best interests of the nation to have the federal government assume the responsibility for maintaining full employment. These two perspectives on the role of government were not unique to that time and can be traced back to the Federalist versus Anti–Federalist philosophies that took root during the founding of the United States.

Pressure groups were perceived as especially powerful before the enactment of the first comprehensive federal lobbying law, the Federal Regulation of Lobbying Act, in August 1946.[11] As discussed in previous chapters, a formidable number of business interests, labor unions, and other pressure groups were intensely engaged in the full employment legislation. The persuasive powers of such groups helped delineate the issues of national policy. Members who did not perceive their districts as especially vulnerable to unemployment might well have opted to follow the advice of interest-group lobbyists to whom they were close. Even a member whose district's traits would have suggested an alternative action might have heeded an interest group because of the advantages that that interest group offered the member. Prior to federal regulation of lobbying, such pressure groups had considerable clout to reward their friends and otherwise influence the debate.

The power of the press to interpret events and shape the debate is another element to be factored in. Although Chapter 3 presents survey research data indicating overwhelming public support for the federal government having a role in job creation and full employment, the press was largely opposed to the legislation. Public opinion research was a relatively new field in the 1940s. Senators and representatives at that time did not track opinion polls as they do today. They were more likely to presume they had been elected to show sound judgment in voting rather than to mirror the views of their constituents. That the campaign against full employment legislation waged in the print media amplified the views of those opposed, albeit a minority view, served to further minimize the public support for the legislation.

Political brokering is a longstanding activity in Congress, and none would doubt that it plays an important function. One form is colloquially known as "back-scratching," where members trade votes on bills they are less concerned with to ensure sufficient support on measures important to them. Another form of political bargaining is the role party leaders play in exerting pressure on members to vote with the majority of their party on issues deemed of national importance. The academic literature defines this broker role of party leaders as part of the "coalition representational" model. One easily can imagine that some arm-twisting occurred over the full employment bill, some of which may have been captured in the explanatory power of the political party variable (Jackson 1974).

Finally, the power of the status quo might well have led some members whose districts might have been described as vulnerable to unemployment to nonetheless vote against the full employment bill, their rationale being, "Better the devil you know than the devil you don't." This folk adage could well have characterized the sentiments of some members who might have concluded that unemployment was a serious problem but lacked trust in a federal policy to resolve it. Though less sophisticated perhaps than the classic Federalist versus Anti-Federalist tension, the power of the status quo is a familiar force in legislative dynamics.

We know there were many reasons for why members of Congress either supported or opposed full employment. The unmeasurable aspects mentioned above offer such plausible explanations of legislative behavior that the explanatory power of the statistical analysis provides a noteworthy contrast. Yet even though the statistical analysis does not account fully for this dramatic change in the role of the federal government, it does enlighten our understanding of this change. This significant legislation passed the U.S. Congress for a complex set of reasons, not least of which were the political party of the members voting on it and the economic characteristics of their congressional districts.

Notes

1. Some of the major works of legislative behavior research that guide these analyses include the following: James T. Patterson, *Congressional Conservatism and the New Deal* (Lexington: University of Kentucky Press, 1967); Duncan MacRae, *Dimensions of Congressional Voting* (Berkeley: University of California Press, 1958); Warren E. Miller and Donald E. Stokes, "Constituency Influence in Congress," *American Political Science Review,* vol. 57, no. 1 (March 1963); Aage Clausen, *How Congressmen Decide: A Policy Focus* (New York: St. Martin Press, 1973); Jerrold Schneider (1979), *Ideological Coalitions in Congress* (Westport, Connecticut: Greenwood Press); John E. Jackson, *Constituencies and Leaders in Congress* (Cambridge, MA: Harvard University Press, 1974); Joshua D. Clinton, Simon Jackman, and Douglas Rivers, "The Statistical Analysis of Legislative Behavior: A Unified Approach," *American Political Science Review*, vol. 988, no. 2 (Clinton, Jackman, and Rivers 2004); and Larry M. Bartels, *Economic Inequality and Political Representation* (Princeton, NJ: Princeton University Press, 2005).
2. For an explanation of how these scores were constructed, see Appendix B.
3. These county-level data are used to construct congressional district–level data according to a rather complex set of procedures. Appendix A describes this process in some detail and also discusses why actual 1940 data are used rather than interpolated 1945 estimates.
4. Looking at senators whose scores deviated from their party reveals some rather interesting patterns. For the purposes here, deviance is defined as Democrats who score negatively on the full employment scale and Republicans who score positively. The lowest rates of unemployment are in states with Democrats who have negative scores on full employment. These same Democrats also represent states that, on average, are the poorest in 1943 and that have experienced the slowest growth in per capita personal income over the previous decade. For the most part, these deviant Democrats are from the South. Republicans who score positively on full employment do not differ meaningfully from their fellow Republicans except in regard to urbanization. These deviant Republicans come from states with the lowest average increase in urbanization from 1920 to 1940. This phenomenon is largely attributable to Republicans from New England states that already had high levels of urbanization. For further analysis, see Appendix C.
5. See Appendix F for methodological references. Tests of significance are not presented as part of these analyses because the data captures the entire population during the span of time under study; however, tests of significance for each exogenous variable are used as a gauge of how directly that variable relates to support for the full employment bill in the multivariate analysis of the House.
6. The relationships among partisan, regional, electoral, economic, and demographic characteristics to one's support for full employment are explored more fully in the analysis of the House action on the legislation.
7. Appendix D provides detailed supporting analysis.
8. Again, Appendix D provides detailed supporting analysis.
9. This multicolinearity undermines the multiple regression assumption of the addi-

tive model, which requires the exogenous variables to be independent of one another.

10. Appendix E presents models of support for full employment that approach it as a sequential process by means of structural equations. The traits of the district are used to predict the party of the candidate who won the most recent election—i.e., the current member of Congress. In turn, the member's party identification is used to predict his or her position on full employment. Of course, this set of relationships is more complex than this simple statement implies and captures other variables as well, such as the 1937 unemployment rate's influence upon the party of the person representing the district as well as upon his or her support for full employment.
11. Enacted as Title III of the Legislative Reorganization Act of 1946, P.L. 79-601, this law requires certain persons, groups, and organizations engaged in lobbying activities to keep detailed financial accounts, file financial statements, and in certain cases register as lobbyists before engaging in lobbying activities. Several key court cases, notably *United States v. Harris*, 347 U.S. 612 (1954), and *United States v. Rumely*, 345 U.S. 41 (1953), narrowed the scope of the law in its early years.

7
The Employment Act of 1946

The spirit was one of optimism as 1946 opened. The United States had defeated the powers of fascism and, in the process, had risen out of the Great Depression. Sacrifice and austerity gave way to pent-up consumer demand. People began having children at a rate that countered virtually a century of decline in the fertility rate. The United States had the deterrent power of the atomic bomb, without the full awareness of its horrors. It was a heady, joyful moment in the nation's history.

The enactment of the Employment Act of 1946 was true to this moment in time. It signaled a confidence that America could alleviate unemployment in peacetime as well as during the war, and that the federal government was ready to stimulate the economy when private enterprise fell short. It was a covenant between the federal government and the people that the United States would not tolerate depressions.

FINAL PUSH FOR FULL EMPLOYMENT

As 1946 opened, President Truman used his bully pulpit to advance the Senate-passed version of the full employment bill. During his radio speech of January 3, he encouraged voters to contact their representatives on behalf of "real" full employment legislation. Truman himself had already written to the congressional conferees urging them to approve no less than the Senate-passed bill (Truman 1961c).[1]

On January 6, the U.S. Chamber of Commerce publicly recommended a permanent government commission on unemployment and business fluctuations. Although the U.S. Chamber of Commerce roundly rejected what it called "totalitarian collectivism," it acknowledged that "numerous techniques and policies for shortening periods of income and job losses and avoiding extreme fluctuations are known." The Chamber apparently recognized that it could not block enactment of some form of the full employment bill and opted to push for a version resembling H.R. 2202, which had become the House-passed S. 380 (Cotton 1946).

In his 1946 State of the Union Message, President Truman continued to push for full employment legislation. In the speech, he asserted, "It is the responsibility of Government to gear its total program to the achievement of full production and full employment." Again, he emphasized his wish that Congress would enact a full employment bill like the one the Senate had passed. Indeed, during the address Truman expressed strong and repeated references to the need for full employment (Truman 1961d).

Public support for a federal role in job creation remained high. In a *Fortune* survey published in February 1946, only 17.7 percent of respondents chose the response "Let business and industry work out the problem without any government interference at all." As Figure 7.1 depicts, a total of 38.1 percent selected the survey responses depicted by the two sections of the pie chart dealing with "continuous public works": 10.3 percent of those chose large-scale continuous public works programs, and 27.8 percent chose public works programs that would ebb and flow with fluctuations in the business cycle. Almost one-third (31.0 percent) selected the survey response "Depend mainly on business and industry to create enough employment normally, and just provide work at those times when industry cannot employ everyone," represented on the pie chart by the phrase "Business & industry with government" (Cantril 1951, p. 904).

The day after Truman's State of the Union address, the conference committee began meeting on the full employment legislation. Sen. Robert Wagner, initially the chair of the conference managers, had become ill a few weeks earlier and was not able to assume the task. This key sponsor of the original bill was replaced by respected Senate majority leader Alben Barkley (D-KY), who also supported the original language.[2] The other Senate conference managers were Murdock, Taylor, Radcliffe, Tobey, Taft, and Buck. The House conferees were led by Manasco and included Cochran, Whittington, Bender, and Hoffman.

From all unofficial accounts, it appears that the conferees engaged in a series of hard-fought struggles. During the first two sessions, no agreements were reached, and it took five sessions just to debate the bill's opening declaration of policy. Meanwhile, rumors abounded not only of infighting between two pivotal administration officials—Vinson

Figure 7.1 Public Opinion on the Government's Role in Employment: February 1946

Which one of these comes closest to expressing your ideas of what the government should do to avoid periods of unemployment after the war?

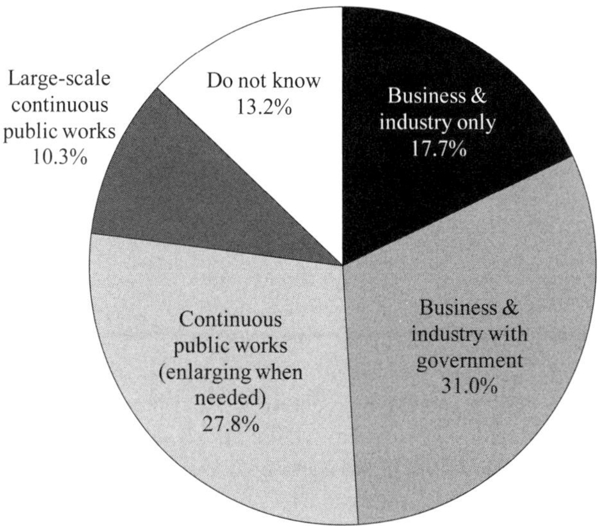

SOURCE: *Fortune*, February 1946 (Cantril 1951, p. 904).

and Snyder—but of administration strategies to co-opt a key Republican conferee (Bailey 1964, pp. 222–227).

The debate focused on two substantive issues: full employment and compensatory spending. Whittington led the House managers in opposing any reference to full employment or to the government's guarantee of employment. Whittington also argued that the spending provisions must be deleted. Barkley, on the other hand, blasted the House-passed version and restated the importance of full employment and compensatory spending. Furthermore, Barkley emphasized President Truman's warning that only the Senate-passed version was acceptable to Truman (Bailey 1964, pp. 222–227).

The conferees finally, on February 3, 1946, hammered out a compromise that essentially resulted in a totally rewritten bill. The conference legislation was briefer than previous versions and used the kind of sweeping language that offended few and defied strict interpretation. The planning structures—i.e., the Council of Economic Advisers and the Joint Committee on the Economic Report—became the crux of the proposal.

The Council of Economic Advisers and the Joint Committee on the Economic Report now were charged with the task of achieving the objectives of the legislation. The policy declaration contained in the bill expressed these objectives and represented the carefully crafted compromise:

> The Congress hereby declares that it is the continuing policy and responsibility of the Federal Government to use all practical means consistent with its needs and obligations and other essential considerations of national policy with the assistance and cooperation of industry, agriculture, labor, and State and local governments, to coordinate and utilize all its plans, functions, and resources for the purpose of creating and maintaining, in a manner calculated to foster and promote free competitive enterprise and the general welfare, conditions under which there will be afforded useful employment for those able, willing, and seeking to work, and to promote maximum employment, production and purchasing power. (U.S. Congress 1946)

Almost all of the interested parties claimed victory. The conservatives were pleased that they had stripped the law of its right-to-employment phrases, its provisions requiring compensatory spending in times of private sector shortfalls, and its full employment language. Liberals were pleased that the bill created structures for economic planning, that it did not require a balanced budget, and that it vested the federal government with the responsibility and the authority to draw on all of its resources and functions to promote maximum employment, production, and purchasing power. Although it was turgid prose, it appeared to be a semantic success.

The House and Senate quickly acted on the conference committee report. Wright Patman, one of the original drafters, was joined by Cochran, Whittington, and Manasco in expressing support for the compromise legislation. The House passed it by a vote of 320 to 84 on February 6, 1946. Two days later the Senate approved the conference report without dissent (*Congressional Record* 1946, pp. 999–1009, 1170).

On February 20, 1946, President Truman signed the Employment Act, making it Public Law 304 of the 79th Congress. It was not the strong bill he had requested, but he expressed the intent to implement it in a manner true to the original language. Reviewing the key components of the initial bill—federal responsibility and structure, economic planning, right to employment, and compensatory spending—it was clear that Truman would be able to do much within the language of the enacted law.

The Employment Act promoted "maximum employment," not "full employment." Though the administration had fought to retain the term, it now said the difference between full employment and maximum employment was the difference between "Tweedledum and Tweedledee" (*Congressional Quarterly* 1946). This comment on the insignificance of the difference was true regarding the Truman administration's application of the law, but it would not hold true in the presidencies to follow.

Maximum employment, unlike full employment, was not a value-laden term. The latter was a panacea to some, an anathema to others. Some called full employment fascism, some called it communism, and some called it the hallmark of a free society. Maximum employment, on the other hand, did not carry such divergent connotations. Nothing in the Employment Act precluded defining maximum employment in Keynesian terms, yet nothing required it. The importance of the Employment Act was that it clarified the federal responsibility to assure maximum employment.

Neither chamber of Congress had been able to muster a majority that would accept the right-to-employment provision, despite the importance Roosevelt had given it in his 1944 State of the Union address. Even many who agreed with the concept in theory were uncertain about a statute in which the federal government guaranteed a job for anyone who wanted one. The Employment Act, nonetheless, stated that the government would maintain "conditions under which there will be afforded useful employment for those able, willing, and seeking to work." In other words, instead of pledging the right to employment, it promised an economic climate of employment opportunities.

The Employment Act did not require compensatory spending. The conservatives' favorite amendment—requirement of a balanced budget and a tax plan to ensure it—also was omitted. The absence of such specific language freed subsequent policymakers to use the most acceptable fiscal and monetary practices to meet the objectives of the act. Clearly, Keynesian fiscal policies such as compensatory spending implicitly fell within the "all practical means" and "all plans, functions, and resources" that the federal government might use. Most significantly, the Employment Act emphasized two key elements that Hansen had highlighted earlier—1) maximum production and 2) purchasing power—and instituted "consumer Keynesianism."

Finally, the Employment Act established the federal structures for economic planning. As stated at the onset, most scholars hail the law for this accomplishment. Moreover, the final law was superior to the initial bill in terms of creating a flexible and accountable apparatus for national economic planning. In this regard, the Employment Act heralded a new era in the federal role.

The dreaded postwar unemployment never swept the United States. Some have subsequently argued that because this unemployment did not materialize, members of Congress retreated on their initial commitment to full employment. The passage of the Employment Act, however, occurred when economic forecasters were still sending mixed messages, when war production workers were being laid off, and when it was too soon to measure the full effect of soldiers returning home (e.g., *Time* 1945b,d,e,h). Thus, it was the wisdom of hindsight that credited members of Congress with such foresight.

Indeed, the passage of the Employment Act had a positive effect by buoying the U.S. economy during this critical period of demobilization. In many ways, the Employment Act offered economic security to American consumers, workers, and business. It might well have been an antidote to the economic pessimism that public opinion surveys found during the war years and might well have provided some of the confidence that fueled postwar consumerism.

IMPLEMENTING THE EMPLOYMENT ACT

Absent the specific requirements of the original full employment legislation, the overarching question becomes, "Would the Employment Act succeed in accomplishing the goals of its initial sponsors?"

Given the compromises that were made to ensure its passage, there was no guarantee that the policies prescribed by the Employment Act would be vigorously pursued by the structures the act created. As Cervantes wrote, "The proof of the pudding is in the eating."

The Employment Act established the Joint Committee on the Economic Report (now commonly referred to as the Joint Economic Committee) with only an advisory role.[3] It had no power to authorize programs, pass laws, or appropriate funds. The Joint Economic Committee's functions included reviewing options and programs to further the government's policy of maximum employment and purchasing power, as well as studying the economic report, which the administration would produce annually. It provided guidance and critical assessment of the economic report to other congressional committees. This legislative mandate enabled the Joint Economic Committee to consider and make recommendations on a whole range of economic policy. The clout of the Joint Economic Committee would hinge on the connectional power of its members—that is, whether members of the committee also had prominent or powerful positions within the legislative bodies.

Sen. Joseph O'Mahoney became the first chairman of the Joint Committee on the Economic Report. O'Mahoney had achieved widespread attention on economic matters when he chaired the Temporary National Economic Committee, created in 1938 to study monopolistic business practices. That congressionally mandated committee had produced a report in 1941 that analyzed 50 years of economic data and found that a few corporations had gathered a growing concentration of wealth and economic power (Temporary National Economic Committee 1941). O'Mahoney had cosponsored the Full Employment Act of 1945 (S. 380) and had presented the economic arguments in support of S. 380 during the Senate floor debate. He was a very influential senator, sitting on the powerful Appropriations Committee and the Judiciary Committee. At that time he chaired the Committee on Indian Affairs, and he later chaired the Committee on Interior and Insular Affairs.[4]

Senator Robert Taft was the ranking member of the Joint Economic Committee and a leading Republican.[5] He led the Republican Policy Committee and served on the Banking and Currency and the Education and Labor Committees. Taft had played a pivotal role in the legislative action that established the Employment Act. He had been outspoken in

Illustration 7.1 Senators Joseph O'Mahoney and Robert Taft

NOTE: The original Associated Press cutline for this photo said, "DISAGREE: Senators Joseph C. O'Mahoney (left) and Robert D. Taft shake hands Jan. 16 despite their disagreement over action on President Truman's report on economic conditions. O'Mahoney suggested that the Senate-House committee act promptly to carry out the President's ideas. Taft said he saw no need for haste."

SOURCE: Joseph O'Mahoney Collection, Box 390, Folder 48, American Heritage Center, University of Wyoming.

his opposition to full employment but ultimately supported S. 380 after his amendments were incorporated.

O'Mahoney's Democratic colleagues on the Joint Economic Committee were similarly well-placed on key authorizing committees. The Senate Democrats were the following three men: Abe Murdock, who served on the Banking and Currency Committee's Full Employment Subcommittee as well as on the Appropriations and Judiciary Committees; James Tunnel, who chaired the Committee on Pensions and also served on the Education and Labor Committee; and Francis Myers, who served on the Patents and Naval Affairs committees (and who would become Democratic whip in 1949). The House Democrats were as follows: Edward Hart, who had chaired the Committee on War Claims and now chaired the House Committee on Un-American Activities; Wright Patman, who was chairman of the Select Committee on Small Business and a member of the Banking and Currency Committee; George Outland, who was also on the Banking and Currency Committee; and Walter Huber, who served on the Census and the Civil Service committees.[6]

The other Republican senators on the Joint Economic Committee were equally representative of other key committees. Senator Styles Bridges (R-NH) was the ranking Republican on the Senate Appropriations Committee and served on the Republican Policy Committee. Senator Robert M. La Follette Jr. served on the Education and Labor Committee.[7] Interestingly, the House Republicans on the Joint Committee all came from one committee—the Committee on Expenditures in the Executive Departments. George Bender was one of Republican House members who sponsored the initial full employment legislation and also an ally of Sen. Robert Taft. Walter Judd had supported the Whittington rewrite of the Employment Act. Robert Rich opposed the legislation throughout the legislative debate.

In the 79th Congress, both sides of the aisle chose their Joint Economic Committee from among its most influential members and key congressional committees. Additionally, most of the selected members had considerable ownership in the Employment Act. The combined clout of the members also signaled that the 79th Congress was ready to go toe-to-toe with the executive branch when it came to the economy and employment policy. As a consequence, the Joint Economic Committee was transformed from an advisory committee with very little statutory authority on paper into a very influential committee through the connectional power of its members.

As it did with the Joint Economic Committee, the Employment Act assigned the Council of Economic Advisers only an advisory role when it created the body. Its statutory duties were to provide economic advice to the president and to help the president write an annual economic report. The president was not required to heed the council's guidance. Compared to the Bureau of the Budget, it was a very small unit within the Executive Office of the President. The power of the council would hinge on its efficacy as an authoritative source about the economy and on the closeness of its relationship with the president.

That Alvin Hansen was not chosen to lead the council is rather significant. Hansen was considered "the American Keynes" and was the foremost scholar and tactician on full employment policies in the United States.[8] His prominence on full employment may well have been the reason he was *not* selected. As discussed in earlier chapters, many credit the demise of the NRPB to its publication of Hansen's *After the War—Full Employment* in January 1942. Hansen was a lightning rod to those who feared an enlarged federal role and to the business community. The economist chosen in his stead later confirmed that "Alvin Hansen, who has been the pioneer of the American branch of the Keynesian movement, was thought of [to be the chair of the council]. He had been a protagonist . . . so there was opposition to him."[9]

Instead, President Truman selected Edwin Nourse, vice president of the Brookings Institution, to be the first chairman of the Council of Economic Advisers. Nourse grew up near Chicago and earned his doctorate in economics from the University of Chicago. He was a noted agricultural economist when he joined the Institute of Economics, which was one of the entities that subsequently merged to form the Brookings Institution. Although Nourse identified himself as neither Democrat nor Republican, he had become personal friends with Henry Wallace when they both lived in Iowa. Nourse's position on the council, however, likely came through Sen. James Murray, one of the original drafters of the full employment bill. According to Norse, Murray "had become interested in what I was doing in the field of economic statesmanship, as relating to the question of what private industry would do in adjusting to the postwar situation."[10] The CED had also consulted with Nourse on economic policy while he was at Brookings. Nourse said the first time he met Harry Truman was at the White House when the president asked him to serve on the Council of Economic Advisers (Knapp 1979).

President Truman chose Leon Keyserling, general counsel of the National Housing Authority, as the vice chairman of the council. Born in Charleston, South Carolina, Keyserling obtained a law degree from Harvard and then studied economics at Columbia University under Rexford Tugwell. He left graduate school before completing his doctorate to work as a legislative assistant to Sen. Robert F. Wagner from 1933 to

1937. During his years with Wagner, he drafted several landmark pieces of New Deal legislation, notably the National Industrial Recovery Act of 1934 and the National Labor Relations Act of 1935. Keyserling was also quite involved in writing the Social Security Act of 1935. He then served in the Roosevelt administration, where he ardently advocated for full employment.[11]

The third member of the council was John D. Clark, dean of the business school at the University of Nebraska. Originally from Wyoming, Clark was a successful businessman with a law degree from Columbia who had been vice president of Standard Oil of Indiana in the 1920s. He left Standard Oil to pursue a doctorate in economics at Johns Hopkins University. People in Washington labeled Clark a conservative. He was, nonetheless, a long-time Democrat who had been a delegate for Woodrow Wilson at the Democratic convention in 1912 and had served in the Wyoming State Legislature (Donovan 1977; Hamby 1973).[12]

The Council of Economic Advisers hired Bertram Gross as staff director. Gross's role in drafting the original language of S. 380 and his experiences with members and staff in Congress gave him considerable clout. That he had established a close working relationship with economists in the Bureau of the Budget and the Federal Reserve while drafting the legislation further enhanced his position.

Meanwhile, public opinion data revealed a growing sense of job security in the months after the Employment Act was enacted. By June 1946, over half of those surveyed—55 percent—said there was no chance that they would be unemployed in the coming year. As Figure 7.2 shows, only 9 percent thought there was a great chance that they would be unemployed in the next year. Just two years earlier, Gallup had asked a sample of the civilian adult population whether they thought they would have a job following the war. In that poll, conducted during July 1944, only 40 percent were "very certain" they would have a job after the war, and 35 percent of the respondents reported that they were "not at all certain" they would have a job after the war (Cantril 1951, p. 903).

Figure 7.2 Public Attitudes on Personal Job Prospects: 1946

During the next year, do you think there is any chance that you (your husband) will be unemployed?

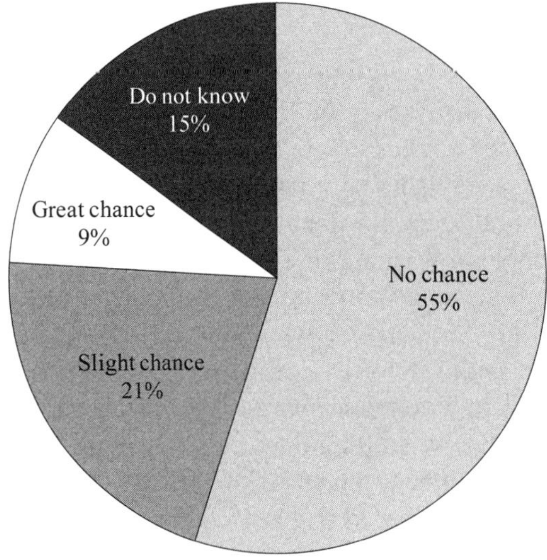

SOURCE: American Institute of Public Opinion, June 5, 1946 (Cantril 1951, pp. 904–905).

EARLY YEARS OF THE EMPLOYMENT ACT

The years immediately after passage of the Employment Act were politically tumultuous in the U.S. Congress. Republicans swept the congressional elections in 1946, picking up 55 seats in the House for a 246-member majority. They also won control of the Senate for the first time since 1928, holding 51 seats to the Democrats' 45. In his Budget Message of January 10, 1947, Truman made clear that "as long as business, employment, and national income continue high, we should maintain tax revenues at levels that will not only meet current expenditures but also leave a surplus for retirement of the public debt. There is no justification now for tax reduction." Republicans in Congress nonetheless moved to cut taxes. True to his word, Truman vetoed tax cuts that the 80th Congress had passed, asserting that the cuts favored the wealthy. Ultimately, the Republicans garnered the votes in Congress to override Truman's veto of their tax cut in legislation passed in 1948.[13]

Much has been written about Truman's campaign to retain the White House in 1948, and a core feature was its populist critique of the 80th Congress, which Truman nicknamed the "Do-Nothing Congress." The Democrats' gain of nine seats in the Senate was enough to give them control of the chamber after the 1948 election. They also picked up 75 seats in the House. The Democrats returned to power just as an economic recession was beginning in late 1948.

The Council of Economic Advisers, led by Nourse, agreed on their assessment of the economic situation as well as the proper course of action to address the unemployment level, which was approaching 6 percent. President Truman and many in Congress supported their actions to reverse the downturn. The recession was short-lived, but internal disputes took their toll on the council. The infighting was not over Keynesian policies, taxes, or deficit financing; rather, it was a personal disagreement between Nourse and Keyserling on whether they should testify before Congress. Nourse viewed his position as solely that of an economic adviser to the president and did not think it appropriate to engage in political affairs. Keyserling argued that the Council of Economic Advisers had an additional responsibility to extend its economic recommendations to Congress. Keyserling proceeded to testify before Congress, and Nourse resigned from the council in 1949.[14]

In 1950, House Republican leader Joseph Martin was among those who led the campaign against "extravagant" deficit spending and the "economic witch doctors" in the Truman administration. Martin further charged that "these socialistic schemers and political medicine men who now infect the executive branch must be run out of Washington." The feisty Keyserling retorted that Martin regarded a certain amount of unemployment as permanent, implying that Martin would be satisfied with a higher level of unemployment. Martin, in turn, sniped that "one of the medicine men" he was referring to was Keyserling (*Washington Post* 1950).

The Republicans picked up a few congressional seats in 1950 and, along with conservative Democrats, clashed with Keyserling, who had become the chairman of the council. The Joint Economic Committee maintained considerable clout and continued to have extensive hearings, expand its staff of experts, and produce its own economic reports. The 82nd Congress cut off almost all appropriations for the Council of Economic Advisers, and the council seemed as if it would expire in early 1953 (Engelbourg 1980).

It was President Dwight D. Eisenhower, elected in 1952, who breathed new life into the Council of Economic Advisers by appointing Arthur F. Burns as chairman. Burns earned his PhD in economics at Columbia University and had already established himself as the leading expert on business cycles while a professor at Columbia and a researcher with the National Bureau of Economic Research (NBER).[15] Eisenhower completed the council by selecting Neil H. Jacoby, a tax specialist who was dean of the School of Business at the University of California, and Walter W. Stewart, an expert on monetary theory who had been a professor at the Institute for Advanced Studies.

The recession of 1953–1954 put the principles of the Employment Act to the test in a Republican administration. Burns clashed vigorously with Secretary of the Treasury George Humphrey on what the proper federal response should be. Humphrey was a wealthy businessman who ran a steel conglomerate in Ohio and who had close ties to Sen. Robert Taft.[16] Although Eisenhower is generally considered to have been an economic conservative, he was persuaded by Burns's advocacy of anti-recession policies in the form of tax cuts and deficit spending, and Burns prevailed in 1954. Council member Neil Jacoby later held that "Keynesian economic thinking played a key role in the recession of 1954 under Eisenhower" (Engelbourg 1980; Sloan 1991).

By the tenth anniversary of the enactment of the Employment Act of 1946, the mainstreams of both political parties in the United States had accepted the principles it embodied. It surprised no one that Wright Patman, vice chairman of the Joint Economic Committee, would praise the act as he detailed the important contributions of the Joint Economic Committee. Senator O'Mahoney, former chairman of that committee, likewise acknowledged the importance of the act and emphasized the unprecedented economic growth over the 10 years since its passage. Especially noteworthy, however, were the observations of Republican congressman Jesse Wolcott, then serving as chairman of the Joint Economic Committee. "A recession in late 1953 and early 1954 was skillfully brought under control," Wolcott said, adding, "I consider this record a tribute to the Employment Act of 1946." Republican senator

Ralph Flanders, a member of the committee who had formerly served as its vice chairman, similarly acknowledged "the respect which we must all accord the operation and usefulness of the Employment Act" (Colm 1956).

There remained in both parties, nonetheless, opposition to the Employment Act among those who opposed a strong federal government and those who reflected conservative corporate interests. Independent research groups, most notably the American Enterprise Institute, thrived as they offered conservative alternatives. Publications such as William F. Buckley's *National Review* served as a sophisticated forum to disseminate the opposing perspective (Bernstein 2001; Phillips-Fein 2009).

VANTAGE POINT OF THE TWENTY-FIRST CENTURY

The United States has experienced almost a dozen recessions since passage of the Employment Act, as Figure 7.3 depicts, but no economic depressions. Even during these recessions, the unemployment rates remained below 8 percent until the 1974–1975 recession. In 1982, the annual unemployment rate reached its highest level since the Great Depression—9.7 percent. There were 10.7 million people unemployed in 1982 and 1983. The recession that began in December 2007 has resulted in comparably high levels of unemployment.

Over this same span of years, the United States experienced dramatic periods of prosperity and economic growth. The low unemployment levels of the 1960s afforded Congress and Presidents Kennedy and Johnson the opportunity to establish education and job training programs aimed at those left behind in the expanding economy. Initially enacted in response to the recession of 1960, the Area Redevelopment Act of 1961 subsidized training for workers in economically depressed areas. The Public Welfare Amendments of 1962 authorized the Community Work and Training Program, which permitted the states to enroll adult recipients of Aid to Families with Dependent Children in "workfare" programs. The Manpower Development and Training Act and the Trade Adjustment Assistance Act, both enacted in 1962, aided workers who were displaced by automation and trade policies. The Economic

Figure 7.3 Unemployment Rates and Recessions, 1946–2010

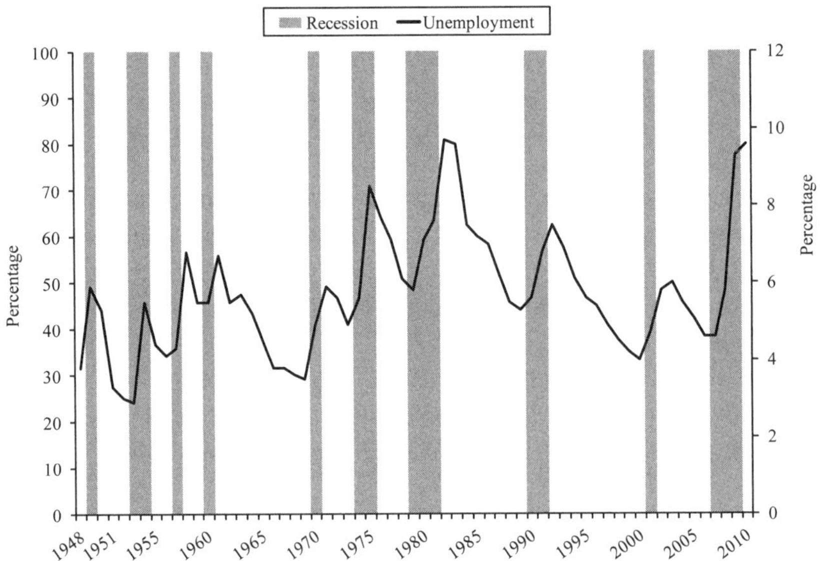

SOURCE: BEA (2012a); BLS (2012); author's calculations.

Opportunity Act of 1964 established a set of employment and job training programs, including Job Corps. Through these programs and other policy initiatives of the 1960s, the activist fiscal policies of the Employment Act were put in full throttle.

The recessions of the 1970s were triggered in part by the sharp increase in oil prices, an international dynamic not envisioned by sponsors of the Employment Act. The rising oil prices fueled inflation, and the anti-inflation policies competed with job creation to be the top economic priority. The presumed relationship between unemployment and inflation, known as the Phillips curve, had been a stable trade-off for policymakers. But by the 1970s, this balancing act no longer appeared valid, and the fiscal and monetary policies based upon the Phillips curve became ineffective. While Republicans had long feared inflation more than unemployment, survey research data had shown that unemployment was a greater concern for the American public than inflation until the 1970s. But as prices began to rise faster than real wages, the balance of public opinion began to tip (Hibbs 1982; Smith 1980; Temin 1998; Weir 1992).

In 1976, Keyserling and Gross, along with many others, came together again to craft legislation aimed at addressing what they perceived to be deficiencies in the Employment Act of 1946. The Full Employment and Balanced Growth Act of 1978 became commonly known as Humphrey-Hawkins, a reference to its sponsors, Rep. Augustus Hawkins (D-CA) and Sen. Hubert Humphrey (D-MN).[17] Originally meant to ratchet up the federal goal to "full employment" from the "maximum employment" of the 1946 Act, as finally enacted Humphrey-Hawkins established goals that competed with full employment. The act's expressed purpose was

> to translate into practical reality the right of all Americans who are able, willing, and seeking to work to full opportunity for useful paid employment at fair rates of compensation; to assert the responsibility of the Federal Government to use all practicable programs and policies to promote full employment, production, and real income, balanced growth, adequate productivity growth, proper attention to national priorities, and reasonable price stability; to require the President each year to set forth explicit short-term and medium-term economic goals; to achieve a better integration of general and structural economic policies; and to improve the coordination of economic policymaking within the Federal Government.

Quite significantly, Humphrey-Hawkins established a dual mandate of full employment and price stability, and it required the Federal Reserve to use monetary policy to pursue full employment as well as curb inflation. Whether the Federal Reserve has acted on its responsibilities for full employment policy remains in dispute. For this and other reasons beyond the scope of this book, the debate leading up to the passage of the Full Employment and Balanced Growth Act of 1978 is considered to be the "last hurrah" of Keynesian dominance in U.S. policymaking, rather than the major step forward its sponsors had hoped it would be (U.S. Congress 2007; Weir 1992).

A last look back at selected economic indicators over the years after enactment of the Employment Act—in addition to the Bureau of Economic Analysis time series on recession and unemployment levels presented in Figure 7.3—sheds a little more light on the subject. While there is a myriad of economic data on which the Employment Act might be judged, Figures 7.4–7.6 offer three varied perspectives with which to assess the legislation's long-term impact. The Congressional Budget Office's capital infrastructure spending trends present a snapshot of the federal government's investment strategies. Internal Revenue Service data on tax rates and receipts shed some light on the tax priorities. The Bureau of Economic Analysis's personal income data as well as income data from the World Top Incomes Database convey a picture of the relative prosperity of Americans over the past 60 years.[18]

The initial spurt of capital infrastructure spending in the post–World War II period occurred during the Eisenhower administration. As Figure 7.4 illustrates, the rate of federal infrastructure spending to the gross domestic product (GDP) had its sharpest rise during the Eisenhower years. The federal interstate highway program remains the premier example of infrastructure spending on public works that reaps multiplicative benefits for the economy and the American people.[19] While it is true that Senator O'Mahoney had cited the construction of Boulder Dam (renamed Hoover Dam in 1947) as the quintessential example of public spending for the common good during the Senate floor debate over S. 380, the highway program brought more benefits because the construction of federal interstate highways reached almost all corners of the nation. Not only did the interstate system open communities up for commerce and ease of travel to work, it helped boost the auto industry. President Eisenhower himself recognized that the federal highway program would "have some effect in leveling out the peaks and valleys in our economic life" (Sloan 1991, p. 134).

Figure 7.4 also depicts the rise in capital infrastructure spending in response to the spike in unemployment during the mid-1970s. Congress and the Carter administration increased capital infrastructure spending generally and as a rate of GDP from 1977 through 1980. The stimulus package included public works, public employment, and an expansion of the Comprehensive Employment and Training Act (CETA). Unemployment dropped correspondingly until the recession of the early 1980s.

It was in the 1980s that policy priorities on unemployment and the federal role in employment stimulation shifted. Unemployment spiked to its highest levels since the Great Depression, rising above 10 percent for several months and staying above 8 percent for two years. In response, Congress and the Reagan administration cut infrastructure

Figure 7.4 Capital Infrastructure Spending, 1956–2009 (2009 dollars)

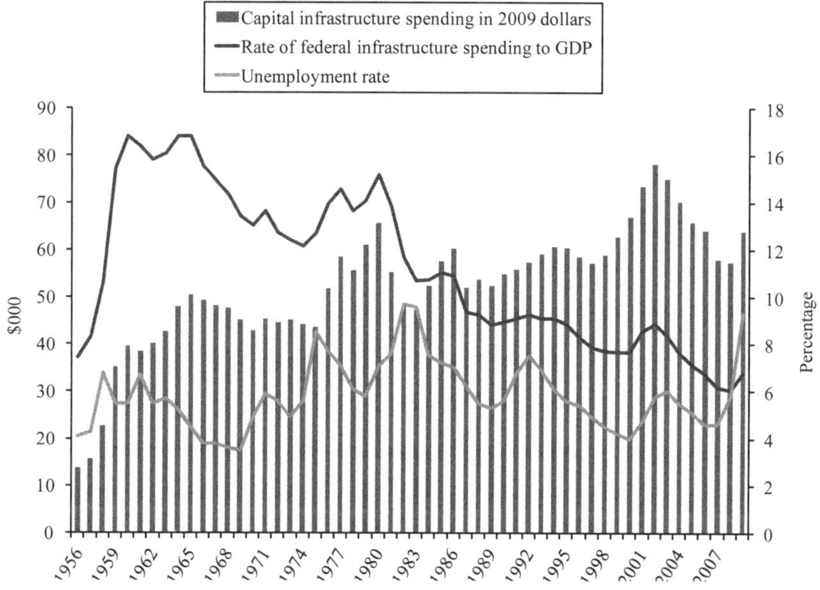

SOURCE: BEA (2012b); BLS (2012); CBO (2010); author's calculations.

spending generally and as a rate to GDP. Although there were limited increases in capital infrastructure spending during the mid-1980s, the Reagan administration advocated the use of tax policy as its main tool to address the recession and high levels of unemployment (Bernstein 2001; Brownlee and Graham 2003).

The relationship between full employment policy and taxation was one of the key features of Hansen's *After the War—Full Employment* report and a major issue of contention during the Senate debate on S. 380. The rates of the 1950s were quite high by contemporary standards, as Figure 7.5 shows, especially for the upper income levels. Many political leaders of the 1940s and 1950s, such as Sen. Robert Taft, argued that tax rates should be increased to balance the budget when additional federal spending was necessary. Taft, for example, voted to increase taxes to pay for the Korean War (Patterson 1972; Sloan 1991).

Walter Heller, chairman of the Council of Economic Advisers for President Kennedy, advocated passing tax cuts during the 1960s. Con-

Figure 7.5 GDP, Federal Tax Receipts, and Tax Rates, 1946–2010

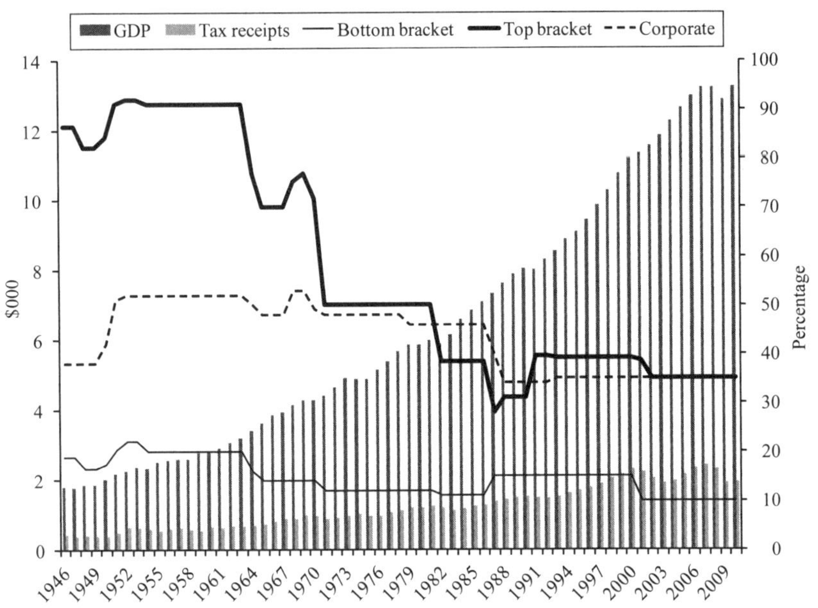

SOURCE: BEA (2012b); IRS (2012); author's calculations.

gress and the Kennedy administration listened: they cut taxes sharply, as Figure 7.5 shows, for the lowest tax bracket as well as the top tax bracket. The tax cut, enacted in early 1964, after Kennedy's death, cut the top marginal income tax rate from 91 percent to 70 percent and reduced the corporate income tax rate from 52 percent to 47 percent. Much has been written about the implementation of Keynesian economics by Heller and his colleagues on the Council of Economic Advisers, Kermit Gordon and James Tobin. In its 1962 report, the council established a 4 percent unemployment level as the interim target for full employment. Heller, Gordon, and Tobin maintained that unemployment could be reduced without increasing inflation (Bernstein 2001).

In the 1980s, Congress and the Reagan administration enacted further tax cuts for upper income earners and corporations. The Tax Reform Act of 1986 reduced the top marginal tax rate to a low of 28 percent. As mentioned above, these cuts were a response to the recession and high levels of unemployment, and their proponents hoped the cuts would have a stimulating effect comparable to the tax cuts of the 1960s. The "New Federalism" articulated by President Reagan and embodied in the tax cuts, moreover, shifted the major responsibility for job creation back to the private sector. As Reagan famously said, "Government is not the solution to our problem; government *is* the problem." The federal role in job creation mandated by the Employment Act was not repealed, but it *was* rendered obsolete (Bernstein 2001; Brownlee and Graham 2003; Jones 1988; Philips 1993).

A critical feature of full employment policy—and ultimately the Employment Act—was to increase purchasing power. Job creation and increased purchasing power went hand-in-glove. The statistical models of legislative support for full employment discussed in Chapter 6 showed that the demographic and economic characteristics of the congressional districts correlated with action on the legislation. More specifically, the districts' unemployment levels in 1937, percentage of working class residents, and percentage of foreign-born and African American residents were among the variables underlying legislative support for the Employment Act. A fundamental issue was whether these hardest-hit segments of the workforce would be reached by these policies.

Personal income has risen substantially since the passage of the Employment Act, as Figure 7.6 shows. Average personal income stood at $8,907 per capita (in 2005 dollars) in 1946 and reached $33,010 per capita (in 2005 dollars) in 2010, increasing by 271 percent over this period. The average personal income plus capital gains of the bottom 90 percent of earners had its largest gains (an 84 percent increase) during the period from 1946 through 1980 and has only increased by 4 percent since 1981. The average personal income plus capital gains of the top 1 percent of earners grew modestly (a 34 percent increase) from 1946 through 1980 but has increased by 138 percent since 1981. The bursting of the high-tech bubble led to a dip in the average personal income of the top 1 percent of earners in the early 2000s.

The difference between the average personal income plus capital gains of the bottom 90 percent of earners and the top 1 percent of earners (both in 2010 dollars) was $304,906 in 1946. By 2007, the difference between the average personal income plus capital gains of the bottom 90 percent of earners and that of the top 1 percent of earners (both in 2010 dollars) was $1,400,905. The time series in Figure 7.6 illustrates the growing income inequality in the United States, which has been

Figure 7.6 Average Personal Income (2005 dollars) and Average Personal Income Plus Capital Gains of the Bottom 90% and Top 1% (2010 dollars)

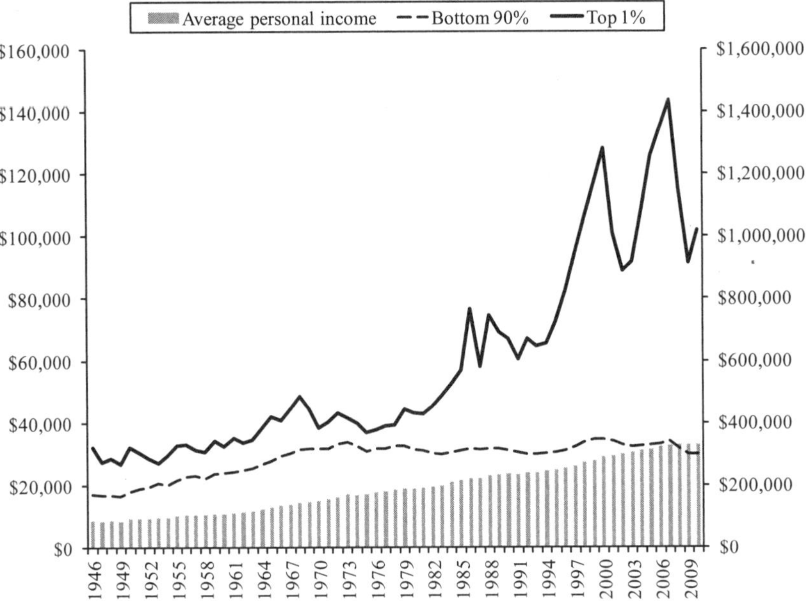

NOTE: Average personal income plus capital gains of the top 1 percent (2010 dollars) is scaled on the right axis, while average personal income (2005 dollars) and average personal income plus capital gains of the bottom 90 percent (2010 dollars) are scaled on the left axis.
SOURCE: BEA (2012b); World Top Incomes Database (2012); author's calculations.

well-documented elsewhere (Atkinson, Piketty, and Saez 2011; Bartels 2008; Piketty and Saez 2003).

More enlightening on income inequality than Figure 7.6 is the research on wage structure during the mid-twentieth century that Claudia Goldin and Robert A. Margo conducted. They found "extraordinary" wage compression by education, job experience, and occupation from 1940 to 1970. Their analysis implies that the segments of the workforce that were hardest-hit in the Great Depression thrived, relatively, in the postwar period. They also found that the wage differentials had returned to 1940 levels by the late 1980s. Goldin and Margo identified the economic and demographic factors that contributed to the changes in wage structure, but they did not explore the policy factors that might have influenced the wage compression. There is abundant research under way on the reasons for the wage compression as well as the reversal of the trends that had prevailed from the 1940s up until the 1980s (Goldin and Margo 1992; Jacobs and Skocpol 2005). The part the Employment Act played in establishing the federal role in job creation—as well as increased production and purchasing power—cannot be measured as the economic factors can be, but the correlates of the Employment Act to these income trends are not likely to be serendipitous.

As it turned out, the Employment Act of 1946 accomplished much of what those who drafted it had envisioned. Although it cannot be said that the act directly created the prosperity of the postwar period, it no doubt had a role in facilitating it. It gave the federal government the mandate as well as the tools to alleviate recessions and high levels of unemployment. And for many years a series of Congresses and presidents drew on that authority to counter recessions and foster job growth.

Notes

1. Harry S. Truman to Sen. Robert Wagner and Rep. Carter Manasco, letters, 20 December 1945, Truman Papers.
2. Barkley entered the House of Representatives in 1913, and Kentucky elected him to the Senate in 1926. Truman chose him as his vice presidential candidate in 1948. Barkley was reelected to the Senate in 1954 after serving as vice president.
3. The committee was initially composed of seven members from the House and seven members from the Senate. The partisan makeup was based on the relative membership of the majority and minority parties in each chamber. According to the Employment Act, the Joint Economic Committee members were to be appointed by the president of the Senate and the Speaker of the House.
4. O'Mahoney also chaired the Joint Economic Committee in the 81st and 82nd Congresses.
5. Taft would become chairman of the Joint Economic Committee when the Republicans gained the majority in the 80th Congress.
6. Tunnel represented Delaware for one term. He defeated a Republican incumbent in 1940 but lost his bid for reelection in 1946. Myers served from Pennsylvania in the House of Representatives from 1939 to 1945 and then in the Senate from 1945 to 1951. He was defeated for reelection in 1950. Hart represented New Jersey from 1935 to 1955. In 1954, he did not seek reelection. Huber represented Ohio from 1945 to 1951.

7. Bridges served as the Republican senator from New Hampshire from 1937 until his death in 1961. He was the Senate minority leader from 1952 to 1953. In 1925, La Follette was elected as a Republican senator from Wisconsin to fill the vacancy caused by the death of his father. He was a founder of the Wisconsin Progressive Party in 1934, and he was reelected to the Senate in 1934 and 1940 as a Wisconsin Progressive. When the Wisconsin Progressive Party folded, he returned to the Republican Party for the 1946 campaign. Joseph McCarthy defeated him for the Republican nomination that year.
8. Hansen subsequently returned to Harvard, where he continued as the Lucius N. Littauer Professor of Political Economy.
9. Edwin G. Nourse, oral history interview conducted in Washington, DC, by Jerry N. Hess, March 7, 1972.
10. Ibid.
11. Keyserling often spoke of a national essay contest he had won earlier in his career in which he proposed full employment policy as the solution to the nation's economic problems. The source for the material in this paragraph is Keyserling, from an oral history interview conducted in Washington, DC, by Jerry N. Hess, May 3, 1971, Harry S. Truman Library and Museum, Independence, MO.
12. In addition to Donovan and Hamby, the material in this paragraph also comes from Keyserling, in an oral history interview conducted in Washington, DC, by Jerry N. Hess, May 3, 1971, Truman Library, Independence, MO.
13. From political and historical perspectives, the clashes between Truman and the 80th Congress over labor law and the rights of workers to organize and to bargain collectively were more significant than the fight over tax cuts. Congress overrode Truman's veto of the Taft-Hartley legislation, which rolled back some of the worker rights that the National Labor Relations Act of 1935 had provided.
14. Keyserling, oral history interview conducted in Washington, DC, by Hess, May 3, 1971, Truman Library, Independence, MO; Nourse, oral history interview conducted in Washington, DC, by Hess, March 7, 1972.
15. Burns would later become Chairman of the Federal Reserve under President Richard Nixon.
16. Humphrey had been a major supporter of Taft's campaign for the Republican nomination for president in 1952. After Eisenhower won the nomination, he chaired the finance committee for the Republican Party in the 1952 general-election campaign.
17. *Full Employment and Balanced Growth Act of 1978*, H.R. 50, 95th Cong. (1978).
18. For further discussion of the World Top Incomes Database, see Atkinson, Piketty, and Saez (2011).
19. The funding for the U.S. Highway Trust Fund mainly comes from gasoline and automobile taxes.

Appendix A
Variables and Their Sources

This appendix describes the variables used in Chapter 6 of this book and where they were obtained. Scores and indices constructed from other measures are discussed in Appendix B.

UNITS OF ANALYSIS

The constituency and economic traits of the congressional districts are plagued by a problem of unit of analysis. The census data are county-level, and the unit of analysis for this research is "member of Congress and congressional district." In 1944, most congressional districts neatly follow county boundaries, but the metropolitan counties have more than one congressional district within their area.

There is no straightforward way to disaggregate the metropolitan counties that have multiple congressional districts. I initially divided the census into two data files: one containing all counties represented by only one congressional district; the other containing all counties represented by more than one congressional district. The former data set is aggregated by congressional district number within each state. For those congressional districts from the same counties, the census data for each district are prorated in equal proportions according to the number of districts. The two data sets are then merged together to form a master file, with all congressional districts represented.

This solution dilutes the impact of a metropolitan congressional district having factors that may be skewed in particular ways. For example, differences in Wayne County, Michigan, between Hamtramck, Inkster, and Grosse Pointe are lost, and the economic, social, and ethnic factors are muted.

"TIMELINESS" OF DATA

After serious consideration and some data manipulation, I decided not to interpolate 1945 estimates for the census variables. The primary reason is conceptual: I assume that the influence of the constituency and of the economic variable precedes the election of the representative and the ultimate outcome on the full employment bill. In this regard, 1940 is a reasonable year for which to draw measures of constituency and economic influences.

A second justification for not calculating 1945 estimates is that, despite the fact that we know that significant demographic, social, and economic changes were occurring during the war years, we also know that these changes did not occur uniformly across local areas of the country. For example, people were shifting from some parts of the country to other areas to work in war production. Economic and demographic change, moreover, occurred at differing paces over the course of the decade in response initially to war mobilization and subsequently to demobilization.

I decided that the question of "change" was best handled by a single variable that provides a measure of these shifts in each congressional district from 1940 to 1950. Although imperfect, the percentage of urban change from 1940 to 1950 serves to operationalize this dynamic. This variable addresses the issue of varying amounts of change in different parts of the country, but it is limited because it also captures changes that took place after the passage of the Employment Act.

Table A.1 Variables Used in the Analysis of the House Vote on Full Employment, and Their Sources

Variable	Source
Unemployment rate, 1937	ICPSR (2013c)
% foreign-born, 1940	ICPSR (2013c)
% African American, 1940	ICPSR (2013c)
% urban, 1940	ICPSR (2013c)
% population change, 1920–1940	ICPSR (2013c)
Occupation categories, 1940 (% distribution of those reporting an occupation by major occupation classes)	ICPSR (2013c)
Median years of school completed for those over 25 years of age, 1940	ICPSR (2013c)
Males	
Females	
Region of the country	ICPSR (2013c)
State	ICPSR (2013c)
% urban change, 1940–1950	ICPSR (2013b)
Median family income, 1950	ICPSR (2013b)
Farm-living-level index, 1940	ICPSR (2013b)
Member's military rank or experience	ICPSR (2013d)
Member's occupation prior to election to Congress	ICPSR (2013d)
Member's college attendance	ICPSR (2013d)
Member's cumulative years served in Congress prior to the 79th Congress (tenure in 1945)	ICPSR (2013d)
Year member was first elected to Congress	ICPSR (2013d)
Member's age when 79th Congress began	ICPSR (2013d)
Member's reason for leaving Congress	ICPSR (2013d)
Congressional district	ICPSR (2013a)
Member's margin of victory, 1944	ICPSR (2013a)
Candidate's % of total vote in most recent election, 1944	ICPSR (2013a)
Member's vote on roll call to recommit S. 380 / H.R. 2202	ICPSR (2013e)
Member's vote on roll call to pass S. 380	ICPSR (2013e)
Member's sponsorship of H.R. 2202	Hand-tabulated from Bailey (1964)

Table A.2 Variables Used in the Analysis of the Senate Vote on Full Employment, and Their Sources

Variable	Source
% urban change, 1920–1940	Hand-tabulated by author from U.S. Census Bureau (1940a)
% working class, 1940	Hand-tabulated by author from U.S. Census Bureau (1940b)
Per capita personal income, 1933	Hand-tabulated by author from U.S. Department of Commerce (1943)
Per capita personal income, 1943	Hand-tabulated from U.S. Department of Commerce (1943)
Unemployment rate, 1940	Hand-tabulated from U.S. Census Bureau (1940b)
% of vote in most recent election	ICPSR (2013a)

Appendix B
Scores and Indices

This book draws on several existing indices and calculates or modifies other scores and indices for use in this research. This appendix details the components of each of these variables. Specific variables and their sources are listed in Appendix A.

FULL EMPLOYMENT SCORE

The full employment score is actually two different measures—a score for the Senate and a score for the House. In the Senate, the score is composed of three roll call votes on S. 380, two that amended it and one that passed it. In the House, the three components consist of sponsorship of the full employment bill, a roll call to recommit the compromise bill, and a roll call on its final passage.

Both of these scores, however, are constructed in the same manner and are fashioned after the roll-call scoring approaches used by many others (Clausen 1973, pp. 12–35; MacRae 1958; Miller and Stokes 1963). In this instance, behaviors deemed to be supporting full employment are assigned the value of 1.0, and behaviors deemed to be opposing full employment are assigned the value of −1.0. In the case of the Senate, voting to amend S. 380 is considered to be in opposition to full employment. In the House, voting to recommit S. 380 is considered an antagonistic action. It almost goes without saying that sponsoring and voting for final passage are supportive of full employment.

After each member was given a 1.0 or −1.0 score for each of the three possible actions, the three values were summed for each member. This sum became the numerator in a ratio that had 3—the total possible behaviors—as the denominator. This ratio was computed for each member to form a score that ranged from −1.0 to 1.0.

PARTISANSHIP SCORE

The partisanship score is an index of support calculated from those 50 roll calls in which a majority of one party opposed a majority of the other party during the first session of the 79th Congress. It forms a ratio, with 1.0 as the perfect partisanship score and −1.0 as the most extreme negative partisanship score. The numerator is the number of times the legislator voted with his or her party's position minus the number of times the legislator voted with the opposing party's position. The denominator is 50, which was the total number of party-line votes (i.e., when the majority of one party votes in contrast to the majority of the other party) that were taken in the U.S. House of Representative during the 79th Congress.

Unlike other scores based upon roll calls, this ratio does not equate nonvoting to voting with the opposition, and the Democratic partisanship score symmetrically complements the Republican partisanship score.

This partisanship score differs from the Rice Index of Party Cohesion on several dimensions. Foremost, this partisanship score is calculated for each member based upon his or her voting record. The Rice Index is calculated for parties according to sessions of Congress and is based upon the degree that members of the same party voted together. This partisanship score also differs from the Index of Party Unlikeness, again because the unit of analysis for the latter is the Congress rather than the member.

IDEOLOGY SCALE

The liberal-conservative ideology scale is based on selected roll-call votes that tap liberal versus conservative cleavages. The *New Republic* published how each member of Congress voted on 10 roll calls occurring during the 79th Congress that the Union for Democratic Action (UDA) identified as critical "progressive" votes in the areas of foreign policy, civil liberties, farm policy, price controls, poll taxes, antiracketeering, and the confirmation of Henry Wallace as commerce secretary (*New Republic* 1946a,b).

As in the case of the partisanship score, nonvoting is not equated with a negative vote. The number of votes against the liberal positions is subtracted from the number of votes with the liberal positions and then divided by the total number of times the member voted. Those members of Congress on record as having voted for all 10 liberal stands scored a perfect +1.0, and those on record as having voted 10 times against the liberal position scored a perfect −1.0.

ADJUSTED LIVING LEVEL

The 1952 County and City Data Book provides a "Farm Living Level Index" for 1940 that is unsophisticated compared to contemporary measures such as the Consumer Price Index, but is used as a relative measure of wealth. It was originally designed to be a measure of wealth that was based on more than simple income—e.g., the nonsalary resources and expenditures of farm households. Analysis reveals that this Farm Living Level Index parallels the median family income in direction and in distribution across areas. It is a valuable index of living levels because it measures the nonincome resources of agricultural families.

I made adjustments to the Farm Living Level Index to deal with the counterpoint—exclusively urban counties. First, the Farm Living Level Index was correlated with median family income, and all congressional districts were ranked according to their median family income. Values were then imputed for exclusively urban congressional districts according to the Farm Living Level Index of those congressional districts that had corresponding median family incomes. These imputed values accounted for less than 5 percent of the cases.

INDICES

New Deal Realignment

This variable is constructed from the "Year First Elected to Congress" variable in the Roster of Congressional Officeholders data set listed in Appendix A. It simply assigns a number "1" to all members of Congress elected in 1932 or later. All other members are coded "0."

Biographical Status

Three variables pertaining to the members' background are ranked and summarized into a score—"biographical status." The three components are 1) member's occupation prior to election to Congress, 2) college that the member attended, and 3) member's military rank. I made subjective decisions regarding the ordinal values of the categories for the three component variables. Each of these three variables is potentially worth three points, so they have equal weight and sum to nine.

Occupation:
- Business (includes agriculture) = 3
- Law, education, and other professional = 2
- Miscellaneous and other = 1
- None, unreported or retired = 0

College attended:
- Ivy League = 3
- Other private colleges = 2
- Major state university = 1
- No college reported = 0

Military rank:
- General, colonel, lt. colonel, major = 3
- Captain, lieutenant = 2
- Enlisted or nonranked = 1
- No military service reported = 0

Percentage Working Class

A summary measure of occupation for 1940 is constructed by summing the categories that are deemed working class. Consistent with the discussion in Chapter 2, this "working class" variable includes people who reported occupations as laborers, operators, domestics, clerical, craftsmen, foremen, service workers, and farm laborers. It excludes business and professional occupations as well as farm owners.

Region

This variable is a traditional grouping of states by geographic area and is the standard ICPSR region variable. The categories are shown in Table B.1 on the following page.

For some analyses, these eight regions were combined into five groupings. In such cases, the Northeast includes the New England and Mid-Atlantic states. The Midwest includes the East North-Central and the West North-Central states. The South and the Border states remain intact, and the Mountain and Pacific states are grouped into the West.

Table B.1 Traditional Grouping of States by Geographic Area, Serving as the Standard ICPSR Region Variable

Region	State	Region	State
New England	Connecticut	South	Alabama
	Maine		Arkansas
	Massachusetts		Florida
	New Hampshire		Georgia
	Rhode Island		Louisiana
	Vermont		Mississippi
			North Carolina
Mid-Atlantic	Delaware		South Carolina
	New Jersey		Texas
	New York		Virginia
	Pennsylvania		Border Kentucky
			Maryland
East North-Central	Illinois		Oklahoma
	Indiana		Tennessee
	Michigan		West Virginia
	Ohio		
	Wisconsin	Mountain	Arizona
			Colorado
West North-Central	Iowa		Idaho
	Kansas		Montana
	Minnesota		Nevada
	Missouri		New Mexico
	Nebraska		Utah
	North Dakota		Wyoming
	South Dakota		
		Pacific	California
			Oregon
			Washington

Appendix C
Profiling Support for S. 380

Appendix C presents further analysis underpinning the discussion of Senate support for S. 380 in Chapter 6. There are clear partisan underpinnings to support for full employment legislation. As Table C.1 presents, the Democratic average on the full employment score is almost twice the overall mean of 0.36. The Republican mean score, however, falls well below the total average score.

Table C.1 Senate Full Employment Mean Scores by Region and Party

Region (*n*)	Mean	Democratic mean	Republican mean
New England (12)	0.62	0.50	0.77
Mid-Atlantic (8)	0.42	1.00	−0.55
East North-Central (10)	−0.06	1.00	−0.33
West North-Central (14)	−0.03	1.00	−0.11
Border (10)	0.33	0.62	−0.67
South (20)	0.42	0.42	
Mountain (16)	0.59	1.00	−1.00
Pacific (6)	0.79	1.00	0.56
National (96)	0.36	0.71	−0.15
Total cases	96[a]	55	40

[a]Democratic and Republican cases do not sum to total because one senator was an Independent.

The regional variation in support for full employment is also quite interesting. The New England and Pacific Coast regions have the most consistently high scores, regardless of party identification. All of the other regions, with the exception of the exclusively Democratic South, have a partisan split in their mean scores on full employment. The East and West North-Central regions are the least supportive of full employment.

It is possible that electoral factors might influence whether a senator would support such an avant-garde (but potentially popular) piece of legislation. One could speculate that senators who are more secure electorally would be more likely to deviate from their party's position on S. 380 because it is easier for them to take risks. The importance that the Democratic Party leadership placed on this bill suggests that the more seasoned legislators supported it. Tenure in office might have had an intervening effect on the importance of electoral factors.

The importance of partisan identification, discussed above, is not forgotten in this context. Republicans came from states that were wealthier, both in 1943 and 1933, and that had experienced less of a percentage increase in urbanization from 1920 to 1940. The difference in state unemployment rates between Democratic and Republican senators, however, is trivial.

These differences are small, but the directions in which they move are consistent and expected. The findings, though based upon simple analyses, hint that less relative wealth and greater vulnerability to unemployment might be linked to support for full employment. These results do not challenge what we might intuitively hypothesize from the earlier discussion of public opinion, but they beg for further scrutiny (Table C.2).

It is enlightening to refine the inquiry by looking at senators whose scores deviated from their party's average score. For the purposes here, deviance is defined as Democrats who score negatively on the full employment scale and Republicans who score positively. Table C.3 presents some rather interesting patterns. The lowest rates of unemployment are in states with Democrats who have negative scores on full employment. These same Democrats also represent states that, on average, are the poorest in 1943 and that have experienced the slowest growth in per capita personal income over the previous decade. For the most part, these deviant Democrats are from the South.

Republicans who score positively on full employment do not differ meaningfully from their fellow Republicans except in regard to urbanization. These deviant Republicans come from states with the lowest average increase in urbanization from 1920 to 1940. This phenomenon is largely attributable to Republicans from New England states that already had high levels of urbanization.

Table C.2 Economic and Demographic Characteristics by Senators' Party

	Mean value	
	Democrat	Republican
Unemployment rate (%)	14.1	14.3
Per capita personal income, 1943 ($)	908	1,043
Per capita personal income, 1933 ($)	280	341
Change in per capita income, 1933–1943 (%)	2.1	2.3
Change in urban population, 1920–1940 (%)	6.2	4.3
Total cases	55	40

Table C.3 Economic and Demographic Characteristics by Party and Full Employment Score

	Mean value	
	Positive	Negative
Democrats		
Unemployment rate (%)	14.9	11.9
Per capita personal income, 1943 ($)	943	923
Per capita personal income, 1933 ($)	285	328
Change in per capita income, 1933–1943 (%)	2.1	1.9
Change in urban population, 1920–1940 (%)	5.8	4.4
Total cases	40	7
Republicans		
Unemployment rate (%)	14.6	14.1
Per capita personal income, 1943 ($)	1,037	1,056
Per capita personal income, 1933 ($)	355	333
Change in per capita income, 1933–1943 (%)	2.2	2.3
Change in urban population, 1920–1940 (%)	3.4	5.0
Total cases	9	24

Appendix D
Profiling Support for H.R. 2202

Appendix D provides a more detailed analysis of House support for H.R. 2202/S. 380, which is discussed in Chapter 6. The size and diversity of the House of Representatives offers the opportunity for more in-depth analysis of the characteristics of its membership than does the 96-member Senate. The 79th House of Representatives consisted of 242 Democrats, 193 Republicans and 1 Progressive. The region with the most representatives in the House was the South, with 22.8 percent. The Mid-Atlantic and East North-Central regions followed, with 21.7 and 19.5 percent, respectively. The smallest delegation came from the Mountain region and constituted only 3.8 percent of those serving in the 79th Congress.

Breaking down party affiliation by region presents some striking patterns. In general, the eastern and midwestern sections of the country were dominated by the Republicans, while the southern and western parts were controlled by the Democrats (see Table D.1). The Mid-Atlantic region was the most balanced, with 57.1 percent Republicans and 42.9 percent Democrats. The most extreme region was the South, which was exclusively represented by Democrats.

The congressional districts had an average district population living in urban areas of 45.3 percent. During the period from 1930 to 1950, congressional districts experienced a mean percentage increase in total population of 25.8 percent. On average, 8.3 percent of the population in the districts was foreign-born and 9.3 percent was African American in 1940. The median number of school years completed by men over the age of 25 was 8.6, and the median number of years in school for women over 25 was 8.2.

Table D.1 Political Party, by Region

	Democratic	Republican	*n*
New England	35.7	64.3	28
Mid-Atlantic	42.9	57.1	98
Border	82.1	17.9	39
South	100.0	0.0	103
East North-Central	30.7	68.3	88
West North-Central	20.5	79.5	44
Mountain	58.8	41.2	17
Pacific	58.8	41.2	34
Total no. of districts	242	193	435

Table D.2 Mean Constituency Traits, by Party and Region

	Democratic	Republican	Total	
% foreign-born	8.2	8.5	8.3	
% African American	14.9	2.0	9.3	
% urban	46.9	43.9	45.3	
% population change	29.4	21.2	25.8	
Years in school, male	8.4	8.8	8.6	
Years in school, female	8.0	8.4	8.2	
	New England	**Mid-Atlantic**	**Border**	**South**
% foreign-born	16.7	16.1	1.2	1.4
% African American	1.4	3.6	10.6	28.6
% urban	67.8	71.5	21.8	21.5
% population change	17.2	16.0	21.8	27.9
Years in school, male	9.2	8.3	7.9	8.2
Years in school, female	8.7	8.4	7.5	7.6
	East North-Central	**West North-Central**	**Mountain**	**Pacific**
% foreign-born	8.5	5.4	6.2	12.2
% African American	3.4	2.2	0.7	1.3
% urban	52.6	30.1	28.1	58.5
% population change	21.0	11.4	35.6	87.2
Years in school, male	8.6	8.8	9.5	9.2
Years in school, female	8.4	8.3	8.6	10.1

As Table D.2 indicates, most of these constituency characteristics did not vary a great deal by the party of the representative elected in the district, though the Democratic districts tended to be slightly more urban and less educated. A notable exception was race. Democratic districts had a considerably larger proportion of African Americans (14.9 percent, in contrast to 2.0 percent for Republican districts).

There were observable differences in constituency traits by region. The New England and Mid-Atlantic congressional districts were the most urban, and the South, West North-Central and Border districts were the least urbanized. While the South and Border districts had means of 28.6 percent and 10.6 percent, respectively, of their populations that were African American, the remaining regions each averaged less than 4 percent African American. Conversely, the South and Border districts had the smallest averages of their population that were foreign-born. The New England, Mid-Atlantic and Pacific districts had the largest average percentages of foreign-born residents.

The economic characteristics, which Table D.3 presents, exhibit interesting differences. Overall, the mean of all districts' adjusted living level was 85, the average 1937 unemployment rate was 10.8 percent, and the average of the workforce reporting working-class occupations was 62.7 percent. The proportion of working class in the district did not vary much by party. The unemployment rate was slightly higher for the Democratic districts. There was a dramatic difference, moreover, in the adjusted living level by party. The Democratic districts averaged a modest 67 score, in contrast to the Republican mean score of 108.5. Thus, the Republicans represented districts that were much more prosperous in terms of standard of living.

Table D.3 Mean District Economic Traits, by Party and Region

	Democratic	Republican	Total	
% unemployed, 1937	11.4	10.1	10.8	
% working class	62.8	62.6	62.7	
Adjusted living level	67.0	108.5	85.0	
	New England	**Mid-Atlantic**	**Border**	**South**
% unemployed, 1937	11.5	12.6	12.6	10.3
% working class	76.4	76.5	54.9	50.5
Adjusted living level	102.4	74.6	60.7	46.7
	East North-Central	**West North-Central**	**Mountain**	**Pacific**
% unemployed, 1937	9.7	9.4	10.0	9.7
% working class	67.1	49.0	55.4	67.1
Adjusted living level	121.1	104.6	81.9	124.8

The regions also differed widely on these economic measures. New England, the Pacific, and the East and West North-Central regions were the wealthiest, according to the adjusted living level, in contrast to the South, Border and Mountain regions. The unemployment rates tended to differ in a pattern across regions that shows the Mid-Atlantic and Border regions with the highest averages and the Pacific and North Central regions with the lowest. New England and the Mid-Atlantic had the largest average proportions of working-class people, while the West North-Central and the South had the lowest percentages of working class.

Table D.4 Mean Electoral Traits, by Party and Region

	Democratic	Republican	Total
% most recent vote	72.2	60.4	66.8
% margin of victory	46.4	21.7	35.2
Tenure in 79th Congress	7.2	6.4	6.9

	New England	Mid-Atlantic	Border	South
% most recent vote	60.1	55.8	65.1	90.5
% margin of victory	20.4	17.5	30.6	81.4
Tenure in 79th Congress	6.7	6.2	6.5	9.2

	East North-Central	West North-Central	Mountain	Pacific
% most recent vote	60.7	60.1	58.5	66.4
% margin of victory	22.1	20.5	17.2	32.9
Tenure in 79th Congress	6.9	6.5	4.2	4.6

The Democratic delegation as a whole appeared more secure electorally, as Table D.4 indicates. On average, the victorious Democratic candidate received 72.2 percent of the votes cast in their 1944 congressional elections. Successful Republican candidates got an average of 60.4 percent of the total votes cast in their districts. The average margin of victory of the two parties further accentuated the Democrats' greater electoral strength over the Republicans: the successful Democratic congressman had a 46.4 percent mean margin of victory, and the successful Republican congressman had a 21.7 percent mean margin of victory. Again, the South's unique electoral features were skewing the Democratic averages, as the regional breakdown reveals.

Democrats' tenure—i.e., mean number of cumulative years served at the beginning of the 79th Congress—was longer than that of the Republicans. The mean number of years' tenure for the Democrats was 7.2, and the mean number of years' tenure for the Republicans was 6.4. However, the South's unusually long tenure in office—an average of more than nine years—drove up the Democratic average.

Despite the fact that the Democrats had more years of tenure in office, they were, on average, younger in age than their Republican peers. The average age of a Democratic congressman was 52.4 years. The Republican representatives' mean age was 53.6. (See Table D.5.)

Differences in background that the members of the two parties and eight regions evidence is summarized in the "biographical status" score presented in Table D.5. Republicans on average had higher status scores than their Demo-

Table D.5 Mean Ideological/Personal Traits, by Party and Region

	Democratic	Republican	Total	
Partisanship score	0.47	0.59		
Ideology score	0.44	−0.57	0.0	
Biographical status	4.1	4.7	4.4	
Age	52.4	53.6	53.0	

	New England	Mid-Atlantic	Border	South
Partisanship score				
Democrats	0.60	0.64	0.57	0.51
Republicans	0.45	0.43	0.73	
Ideology score	−0.1	0.1	0.2	0.0
Biographical status	4.2	4.9	4.6	4.1
Age	52.8	52.9	52.7	52.9

	East North-Central	West North-Central	Mountain	Pacific
Partisanship score				
Democrats	0.68	0.63	0.59	0.67
Republicans	0.67	0.64	0.70	0.40
Ideology score	−0.1	−0.4	0.0	0.3
Biographical status	4.3	4.3	4.2	4.0
Age	54.6	52.6	53.3	51.0

NOTE: Blank = not applicable. South region is blank for the Republicans because there were no Republican representatives from the South.

cratic counterparts. The Mid-Atlantic region scored highest on this measure, while the Pacific region averaged the lowest value on this summary scale.

A look at the components of the biographical score provides a fuller explanation of the regional and party differences in status. The Democratic members were preponderantly lawyers before entering Congress, 61 percent being from the legal profession. While the Republican delegation consisted of 45.7 percent lawyers, it had larger proportions of professionals (excluding lawyers), businessmen, and agricultural occupations than the Democratic delegation. Across every region, law was the most prevalent occupation listed by the House members of the 79th Congress. The percentage of lawyers ranged from an overwhelming 82.5 percent of the congressmen from the South to 35.3 percent of both the Mountain and Pacific regions. Some 38.8 percent of the Mid-Atlantic region's delegation reported that they had been businessmen before their election to Congress. Some 23.5 percent of the congressmen from the Mountain region were businessmen, and an equal percentage were in agricultural occupations. The Mountain region led the nation in the proportion of its delegation from agriculture.

The congressional delegations also differed in terms of educational background, another component of biographical status. Although there was only a slight difference between Republicans and Democrats on the percentage who had not attended college, the Democrats being 1.2 percent higher, there were noticeable variations in what kind of college the member had attended. Republicans had attended Ivy League colleges at a rate three times greater than Democrats. There were also regional differences in college attendance. New England had the largest proportion of a delegation that had not attended college and the largest proportion that had attended an Ivy League college, both percentages being 32.1. The Border and the South had the smallest percentage of delegations that had not attended college, with 5.1 and 7.8 percent, respectively. Over 43 percent of the southern delegation had attended a state college, the largest percentage in the nation.

The congressional delegations of the two parties exhibited varying levels of partisan loyalty, as Table D.5 presents. During the period the 79th Congress was in session prior to the election of 1946, the Democratic members had an average partisanship score of 0.58 and the Republican members a score of 0.56 (not shown). However, the scores based on party votes for the entire span of the 79th Congress reveal a noticeable change in partisan voting following the 1946 campaign, with the result being that the Republican delegation's average partisanship score increased to 0.59 and the Democratic membership's average score fell to 0.47.

The sharpest contrast between the two parties, however, was displayed by their ideology scores. The Democratic delegation registered an average ideology score of 0.44 during the 79th Congress. The Republican membership scored an average of −0.57 on the same set of roll calls identified by the UDA. This finding substantiated that the ideological differences expressed by the party platforms were manifested in congressional voting behavior as well.

The regions also exhibited differences in average ideology scores. The most conservative region, the West North-Central, had a −0.41 mean ideology score. The Pacific region, with a 0.28 average, fell at the other end of the spectrum. Only one other region had a mean score greater than plus or minus 0.1; most of the regions cluster near the national average of −0.004.

The regional differences in ideology scores became much sharper when the Republicans and Democrats were observed separately (not shown). The Democratic regional mean scores ranged from 0.01 in the South to 0.92 in the East North-Central. The Republican mean scores, while not varying as widely as the Democratic scores, spanned from −0.72 in the West North-Central to

−0.42 in the Pacific. When one looks at the difference between the Democratic and Republican scores within a region, one sees that the most divergent region was the East North-Central, with average scores ranging from 0.92 for the Democrats to −0.55 for the Republicans.

Just as ideology varied across regions and parties, so too did partisanship. The South was the least partisan region, averaging a Democratic partisanship score of 0.51. The East North-Central, consistent with its liberal ideology score, had the highest mean Democratic partisanship score, 0.68. On the Republican side, the Mountain region had a mean partisanship score of 0.70, making it the highest. The lowest average Republican partisanship score was 0.40 in the Pacific region.

Table D.6 Support for Full Employment, by Regional Delegation

	% sponsored H.R. 2202	% final roll call "yes"
New England	29	43
Mid-Atlantic	34	53
Border	31	52
South	4	28
East North-Central	30	47
West North-Central	12	45
Mountain	38	41
Pacific	64	62

In terms of the constituency measures, there should be differences between supporters and opponents of the full employment bill. Specifically, districts with more foreign-born and African Americans should be more likely to elect supporters of the legislation—if these groups are enfranchised—since these were groups more likely to be disadvantaged and therefore more likely to have supported an activist federal role. Likewise, supporters should be more likely to come from districts that have experienced more demographic change and are more urbanized, since they might have a greater appreciation for the interdependence of social and economic phenomena and thus have been more apt to support economic planning. The districts' educational attainment may not yield differences in support for full employment, because better-educated constituencies, though more equipped to understand the sophisticated logic of full employment, may also reflect more prosperous areas less sympathetic to the legislation.

The economic measures should display the sharpest differences between supporters and opponents of the legislation. Those who support the full employment bill should represent districts with higher 1937 rates of unemployment than their opponents, assuming they would least want to repeat the experience. Districts with a higher percentage of their population who are working-class, a segment of the population vulnerable to unemployment when war production ends, should be more likely to have elected supporters of full employment. On the other hand, opponents to the full employment bill should represent districts that are wealthier according to the adjusted living level, since these might be the areas most likely to benefit from the status quo.

At this juncture, it is difficult to speculate on how electoral measures might vary between the supporters and opponents. While more junior members of Congress might be more likely to support an idea as innovative as full employment, the support of the Democratic leadership for the bill would balance the less tenured members, leading to little variation among Democratic members on the tenure variable. Moreover, electoral variables should have little bearing in the South, because of its unique political dynamics. If the electoral measures have any effect, it may be seen in the New Deal realignment cohort.

Since the full employment bill was championed by the liberal community, those in Congress who have higher liberal scores on the ideology scale should be more likely to support the legislation. The opponents, on the other hand, should be more pervasive among members with higher status scores on the biographical measures than those who advocated full employment legislation. This statement assumes that higher-status people are more apt to benefit from less government involvement in maintaining economic well-being and that higher-status members are more likely to be associated with business elements, most of which opposed the full employment bill.

One simple way of approaching the hypotheses discussed above is to see if members vary in their support of the legislation according to whether their economic, constituent, electoral, ideological, and personal features were above or below average. On the basis of each variable's mean value, the members were grouped into a high or low category. By comparing the percentage of the members who fell into the high or low categories according to sponsorship, some interesting patterns emerge.

Since sponsors make up 26 percent of all members, a null hypothesis would be reflected in the sponsors falling into the high and low categories in approximately the same percentages. Likewise, the 74 percent of the members who did not sponsor H.R. 2202 should be distributed evenly in each of the high and low categories if the measures of economic, electoral, constituent, ideological, and personal features did not capture meaningful differences among members.

The constituency features of the sponsors' districts differed from those of the nonsponsors in several key ways, as Table D.7 reveals. Sponsors came from districts that were much more urban than those who chose not to sponsor

Table D.7 Percentage with Selected Features, by Sponsorship

	Yes		No	
	High	Low	High	Low
Economic				
% unemployed, 1937	35.3	18.3	64.7	81.7
% working-class	41.5	8.1	58.5	91.9
Adjusted living level	34.8	12.7	65.2	87.3
Constituency				
% foreign-born	45.3	11.5	54.7	88.5
% African American	15.6	30.5	84.4	69.5
% urban	47.7	12.0	52.3	88.0
% population change	32.5	22.9	67.5	77.1
Years in school—male	30.0	21.6	70.0	78.4
Years in school—female	25.0	27.3	75.0	72.7
Electoral				
% margin of victory	16.2	31.6	83.8	68.4
Tenure in 79th Congress	23.3	28.1	76.7	71.8
Ideological/personal				
Age	24.4	28.1	75.6	75.6
Biographical status	18.1	32.0	81.9	68.0
Ideology	54.4	3.4	45.6	96.6
Total cases	114		319	

the bill. The districts with below-average foreign-born citizens were less likely to be represented by sponsors of the legislation. Sponsors were more apt to come from districts with a smaller percentage of African Americans.

All three of the economic measures appear to differentiate the sponsors from those who did not sponsor the legislation. The percentage of the sponsors coming from districts with above-average proportions of working-class people was especially noteworthy, as Table D.7 indicates. Not surprisingly, sponsors represented districts that had a higher rate of unemployment in 1937 than nonsponsors. However, the predicted difference between sponsors and nonsponsors according to wealth, as measured by the adjusted living level index, is challenged by Table D.7.

As hypothesized, members who had higher scores on the biographical status measure were less likely to sponsor the bill. Moreover, sponsors of the legislation exhibited ideology scores that were much more liberal than those who did not endorse full employment officially. Sponsors had average ideology scores of +0.77—i.e., quite liberal—while those not on record averaged a −0.28 ideology score.

Tables D.8 and D.9 reveal that there are partisan underpinnings to this relationship among these measures as well. Sponsors made up almost 43 percent of all Democrats and only 5 percent of all Republicans. For the Democrats, all of the constituency measures but district population change appeared to distinguish sponsors from nonsponsors. Percentage working class, the adjusted living level, ideology score, tenure, and margin of victory all suggested differences in likelihood of supporting full employment.

Table D.8 Percentage with Selected Features, by Sponsorship and Party: Democrats

	Yes		No	
	High	Low	High	Low
Economic				
% unemployed, 1937	49.6	34.9	50.4	65.1
% working-class	65.9	14.0	34.1	86.0
Adjusted living level	72.8	16.4	27.2	83.6
Constituency				
% foreign-born	77.2	18.4	22.8	81.6
% African American	15.9	66.7	84.1	33.3
% urban	71.8	21.6	28.2	78.4
% population change	46.9	40.3	53.1	59.7
Years in school—male	65.0	27.5	35.0	72.5
Years in school—female	56.8	36.9	43.2	63.1
Ideological/personal				
Ideology score	57.2	1.6	42.8	98.4
Age	42.1	43.7	57.9	56.3
Biographical status	39.2	44.6	60.8	55.4
Electoral				
Tenure in office	33.3	50.0	66.7	50.0
Margin of victory	19.7	64.8	80.3	35.2
Total cases	104		138	

Moreover, Democrats who sponsored the bill had an average ideology score of 0.86, while the remaining Democrats scored an average of 0.13. Although Republican sponsors were more liberal than those Republicans who did not endorse the bill, scoring an average −0.11 in contrast to an average of −0.59, they were best described as moderate rather than liberal.

An interesting pattern emerged in terms of the electoral characteristics of those who sponsored H.R. 2202. Sponsors on average had less tenure in Congress—specifically a mean of 5.0 years of cumulative service in the House as

Table D.9 Percentage with Selected Features, by Sponsorship and Party: Republicans

	Yes		Yes	
	High	Low	High	Low
Economic				
% unemployed, 1937	8.5	3.3	91.5	96.7
% working-class	8.9	1.1	91.1	98.9
Adjusted living level	6.5	0.0	93.5	100.0
Constituency				
% foreign-born	9.0	2.0	91.0	98.0
% African American	11.1	4.9	88.9	95.1
% urban	12.7	0.8	87.3	99.2
% population change	7.1	4.4	92.9	95.6
Years in school—male	5.6	4.2	94.4	95.8
Years in school—female	4.4	6.5	95.6	93.5
Ideological/personal				
Ideology score	20.0	4.0	80.0	96.0
Age	5.1	5.4	94.9	94.6
Biographical status	2.9	8.0	97.1	92.0
Electoral				
Tenure in office	5.3	5.2	94.7	94.8
Margin of victory	3.2	5.6	96.8	94.4
Total cases	10		181	

compared to 7.6 years for those not on record. The endorsers also happened to be slightly younger. These official advocates, moreover, had secured smaller margins of victory in their most recent election. Most interestingly, sponsors were more likely to have been elected in 1932 or later—i.e., they were part of the New Deal realignment.

A further breakdown by region revealed that the South, with its unique electoral returns (due to the predominance of the Democratic Party, which resulted in competitive primaries and many "no contest" general elections), had skewed the electoral data on sponsorship because so few Southerners had sponsored the bill.

THE FINAL VOTE

The partisan differences exhibited in the sponsorship of H.R. 2202 were not quite as sharp when compared with supporting the final roll call. Nonetheless, 77 percent of those voting for the bill were Democrats and 23 percent were Republicans. Of all the Democratic members of Congress, 79 percent voted for the final bill. A total of 30 percent of the Republican members did so.

Their respective partisanship scores indicated that the party differences had become much more muted by the final vote. Democrats voting "yes" have a partisanship measure of 0.50, and Republicans voting "yes" have a measure of 0.43. Democrats who voted "no" have an average partisanship measure of 0.41, while Republican "no" voters have a mean score of 0.69 for partisanship. These figures suggest that support for the legislation among the Democrats was not overwhelmingly related to the strength of partisanship (a 0.09 difference of means), but that opposition to the bill among the Republicans was associated more closely with strong partisanship (a 0.26 difference of means).

The ideology scores for the final vote very much resembled the scores for sponsorship. Those who favored the legislation had a mean score of 0.48, and those who opposed had a mean score of −0.64. Democrats who voted for the bill had an average ideology score of 0.79, while Republican supporters had an average score of −0.15 on ideology.

When the opponents were split along party lines, the partisan differences were also quite striking. Democrats against the bill had a mean partisanship score of −0.11, and Republican had a mean partisanship score of −0.64. A comparison of the ideology scores on sponsorship with the roll call on H.R. 2202 implies that the final bill had a broader base of support among the Democrats, but that both the sponsorship of the original bill and final vote on the compromise bill split the Republicans along sharp ideological lines.

The members of Congress who voted for the final legislation, like those who initially sponsored it, tended on average to be younger than their colleagues on the other side of the fence. Likewise, they had slightly fewer years of service in the House. The margin-of-victory measure indicates that supporters were more secure electorally than opponents.

An investigation of the final vote by region discloses a critical aspect: the compromise legislation had picked up the support of the South. Only a few in this bloc of Democrats had endorsed the first version of the bill, but a clear majority voted "yes" on the roll call. This regional delegation was noted for lower than average partisanship scores as well as more conservative ideology scores, so its inclusion with the final supporters has diluted these measures in a way one would have expected from a base-broadening outcome.

Constituency and economic variables presented in Table D.10 reveal the effects of broadening the base by way of compromise. Although the initial bill's supporters tended to be from districts that were more urban and had more foreign-born, the differences were less pronounced. Now, following the com-

Table D.10 Percentage with Selected Features, by Final Vote

	Yes		No	
	High	Low	High	Low
Economic				
% unemployed, 1937	65.2	51.5	20.6	35.8
% working-class	62.3	52.8	24.6	33.5
Adjusted living level	52.4	66.9	33.3	21.1
Constituency				
% foreign-born	62.6	54.3	23.7	32.5
% African American	73.8	51.8	12.3	35.0
% urban	66.7	52.1	21.3	33.6
% population change	61.0	56.3	24.7	30.8
Years in school, male	53.3	63.7	34.6	21.1
Years in school, female	50.0	64.1	38.3	21.2
Ideological/personal				
Ideology score	79.5	40.3	9.2	44.5
Age	53.7	61.8	33.7	24.1
Biographical status	55.4	59.8	32.2	26.2
Electoral				
% most recent vote	67.1	53.2	18.8	33.8
% margin of victory	66.2	53.7	18.9	33.7
Tenure in 79th Congress	60.4	56.6	25.2	30.7
Total cases	251		124	

promise, supporters came from districts that on average had a higher percentage of African American residents, completely reversing the previous relationship. Moreover, the supporters represented districts that were poorer according to the adjusted living level than those who opposed the final bill.

The patterns become more intriguing when the data are further analyzed according to party, in Tables D.11 and D.12. For the Democrats, the matter of whether they fell into the high or low groups on the various measures appeared trivial, with the exception of the ideology score. Republican supporters, on the other hand, were from districts that were much more working-class, urban, African American, and foreign-born than Republican nonsupporters.

In sum, the typical sponsor was a liberal Democrat elected during the New Deal realignment from a district that was more working-class, had experienced urbanization and an influx of immigrants, and had been hardest hit by the Great Depression. The members who voted for the final measure were generally nondescript in contrast to the sponsors, but they still were characterized as Democrats and some Republicans who represented districts that had more

Table D.11 Percentage with Selected Features, by Final Vote and Party: Democrats

	Yes		No	
	High	Low	High	Low
Economic				
% unemployed, 1937	79.7	78.9	6.8	11.0
% working-class	80.7	77.6	6.7	11.2
Adjusted living level	80.7	78.1	7.9	9.4
Constituency				
% foreign-born	78.2	80.1	8.9	8.5
% African American	77.9	80.6	9.7	7.8
% urban	82.5	77.0	6.8	10.1
% population change	76.5	81.3	11.2	6.9
Years in school, male	85.0	75.4	6.0	10.6
Years in school, female	82.4	78.0	8.1	8.9
Ideological/personal				
Ideology score	82.8	69.4	5.0	19.4
Age	78.5	80.0	8.4	8.9
Biographical status	81.1	78.6	6.8	9.5
Electoral				
Margin of victory	76.1	82.4	9.4	8.0
Tenure in office	81.4	77.9	5.9	10.7
Total cases	192		21	

foreign-born, more African Americans, and more working-class people who were more likely to have been unemployed in 1937.

CLOSING OBSERVATIONS

An interesting pattern emerged when these regional, ideological, and partisanship data were viewed together. The three highest average Democratic partisanship scores and the three highest average Democratic ideology scores were in the eastern regions of the country, where the Democrats were in the minority. The lowest Democratic partisanship and ideology scores were in the South and the Border regions, where the Democrats had an overwhelming majority. Of the three regions in which the Republicans were the minority delegations, two regions had the highest Republican partisanship scores. These two regions also had the second and third most extreme ideology scores for the Republicans. Excluding the Pacific region, which had extremely low Republi-

Table D.12 Percentage with Selected Features, by Final Vote and Party: Republicans

	Yes		No	
	High	Low	High	Low
Economic				
% unemployed, 1937	38.0	26.7	46.5	58.3
% working-class	37.6	23.3	48.5	60.0
Adjusted living level	31.4	28.9	52.3	60.5
Constituency				
% foreign-born	44.9	18.6	40.4	65.7
% African American	22.2	31.3	44.4	54.4
% urban	43.7	23.3	42.3	60.8
% population change	33.9	29.6	48.2	56.3
Years in school, male	31.5	29.2	54.5	52.1
Years in school, female	28.9	33.8	57.9	48.1
Ideological/personal				
Ideology score	40.0	30.1	60.0	53.4
Age	26.5	35.5	61.2	46.2
Biographical status	36.9	23.9	50.5	58.0
Electoral				
Margin of victory	29.0	31.3	54.8	53.8
Tenure in office	22.8	34.3	59.6	51.5
Total cases	59		103	

can partisanship and ideology scores, the three lowest Republican average partisanship and ideology scores were in the eastern regions, where Republicans constituted a majority of the congressional delegations. However, the most extreme Republican ideology score, as well as one of the highest partisanship scores, was in the West North-Central, the region most dominated by the Republicans. This last finding notwithstanding, these data suggest that minority delegations were less moderate than majority delegations in their overall voting behavior.

Appendix E
A Structural Model Approach

This appendix uses sequential equations to posit structural models for support of full employment legislation in the House. It is intuitively clear that the forces of constituency, economic factors, personal ideology, party, and electoral security all did not converge simultaneously in 1945 to influence the outcome of the full employment bill. The economic traits of the district and the constituency characteristics already had affected the type of person elected to Congress, particularly the question of whether the representative was a Democrat or Republican. These district characteristics may also have a further effect on the likelihood that the representative supported the full employment bill, an effect that is distinct from the party of the member, as the earlier analysis of those who deviated from their party's position suggests.

The most appropriate models of support for full employment are those that approach it as a sequential process. The traits of the district are used to predict the party of the candidate who won the most recent election—i.e., the current member of Congress. In turn, the member's party identification is used to predict his or her position on full employment. Of course, this set of relationships is more complex than this simple statement implies, and it captures other variables as well, such as the 1937 unemployment rate's influence upon the party of the person representing the district as well as upon his or her support for full employment.

One way of depicting this set of relationships is presented in Figure E.1. This general model assumes that the influence of the district traits—economic and constituency—upon party moves in one direction. That is, the district traits affect party, but party does not affect the district traits. Moreover, the general model assumes that electoral security measures and biographical status of the member do not affect the party of the representative elected by the district. Finally, this model assumes that support for the full employment bill does not "feed back" on the district, electoral, or personal characteristics. In other words, support for full employment does not influence the district, electoral, or personal characteristics that were measured before the vote.[1]

In such models, a long-standing method used in various disciplines involves structural equations. Essentially, this approach is based upon a series of multiple regression equations that refines the information on each exogenous variable's direct and indirect effects on the dependent variable.[2] Another advantage of using structural equations is that the method enables us to address

Figure E.1 Basic Model of Support for Full Employment: Model A

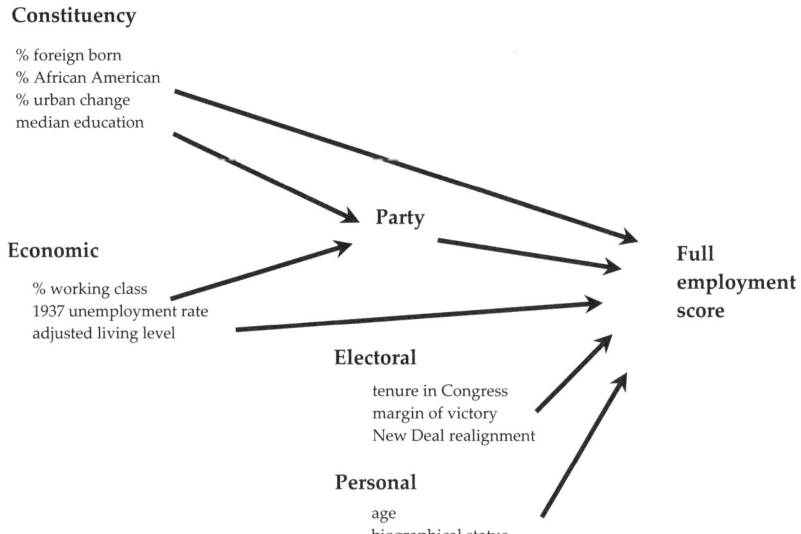

the push for full employment as a sequential process and, thus, to place support for full employment in a context that comes a bit closer to the actual dynamics.

As the structural equation model is constructed, party becomes an endogenous variable—i.e., one that is dependent on external forces. The multiple regression of party upon the districts' constituency and economic variables reveals several interesting relationships. Wealth, as measured by the adjusted living level, is strongly and negatively associated with a Democratic representative. The percentage of the district's population that is African American and the percentage that is foreign-born are also good predictors of electing a Democratic member of Congress. The districts' percentage of working-class citizens and percentage of urban change are significant as well.

Several interesting patterns emerge in the first structural equation model (Model A) when the indirect effects of the district traits through party are compared with these traits' direct effects on support for full employment (Table E.1). Percentage working-class, which has one of the highest simple correlation coefficients with full employment, appears to have more of an indirect effect through party than a direct effect on the full employment scale. Most of the effect of urban change is felt through party, as are the effects of race and ethnicity. The unemployment rate, on the other hand, has some direct effect on support for full employment over and above its effect on party.

Table E.1 Modeling Support for Full Employment in the House: Model A—Direct and Indirect Effects

	Total	Direct	Indirect
New Deal realignment	0.00	0.00	
Margin of victory	−0.06	−0.06	
Age	−0.04	−0.04	
Tenure in Congress	−0.02	−0.06	
Biographical status	−0.02	−0.02	
Political party	0.70**	0.70**	
% urban change	0.13**	0.00**	0.12**
% foreign-born	0.32**	0.11**	0.21**
% African American	0.20**	−0.03**	0.23**
% working-class	0.25	0.08	0.13
Living level index	−0.27**	0.07**	0.34**
% unemployed, 1937	0.12**	0.10**	0.02**
Median education	0.10	0.06	0.04
Multiple correlation coefficient	0.72		
Proportion of explained variance	0.52		

NOTE: **Statistically significant at the 0.05 level. Blank indicates no indirect effects were calculated.

The research of this period maintains that the region of the country has an important influence on legislative behavior and that there are regional differences in party structure and composition. There is consensus, for example, that the South was unique in terms of its political culture, and there are suggestions that other regions had distinctly partisan features. One way of analyzing the effect of region upon party and, in turn, on support for full employment is presented in Figure E.2 as Model B. Results of this second set of structural equations (Model B) are presented in Table E.2.[3]

The differences between Model A and Model B are generally modest, but the regional groupings have altered some of the effects. Party remains the leading predictor, with foreign-born and working-class exhibiting notable increases of direct and indirect effects. The percentage of urban change decreases in effect to a trivial level when the regional groupings are included in the analysis. One regional grouping, the Northeast, displays strong negative effects on support for the legislation. The South, as one might expect, has a noteworthy positive effect on party and a negative effect on support for full employment.

One of the goals in selecting a model is a balance between explanatory power and simplicity. The models presented above are useful in that they explain half of the variance in support for full employment. Their size, how-

Figure E.2 Support for Full Employment in the House: Model B

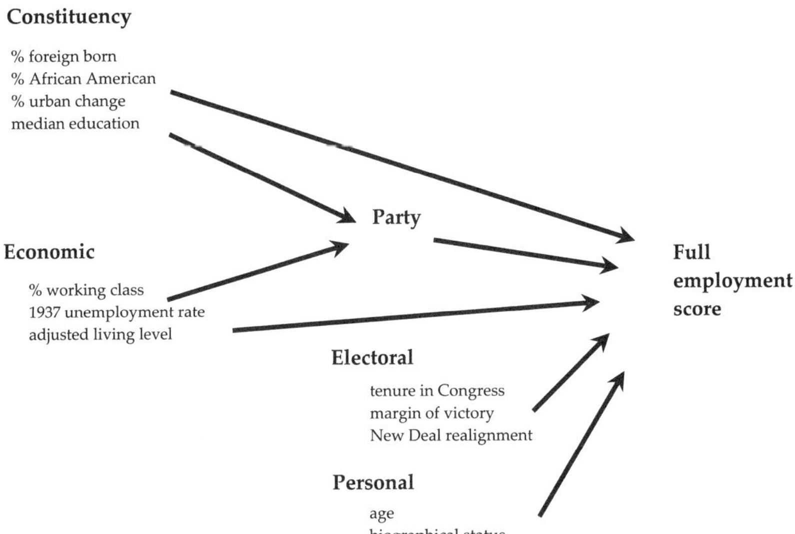

ever, limits their use because it is difficult to unravel the relationships among all of the variables. In winnowing the variables for inclusion in a model, a standard practice is used: drop out those variables that are not statistically significant.

The model presented in Table E.3 as Model C strives for parsimony yet still explains just over half of the variance in support for full employment, virtually matching the more complex model's explanatory power. Party continues to dominate the equation. Now, in this model, the percentage foreign-born has the second largest total effect, though most of it comes through party. The adjusted living level has a noteworthy negative overall effect due to its strong inverse relationship with party. The percentage of working class increases in its influence, both on indirect effects through party and on direct effects on the full employment score. The unemployment rate remains much as it did in the previous models—a modest indirect effect through party coupled with a modest direct effect on support for full employment (Table E.3).

The models of support for full employment were replicated with the ideology score made of the 10 roll call votes that the UDA labeled as key liberal votes, and the results were found to be quite similar.[4]

Table E.2 Modeling Support for Full Employment in the House: Model B—Regional Groupings, Direct and Indirect Effects

	Total	Direct	Indirect
Margin of victory	−0.01	−0.01	
Tenure in Congress	−0.08	−0.08	
Political party	0.69**	0.69**	
% urban change	0.00	−0.03	0.02
% foreign-born	0.58**	0.15**	0.43**
% African American	0.19	0.04	0.15
% working-class	0.40**	0.14**	0.26**
Living level index	−0.22	−0.02	−0.20
% unemployed, 1937	0.15	0.08	0.07
Age	0.05	0.05	
Median education	−0.05	0.06	−0.01
Biographical status	−0.01	−0.01	
New Deal realignment	−0.03	−0.03	
Northeast	−0.59**	−0.17**	−0.42**
Midwest	−0.26	−0.06	−0.20
South	0.11**	−0.23**	0.34**
West	0.12	−0.06	0.18
Multiple correlation coefficient	0.74		
Proportion of explained variance	0.55		

NOTE: **Statistically significant at the 0.05 level. Blank indicates no indirect effects were calculated.

COMPARING THE MODELS OF FULL EMPLOYMENT WITH IDEOLOGY

As stated at the outset of this book, the drive for full employment legislation is a case study in the process of redefining the federal role and responsibility. The degree to which congressional action on the full employment bill is similar to the broader phenomenon may be observed, although the crudeness of the measures and limits of the data must be kept continually in mind. The ideology score offers a plausible measure of how members define the federal role and responsibility, because the roll calls that make up the liberal-conservative scale address other key components of this general issue.

One approach is to compare these models of support for full employment with models in which the ideology score is the dependent variable. Essentially, Models A and B are replicated with the ideology score replacing the full

Table E.3 Modeling Support For Full Employment in the House: Model C—A Simpler Model, Direct and Indirect Effects

	Total	Direct	Indirect
Political party	0.70**	0.70**	
% urban change	0.12**	0.00**	0.12**
% working-class	0.24**	0.09**	0.15**
Living level index	−0.25**	0.09**	−0.34**
% unemployed, 1937	0.16**	0.11**	0.06**
Median education	0.08**	0.07**	0.01**
% foreign-born	0.31**	0.10**	0.21**
% African American	0.16**	−0.06**	0.22**
Multiple correlation coefficient	0.71		
Proportion of explained variance	0.51		

NOTE: **All variables are statistically significant at the 0.05 level. Blank indicates no indirect effects were calculated.

employment score as the dependent variable. The results of this replication, presented in Tables E.4 and E.5 as Models D and E, are powerful as well as fascinating.[5]

In general, the models are quite similar; however, the ideology models have more explanatory power.[6] As before, party remains the most powerful

Table E.4 Modeling Support For Ideology: Model D—Direct and Indirect Effects

	Total	Direct	Indirect
New Deal realignment	−0.02	−0.02	
Margin of victory	−0.17**	−0.17**	
Age	0.02	0.02	
Tenure in Congress	−0.04	−0.04	
Biographical status	−0.05**	−0.05**	
Political party	0.87**	0.87**	
% urban change	0.16**	0.01**	0.15**
% foreign-born	0.32**	0.08**	0.26**
% African American	0.29**	−0.08**	0.29**
% working-class	0.32**	0.15**	0.17**
Living level index	−0.30**	0.12**	−0.42**
% unemployed, 1937	0.12**	0.09**	0.03**
Median education	0.02	−0.03	0.05
Multiple correlation coefficient	0.87		
Proportion of explained variance	0.76		

NOTE: **Statistically significant at the 0.05 level. Blank indicates no indirect effects were calculated.

Table E.5 Modeling Support for Ideology: Model E—Regional Groupings, Direct and Indirect Effects

	Total	Direct	Indirect
Realignment	−0.05	−0.05	
Margin of victory	−0.11	−0.11	
Age	0.00	0.00	
Tenure in Congress	−0.05	−0.05	
Status	−0.03**	−0.03**	
Political party	0.89**	0.89**	
% urban change	0.03**	0.01**	0.02**
% foreign-born	0.53**	0.10**	0.43**
% African American	0.13**	−0.02**	0.15**
% working class	0.46**	0.20**	0.26**
Living level index	−0.20**	0.00**	−0.20**
% unemployed, 1937	0.15**	0.08**	0.07**
Education	−0.02	−0.01	−0.01
Northeast	−0.53	−0.11	−0.42
Midwest	−0.20	0.00	−0.20
South	0.10	−0.24	0.34
West	0.10	−0.08	0.18
Multiple correlation coefficient	0.88		
Proportion of explained variance	0.78		

NOTE: ** Statistically significant at the 0.05 level. Blank indicates no indirect effects were calculated.

predictor. Foreign-born, urban change, working-class, race, and adjusted living level all exhibit effects upon ideology much as they do with full employment. The most noteworthy differences are the negative direct effects of margin and victory and, to a lesser extent, of biographical status. Once again, percentage urban change decreases when the regional groupings are included, but the percentage working class increases in its total effects.

The similarity of these models lends support to a fundamental assumption of this book: the dynamics of support for full employment resemble the forces that pushed for a general strengthening of the federal role and responsibility.

Appendix Notes

1. Appendix F discusses the statistical issues involving recursive models.
2. See Appendix F for a fuller and more technical discussion of the methodology.
3. See Appendix F for the reason the Border states were dropped from the equation.
4. The models also yield coefficients that are comparable in explanatory power to statistical analyses of other legislative issues considered during other periods by Congress. For examples drawing on a range of statistical techniques, see Bartels (2005), Clinton (2006), Khan (2005), Nelson (2002), and Sanders (1997).
5. One should be extremely circumspect when comparing models with different dependent variables. Appendix F discusses the statistical problems inherent in such analyses and the strict limitations of the comparisons.
6. This larger explained variance may be due to the differences in the statistical variances of the two dependent variables—full employment score and ideology score—and not indicative of theoretical importance.

Appendix F
Methodology and Research Design

This appendix provides a review of the methodology and research design used in this book. It describes the statistics that are employed in this analysis and raises concerns pertinent to the application of these techniques. Citations of statistical sources are included for reference and for further explanation.

OVERVIEW OF STATISTICS EMPLOYED

Correlation measures the degree to which two variables are linearly related. Unlike the covariance, the correlation coefficient neutralizes any differences in scales (e.g., X might be measured in dollars and Y might be measured in percent) that might exist for the two variables. The correlation coefficient always varies between -1.0 and $+1.0$, with the extremes representing perfectly linear relationships. If X and Y are independent, then the correlation is zero.

Multiple Regression is a type of linear model that enables us to measure the effects of several independent (i.e., exogenous) variables upon a dependent variable. By estimating the parameters of the linear model, this technique provides us with four important pieces of information, including 1) the amount of unit change in Y (the dependent variable) attributable to each of the independent variables (such as the beta parameters or the amount of variance in Y explained by each of the independent variables), 2) the partial correlation coefficients, 3) the amount of variance in Y explained by the combined effects of the independent variables (such as the multiple correlation coefficient), and 4) the statistical significance of the model.

The equation for multiple regression may be expressed as

$$Y = a + bx + bz + e\ ,$$

where a is the intercept (as if plotting a line), bx is the beta coefficient of X (the slope of the line of X on Y), bz is the beta coefficient of Z (the slope of the line of Z on Y), and e is the random error term. When we standardize the model, we set a, alpha, at zero (Wonnacott and Wonnacott 1977, pp. 359–365).

Generally, regression equations require continuous or interval-level variables in order to measure how unit change in the independent variables affects unit change in the dependent variable. Thus, party and New Deal realignment are converted to 0/1 variables, and indices and scores are calculated to gauge biographical status and ideology. If one has ordinal or nominal data, then three other techniques are more appropriate: 1) analysis of variance techniques, such as Multiple Classification Analysis (MCA); 2) contingency table analysis techniques, such as chi-squared or Leo Goodman's ECTA statistics; and 3) logistic regression techniques.

Political party is a dichotomous variable that generally should not be used as a dependent variable in a regression equation. One option would be to use partisanship score, which is a continuous-level variable; however, it is problematic as a subsequent predictor of the full employment score because both are composed of roll call votes. The more statistically sound approach is to use LOGIT or PROBIT, which are both regression techniques designed to handle dichotomous dependent variables. This solution poses problems, nonetheless, with the overall set of structural equations, because they must be parallel—that is, they must use identical methods of calculation.

I have run the regression equations predicting political party using LOGIT and using ordinary least squares (OLS). The results are quite similar, due largely to the fact that the distribution of party is not skewed—in other words, there is a fairly even balance of Democrats and Republicans in the 79th Congress. Thus, I am presenting the OLS results for the sake of consistency with the overall model.

As is apparent from the equations, regression techniques assume an additive model, and thus the exogenous variables must be independent of each other. Given the nature of social science data and its accompanying problems of measurement, it is sometimes difficult to have purely independent exogenous variables. Multicolinearity, which exists when some of the exogenous variables are correlated with each other, is not uncommon. Multicolinearity may occur in instances where the exogenous variables are not truly causally related and result from definitional and measurement problems. Or, the model may be misspecified, such as by omitting variables. In resolving the problem of multicolinearity, one should bear in mind the following caveat: "If minor changes in the model specification or the definition of variables yield large changes in the estimated coefficients, the model should be treated with some caution" (Hanushek and Jackson 1977, pp. 86–96).

Structural equations are more complex forms of linear models that draw on a multiequation approach to represent an underlying behavioral structure. One may consider the model as a series of multiple regression equations, in some instances simultaneous equations. The model determines or predicts the endogenous (i.e., dependent) variables. The exogenous (i.e., independent) variables are determined outside of the model. The other predetermined variables are lagged endogenous variables that have values established prior to the current observation.

One major advantage of structural equations is that they enable one to measure not only the direct effects of the independent variables but also the indirect effects of secondary explanatory variables upon the dependent variable through a primary explanatory variable. These indirect effects may reinforce the direct effects of the primary explanatory variable or negate the direct effects. Structural equations help us measure the reciprocal influences that may characterize the set of variables at hand (Hanushek and Jackson 1977, pp. 217–218).

Recursive models are those that are both hierarchical and have independent error terms across equations. If the error terms are correlated, the ordinary least squares (OLS) assumptions are violated, resulting in biased and inconsistent parameter estimates. "The decision to use a recursive model should not be taken lightly, or simply for the purpose of convenience," William Berry writes. "Unless one is convinced that 1) causation among the factors is strictly unidimensional and 2) the factors constituting the error terms in the model are fundamentally different for each equation, recursive models should not be used" (Berry 1984, p. 15; Hanushek and Jackson 1977, pp. 217–218).

One may argue that the models presented in this chapter are recursive because, to paraphrase Otis Dudley Duncan, all causal linkages run one way and no two variables feed back on each other. Duncan also warns that "letting the data decide which way the causal arrow runs"—for example, opting in certain situations for a nonrecursive model—leads to underidentification, not causal inference (Duncan 1975, pp. 25–50, 81–90).

An important caveat is that the independent stochastic assumption cannot be made in the case of these models. An alternative approach to the recursive model would be to draw on instrumental variables with a two-stage least squares method. At this point, nonetheless, a recursive model is assumed, with the risk that it might lead to overstatement.

DISCUSSION OF PROCEDURES

Tests of significance are not presented as part of these analyses because the data captures the entire population during the span of time under study. The question of sampling and the likelihood that these results would be manifested by a different sample of cases is germane to this research. The one notable exception is the use of statistical significance to winnow down the number of variables in the model of support for the full employment bill. The latter practice is commonly done, but in this instance the tests of significance for each exogenous variable are used as a gauge of the relative importance of their relationship in terms of support for the full employment bill.

The linear models presented in Appendix E are obtained through a series of OLS equations. One set of equations consists of congressional district traits regressed upon party. The other set regresses party and all exogenous variables on the full employment score. The results of these first equations are seen in Model A.

Those variables that are not statistically significant at the 0.05 level with either party or the full employment score are then dropped from the analysis. A new set of equations is run again with those variables that are statistically significant—Model C. The equations for Model A are repeated with the regional groupings included and presented as Model B. All five of the regional groupings cannot be included in the model because they would sum to the whole country and result in a singular matrix. The Border region is arbitrarily dropped from the analysis. The Model A equations are also used to predict ideology and are seen in Model D and Model E (regional groupings).

One should not strictly compare the regression coefficients from Models A and B with Models D and E because the latter models have a new dependent variable—ideology. Since the dependent variable in any regression equation is the crux of the analysis, changing it alters the relative effects that independent or exogenous variables have upon it. The ideology scale has, among other unique attributes, a variance and standard deviation that differs from the attributes of the full employment score; attributes such as the dependent variable's variance are essential components in the calculations that produce the regression coefficients.

It is reasonable, nevertheless, to make general observations about the similarity of the two sets of models. The relative importance of exogenous variables *within* each of the models may be assessed, and the overall models may be compared with that in mind.

Table F.1 Models A and B, Estimated Equations for Full Employment with Unstandardized Coefficients

Model A

$$Y_2 = a + b_1 + b_2 + b_3 + b_4 + b_5 + b_6 + b_7 + b_8 + b_9 + b_{10} + b_{11} + b_{12} + b_{13}$$

$$Y_2 = -1.11 - 0.00 - 0.01 + 1.02 - 0.00 + 0.01 - 0.00 + 0.00 + 0.00 + 0.01 - 0.00 + 0.03 - 0.01 - 0.00$$

$$Y_1 = a + b_4 + b_5 + b_6 + b_7 + b_8 + b_9 + b_{11}$$

$$Y_1 = 0.24 + 0.00 + 0.01 + 0.01 + 0.01 - 0.01 + 0.00 + 0.02\ ;$$

Model B

$$Y_2 = a + b_1 + b_2 + b_3 + b_4 + b_5 + b_6 + b_7 + b_8 + b_9 + b_{10} + b_{11} + b_{12} + b_{13} + b_{14} + b_{15} + b_{16} + b_{17}$$

$$Y_2 = -0.93 - 0.00 - 0.01 + 1.00 - 0.00 + 0.01 + 0.00 + 0.00 - 0.00 + 0.01 - 0.00 + 0.03 - 0.00 - 0.05 - 0.28 - 0.10 - 0.41 - 0.15$$

$$Y_1 = a + b_4 + b_5 + b_6 + b_7 + b_8 + b_9 + b_{11} + b_{14} + b_{15} + b_{16} + b_{17}$$

$$Y_1 = 0.03 + 0.00 + 0.03 + 0.01 + 0.01 - 0.00 + 0.01 - 0.00 - 0.46 - 0.22 + 0.41 + 0.32\ ,$$

where

Y_1 = Political party
Y_2 = Full employment score
b_1 = Margin of victory
b_2 = Tenure in Congress
b_3 = Political party
b_4 = % urban change
b_5 = % foreign-born
b_6 = % African American
b_7 = % working-class
b_8 = Adjusted living level
b_9 = % unemployed, 1937
b_{10} = Age of member
b_{11} = Median education
b_{12} = Biographical status
b_{13} = New Deal realignment
b_{14} = Northeast
b_{15} = Midwest
b_{16} = South
b_{17} = West

Table F.2 Model C, Estimated Equations for Full Employment with Unstandardized Coefficients

Model C

$$Y_2 = a + b_1 + b_2 + b_3 + b_4 + b_5 + b_6 + b_7 + b_8$$

$$Y_2 = -1.52 + 0.102 - 0.00 + 0.00 + 0.00 + 0.02 + 0.03 + 0.01 - 0.00$$

$$Y_1 = a + b_2 + b_3 + b_4 + b_7 + b_8$$

$$Y_1 = 0.42 + 0.00 + 0.01 - 0.01 + 0.02 + 0.01\ ,$$

where

Y_1 = Political party

Y_2 = Full employment score

b_1 = Political party

b_2 = % urban change

b_3 = % working-class

b_4 = Adjusted living level

b_5 = % unemployed, 1937

b_6 = Median education

b_7 = % foreign-born

b_8 = % African American

Table F.3 Models D and E, Estimated Equations for Ideology with Unstandardized Coefficients

Model D

$$Y_2 = a + b_1 + b_2 + b_3 + b_4 + b_5 + b_6 + b_7 + b_8 + b_9 + b_{10} + b_{11} + b_{12} + b_{13}$$

$$Y_2 = -1.11 - 0.00 - 0.00 + 1.16 + 0.00 + 0.00 - 0.00 + 0.01 + 0.00 + 0.02 + 0.00 - 0.01 - 0.02 - 0.04$$

$$Y_1 = a + b_4 + b_5 + b_6 + b_7 + b_8 + b_9 + b_{11}$$

$$Y_1 = 0.24 + 0.00 + 0.01 + 0.01 + 0.01 - 0.01 + 0.00 + 0.02\ ;$$

Model E

$$Y_2 = a + b_1 + b_2 + b_3 + b_4 + b_5 + b_6 + b_7 + b_8 + b_9 + b_{10} + b_{11} + b_{12} + b_{13} + b_{14} + b_{15} + b_{16} + b_{17}$$

$$Y_2 = -0.98 - 0.00 - 0.00 + 1.18 + 0.00 + 0.01 - 0.00 + 0.01 + 0.00 + 0.01 + 0.00 - 0.01 - 0.01 - 0.09 - 0.16 + 0.00 - 0.38 - 0.18$$

$$Y_1 = a + b_4 + b_5 + b_6 + b_7 + b_8 + b_9 + b_{11} + b_{14} + b_{15} + b_{16} + b_{17}$$

$$Y_1 = 0.03 + 0.00 + 0.03 + 0.01 + 0.01 - 0.00 + 0.01 - 0.00 - 0.46 - 0.22 + 0.41 + 0.32\ ,$$

where

Y_1 = Party

Y_2 = Full employment score

b_1 = Margin of victory

b_2 = Tenure in Congress

b_3 = Political party

b_4 = % urban change

b_5 = % foreign-born

b_6 = % African American

b_7 = % working-class

b_8 = Adjusted living level

b_9 = % unemployed, 1937

b_{10} = Age of member

b_{11} = Median education

b_{12} = Biographical status

b_{13} = New Deal realignment

b_{14} = Northeast

b_{15} = Midwest

b_{16} = South

b_{17} = West

References

Ackerman, William C. 1945. "The Dimensions of American Broadcasting." *Public Opinion Quarterly* 9(1): 1–18.

Alwin, Duane F., and Robert M. Hauser. 1975. "The Decomposition of Effects in Path Analysis." *American Sociological Review* 40(1): pp. 37–47.

Atkinson, Anthony B., Thomas Piketty, and Emmanuel Saez. 2011. "Top Incomes in the Long Run of History." *Journal of Economic Literature* 49(1): 3–71.

Atleson, James B. 1998. *Labor and the Wartime State: Labor Relations and Law during World War II.* Champaign, IL: University of Illinois Press.

Austin, Erik W. 1986. *Political Facts of the United States since 1789.* New York: Columbia University Press.

Bailey, Stephen Kemp. 1964. *Congress Makes a Law: The Story behind the Employment Act of 1946.* New York: Vintage.

Barber, William J. 1987. "The Career of Alvin H. Hansen in the 1920s and 1930s: A Study in Intellectual Transformation." *History of Political Economy* 19(2): 191–205.

Bartels, Larry M. 2005. *Economic Inequality and Political Representation.* Princeton, NJ: Princeton University.

———. 2008. *Unequal Democracy: The Political Economy of the New Gilded Age.* New York: Russell Sage.

Berinsky, Adam J. 2006. "American Public Opinion in the 1930s and 1940s: The Analysis of Quota-Controlled Sample Survey Data." *Public Opinion Quarterly* 70(4): 499–529.

Bernanke, Ben S. 2000. *Essays on the Great Depression.* Princeton, NJ: Princeton University Press.

Bernstein, Barton J., ed. 1968. *Towards a New Past: Dissenting Essays in American History.* New York: Pantheon.

Bernstein, Barton J., and Allen J. Matusow, eds. 1966. *The Truman Administration: A Documentary History.* New York: Harper and Row.

Bernstein, Irving. 1985. *A Caring Society: The New Deal, the Worker, and the Great Depression: A History of the American Worker, 1933–1941.* Boston: Houghton Mifflin.

Bernstein, Michael A. 2001. *A Perilous Progress: Economists and Public Purpose in Twentieth-Century America.* Princeton, NJ: Princeton University Press.

Berry, William D. 1984. *Nonrecursive Causal Models.* Quantitative Applications in the Social Sciences 37. Thousand Oaks, CA: Sage.

Beveridge, William Henry, Baron. 1944. *Report on Full Employment in a Free Society*. London: Allen and Unwin.

Bird, Caroline. 1966. *The Invisible Scar: The Great Depression, and What It Did to American Life, from Then until Now*. New York: David McKay Co.

Blumberg, Barbara. 1979. *The New Deal and the Unemployed: The View from New York City*. Lewisburg, PA: Bucknell University Press.

Brinkley, Alan. 1996. *The End of Reform: New Deal Liberalism in Recession and War*. New York: Vintage Books.

Brownlee, W. Elliot, and Hugh Davis Graham. 2003. *The Reagan Presidency: Pragmatic Conservatism and Its Legacies*. Lawrence, KS: University Press of Kansas.

Bureau of Economic Analysis (BEA). 2012a. *National Economic Accounts*. Washington, DC: Bureau of Economic Analysis. http://www.bea.gov/national/index.htm#personal (accessed October 8, 2012).

———. 2012b. *National Income and Product Accounts Tables*. Washington, DC: Bureau of Economic Analysis. http://www.bea.gov/iTable/iTable.cfm?ReqID=9&step=1 (accessed October 8, 2012).

Bureau of Labor Statistics (BLS). 2012. *Databases, Tables & Calculators by Subject*. Washington, DC: Bureau of Labor Statistics. http://www.bls.gov/data (accessed October 8, 2012).

Burns, James MacGregor. 1956. *Roosevelt: The Lion and the Fox. Vol. 1, 1882–1940*. New York: Harcourt, Brace and World.

Caldwell, Bruce. 2007. "Introduction." In *The Road to Serfdom: Text and Documents; the Definitive Edition*, by F.A. Hayek, edited by Bruce Caldwell. Vol. 2, *The Collected Works of F.A. Hayek*. Chicago: University of Chicago Press, pp. 1–33. First published 1944 by the University of Chicago.

Cantril, Hadley. 1951. *Public Opinion, 1935–1946*. With Mildred Strunk. Princeton, NJ: Princeton University Press.

Chicago Daily Tribune. 1943. "Plan for Post-War Depression." Editorial, August 8, p. 16.

Clausen, Aage R. 1973. *How Congressmen Decide: A Policy Focus*. New York: St. Martin's Press.

Clinton, Joshua D. 2006. "Representation in Congress: Constituents and Roll Calls in the 106th House." *Journal of Politics* 68(2): 397–409.

Clinton, Joshua D., Simon Jackman, and Douglas Rivers. 2004. "The Statistical Analysis of Legislative Behavior: A Unified Approach." *American Political Science Review* 98(2): 355–370.

Collins, Robert M. 1982. "American Corporatism: The Committee for Economic Development, 1942–1964." *Historian* 44(2): 151–173.

Colm, Gerhard. 1944. *Postwar Employment: A Report*. Gerhard Colm Papers. Independence, MO: Harry S. Truman Library and Museum.

———. 1945. "The Problem of Estimating Future Expenditures by Consumers, Business, and State and Local Governments." Unpublished paper. Gerhard Colm Papers. Independence, MO: Harry S. Truman Library and Museum.

———, ed. 1956. *The Employment Act, Past and Future: A Tenth Anniversary Symposium*. NPA Special Report No. 41. Washington, DC: National Planning Association.

Congressional Budget Office (CBO). 2010. *Public Spending on Transportation and Water Infrastructure*. Washington, DC: Congressional Budget Office. http://www.cbo.gov/publication/21902 (accessed October 8, 2012).

Congressional Quarterly. 1945. "Full Employment Bill." *Congressional Quarterly* 1(July–September): 487.

———. 1946. "Conference Report on Full Employment." *Congressional Quarterly* 2(January–March): 72.

Congressional Record. 1945a. 79th Cong., 1st sess. Vol. 91, pt. 1. Washington, DC: U.S. Government Printing Office.

———. 1945b. 79th Cong., 1st sess. Vol. 91, pt. 7. Washington, DC: U.S. Government Printing Office.

———. 1945c. 79th Cong., 1st sess. Vol. 91, pt. 9. Washington, DC: U.S. Government Printing Office.

———. 1946. 79th Cong., 2nd sess. Vol. 92, pt. 1. Washington, DC: U.S. Government Printing Office.

Converse, Jean M. 1987. *Survey Research in the United States: Roots and Emergence, 1890–1960*. Berkeley, CA: University of California Press.

Cornell, Saul. 1999. *The Other Founders: Anti-Federalism and the Dissenting Tradition in America, 1788–1828*. Chapel Hill, NC: University of North Carolina Press.

Cotton, Felix. 1946. "Chamber Favors Commission to Advise U.S. on Economics." International News Service, *Washington Post*, January 7, p. 4.

Davis, Christopher M. 2003. "The Speaker of the House and the Committee on Rules." In *The Cannon Centenary Conference: The Changing Nature of the Speakership*, Walter J. Oleszek, ed. Washington, DC: U.S. Government Printing Office, pp. 141–157.

Degler, Carl. 1970. *Out of Our Past*. Rev. ed. New York: Harper and Row. First published 1959 by Harper and Brothers.

Deschler, Lewis. 1976. *Deschler's Rules of Order*. New York: Prentice Hall.

Donovan, Robert J. 1977. *Conflict and Crisis: The Presidency of Harry S. Truman, 1945–1948*. New York: W.W. Norton.

Dornbusch, Rudiger, and Stanley Fischer. 1981. *Macro-Economics*. 2nd ed. New York: McGraw-Hill.

Duncan, Otis Dudley. 1975. *Introduction to Structural Equation Models*. New York: Academic Press.

Ebenstein, Alan. 2001. *Friedrich Hayek: A Biography*. New York: Palgrave.
Elder, Glen H. Jr. 1974. *Children of the Great Depression: Social Change in Life Experience*. Chicago: University of Chicago Press.
Engelbourg, Saul. 1980. "The Council of Economic Advisers and the Recession of 1953–1954." *Business History Review* 54(2): 192–214.
Flamm, Michael. 1994. "The National Farmers Union and the Evolution of Agrarian Liberalism, 1937–1946." *Agricultural History* 68(3): 54–80.
Franklin D. Roosevelt Presidential Library and Museum. 2012. *1944 State of the Union Address: FDR's "Second Bill of Rights" or "Economic Bill of Rights" Speech*. Hyde Park, NY: Franklin D. Roosevelt Presidential Library and Museum. http://www.fdrlibrary.marist.edu/archives/stateoftheunion.html (accessed June 26, 2012).
Freidel, Frank. 1965. *The New Deal in Historical Perspective*. Service Center for Teachers of History, Publication No. 25. 2nd ed. Washington, DC: American Historical Association.
Furniss, Norman, and Timothy Tilton. 1977. *The Case for the Welfare State: From Social Security to Social Equality*. Bloomington, IN: Indiana University Press.
Gallup, George A. 1944. "Public Pessimistic on Postwar Prospects for Employment." *Washington Post*, December 27, p. 6.
———. 1945. "Poll Shows Public Split on Employment Issue." *Los Angeles Times*, September 17, p. 2.
———. 1972. *The Gallup Poll: Public Opinion, 1935–1971*. Vol. 1, *1935–1948*. New York: Random House.
Garraty, John A. 1979. *Unemployment in History: Economic Thought and Public Policy*. New York: Harper and Row.
General Motors. 1945. *The Road to Serfdom in Cartoons*. Thought Starter Series, No. 118. Detroit: General Motors. Originally published by *Look* magazine. http://mises.org/books/TRTS/ (accessed July 18, 2012).
Goldin, Claudia, and Robert A. Margo. 1992. "The Great Compression: The Wage Structure in the United States at Mid-Century." *Quarterly Journal of Economics* 107(1): 1–34.
Goldman, Eric F. 1952. *Rendezvous with Destiny: A History of Modern American Reform*. New York: Knopf.
Graham, Otis L. Sr. 1976. *Toward a Planned Society: From Roosevelt to Nixon*. New York: Oxford University Press.
Hamby, Alonzo L. 1973. *Beyond the New Deal: Harry S. Truman and American Liberalism*. New York: Columbia University Press.
Hansen, Alvin H. 1942. *After the War—Full Employment*. National Resources Planning Board. Washington, DC: U.S. Government Printing Office.
Hanushek, Eric A., and John E. Jackson. 1977. *Statistical Methods for Social Scientists*. New York: Academic Press.

Hawley, Ellis W. 1966. *The New Deal and the Problem of Monopoly: A Study in Economic Ambivalence*. Princeton, NJ: Princeton University Press.

Hazlitt, Henry. 1944. "An Economist's View of Planning." *New York Times Book Review*, September 24, p. 1.

Heller, Francis H. 1982. *Economics and the Truman Administration*. Lawrence, KS: University Press of Kansas.

Hibbs, Douglas A. 1982. "Public Concern about Inflation and Unemployment in the United States: Trends, Correlates, and Political Implications." In *Inflation: Causes and Effects*, Robert E. Hall, ed. Cambridge, MA: National Bureau of Economic Research, pp. 211–232.

Hofstadter, Richard. 1955. *The Age of Reform: From Bryan to F.D.R.* New York: Random House.

Internal Revenue Service (IRS). 2012. *SOI Tax Stats—Individual Time Series Statistical Tables*. Washington, DC: Internal Revenue Service. http://www.irs.gov/uac/SOI-Tax-Stats---Individual-Time-Series-Statistical-Tables (accessed October 8, 2012).

Inter-university Consortium for Political and Social Research (ICPSR). 2013a. *Candidate and Constituency Statistics of Elections in the United States, 1788–1978*. Ann Arbor, MI: Inter-university Consortium for Political and Social Research. http://www.icpsr.umich.edu/icpsrweb/ICPSR/index.jsp (accessed January 15, 2013).

———. 2013b. *County and City Data Book (United States) Consolidated File, 1944–1977*. Ann Arbor, MI: Inter-university Consortium for Political and Social Research. http://www.icpsr.umich.edu/icpsrweb/ICPSR/index.jsp (accessed January 15, 2013).

———. 2013c. *Historical, Demographic, Economic, and Social Data: The United States, 1790–1970*. Ann Arbor, MI: Inter-university Consortium for Political and Social Research. http://www.icpsr.umich.edu/icpsrweb/ICPSR/index.jsp (accessed January 15, 2013).

———. 2013d. *Roster of the United States Congressional Officeholder and Biographical Characteristics of the Members of the United States Congress, 1789–1980*. Ann Arbor, MI: Inter-university Consortium for Political and Social Research. http://www.icpsr.umich.edu/icpsrweb/ICPSR/index.jsp (accessed January 15, 2013).

———. 2013e. *United States Congressional Roll Call Records*. Ann Arbor, MI: Inter-university Consortium for Political and Social Research. http://www.icpsr.umich.edu/icpsrweb/ICPSR/index.jsp (accessed January 15, 2013).

Jackson, John E. 1974. *Constituencies and Leaders in Congress: Their Effects on Senate Voting Behavior*. Cambridge, MA: Harvard University Press.

Jacobs, Lawrence R., and Theda Skocpol, eds. 2005. *Inequality and American Democracy: What We Know and What We Need to Learn*. New York: Russell Sage.

Jones, Charles O., ed. 1988. *The Reagan Legacy: Promise and Performance.* Chatham, NJ: Chatham House.

Keyssar, Alexander. 1986. *Out of Work: The First Century of Unemployment in Massachusetts.* Cambridge: Cambridge University Press.

Khan, Haroon A. 2005. "Determinants of Congressional Support for NAFTA and Clinton's Economic Package." *Journal of Developing Areas* 38(2): 143–154.

Kinder, Donald R., and D. Roderick Kiewiet. 1979. "Economic Discontent and Political Behavior: The Role of Personal Grievances and Collective Economic Judgments in Congressional Voting." *American Journal of Political Science* 23(3): 495–527.

Klein, Lawrence R. 1947. *The Keynesian Revolution.* New York: Macmillan.

Knapp, Joseph G. 1979. *Edwin G. Nourse: Economist for the People.* Danville, IL: Interstate Printers and Publishers.

Kriesberg, Martin. 1945. "What Congressmen and Administrators Think of the Polls." *Public Opinion Quarterly* 9(3): 333–337.

Lazarsfeld, Paul F., and Patricia L. Kendall. 1948. *Radio Listening in America: The People Look at Radio—Again.* New York: Prentice Hall.

Leuchtenberg, William E. 1963. *Franklin D. Roosevelt and the New Deal: 1932–1940.* New American Nation Series. New York: Harper and Row.

Los Angeles Times. 1943. "Postwar Jobs for 58,000,000 Seen as Task Facing Nation," March 12, p. 17.

Lubell, Samuel. 1965. *The Future of American Politics.* 3rd ed. New York: Harper and Row. First published 1952 by Harper and Brothers.

MacRae, Duncan. 1958. *Dimensions of Congressional Voting.* Berkeley, CA: University of California Press.

Markowitz, Norman D. 1973. *The Rise and Fall of the People's Century: Henry A. Wallace and American Liberalism, 1941–1948.* New York: Free Press.

McElvaine, Robert S. 1983. *The Great Depression: America, 1929–1941.* New York: Times Books.

Miller, Warren E., and Donald E. Stokes. 1963. "Constituency Influence in Congress." *American Political Science Review* 57(1): 45–56.

Moley, Raymond. 1942. "The Gentle Art of Prevision: Planning the Post-War Period Is a Major Concern for Busy New Dealers." *Wall Street Journal,* April 22, p. 6.

Neary, Edward Henry. 1945. Letter to the editor. *Wall Street Journal,* April 23, p. 6.

Nelson, Jon P. 2002. "'Green' Voting and Ideology: LCV Scores and Roll-Call Voting in the U.S. Senate, 1988–1998." *Review of Economics and Statistics* 84(3): 518–529.

New Republic. 1946a. "Record of the House." *New Republic* 114(6): 211–215.

———. 1946b. "Record of the Senate." *New Republic* 114(6): 218–220.

New York Times. 1943. "Industry Accepts Call to Find Jobs." *New York Times*, August 2, p. 17.

Newsweek. 1943. "Business Planners Concentrate on Free Enterprise and Turn Deaf Ear to Cries for 'Normalcy.'" *Newsweek* 21(15): 31–32.

———. 1945a. "Selling F.E." *Newsweek* 26(7): 26.

———. 1945b. "Sort of Leery." *Newsweek* 26(15): 36.

Patterson, James T. 1967. *Congressional Conservativism and the New Deal*. Lexington, KY: University of Kentucky Press.

———. 1972. *Mr. Republican: A Biography of Robert A. Taft*. Boston: Houghton Mifflin.

Perrett, Geoffrey. 1985. *Days of Sadness, Years of Triumph: The American People, 1939–1945*. Madison, WI: University of Wisconsin Press.

Philips, Kevin. 1993. *Boiling Point: Democrats, Republicans, and the Decline of Middle-Class Prosperity*. New York: Random House.

Phillips-Fein, Kim. 2009. *Invisible Hands: The Businessmen's Crusade against the New Deal*. New York: Norton.

Piketty, Thomas, and Emmanuel Saez. 2003. "Income Inequality in the United States, 1913–1998." *Quarterly Journal of Economics* 118(1): 1–39.

Riesel, Victor. 1946. "Labor Is Big Business." *Reader's Digest* 48(296): 118–120.

Robey, Ralph. 1945a. "Clever Trick Designed Just to Fool You." *Newsweek* 26(July 23): 66.

———. 1945b. "Gambling at a New High, with Your Money: Murray Full Employment Bill." *Newsweek* 26(July 9): 72.

Romer, Christina D. 1992. "What Ended the Great Depression?" *Journal of Economic History* 52(4): 757–784.

Roosevelt, Franklin Delano. 1941a. "Annual Message to the Congress. January 3, 1938." In *The Public Papers and Addresses of Franklin D. Roosevelt. 1938 vol., The Continuing Struggle for Liberalism: With a Special Introduction and Explanatory Notes by President Roosevelt*. New York: Macmillan, pp. 1–13.

———. 1941b. "Reaffirming Policy of Full Participation in the Defense Program by All Persons, Regardless of Race, Creed, Color, or Nation Origin, and Directing Certain Action in Furtherance of Said Policy." Exec. Order No. 8802, June 25. *Federal Register* 6(125): 3109.

———. 1943. "Further Amending Executive Order No. 8802 by Establishing a New Committee on Fair Employment Practice and Defining Its Posers and Duties." Exec. Order No. 9346, May 27. *Federal Register* 8(106): 7183–7184.

———. 1950. "Unless There Is Security Here at Home, There Cannot Be Lasting Peace in the World—Message to the Congress on the State of the Union. January 11, 1944." In *The Public Papers and Addresses of Franklin D. Roosevelt. 1944–45 vol., Victory and the Threshold of Peace: Compiled with Special Material and Explanatory Notes by Samuel I. Rosenman*. New York: Harper, pp. 32–44.
Salmond, John A. 2002. *The General Textile Strike of 1934: From Maine to Alabama*. Columbia, MO: University of Missouri Press.
Sanders, Francine. 1997. "Civil Rights Roll-Call Voting in the House of Representatives, 1957–1991: A Systematic Analysis." *Political Research Quarterly* 50(3): 483–502.
Schneider, Jerrold E. 1979. *Ideological Coalitions in Congress*. Westport, CT: Greenwood Press.
Sloan, John W. 1991. *Eisenhower and the Management of Prosperity*. Studies in Government and Public Policy Series. Lawrence, KS: University Press of Kansas.
Smith, Tom W. 1980. "America's Most Important Problems—A Trend Analysis, 1946–1976." *Public Opinion Quarterly* 44(2): 164–180.
Spritzer, Donald E. 1985. *Senator James E. Murray and the Limits of Post-War Liberalism*. New York: Garland.
Steinbeck, John. 1939. *The Grapes of Wrath*. New York: Viking.
Strom, Sara. 2003. "Unemployment and Families: A Review of the Research." *Social Service Review* 77(3): 399–430.
Sullivan, Mark. 1945. Editorial column. *Washington Post*, June 22.
Sundquist, James. 1968. *Politics and Policy: The Eisenhower, Kennedy, and Johnson Years*. Washington, DC: Brookings Institution Press.
Temin, Peter. 1998. "The Causes of American Business Cycles: An Essay in Economic Historiography." NBER Working Paper No. 6692. Cambridge, MA: National Bureau of Economic Research.
Temporary National Economic Committee. 1941. "Publications of the Temporary National Economic Committee." *American Economic Review* 31(2): 347–350.
Time. 1932. "Garner *v.* Wagner *v.* Hoover." *Time* 20(1): 10.
———. 1942. "Farmers: Patton Is Willing. Farmers Union's Support for the President's Anti-Inflation Program." *Time* 40(11): 22.
———. 1943. "Business and Finance." *Time* 42(16): 77–82.
———. 1945a. "'I Object.'" *Time* 46(7): 19.
———. 1945b. "National Affairs." *Time* 46(13): 15–20.
———. 1945c. "National Affairs." *Time* 46(14): 19–25.
———. 1945d. "National Affairs." *Time* 46(16): 13–18.
———. 1945e. "National Affairs." *Time* 46(22): 19–25.

———. 1945f. "Out-dealing the New Deal? First Peacetime Message to Congress." *Time* 46(12): 20.

———. 1945g. "Transition: C.E.D. v. Normalcy." *Time* 46(17): 82–83.

———. 1945h. "Transition: Sudden Shift." *Time* 46(8): 23–24.

Truman, Harry S. 1961a. "The President's News Conference of August 16, 1945." In *The Public Papers of the Presidents of the United States: Harry S. Truman, Containing the Public Messages, Speeches, and Statements of the President, April 12 to December 31, 1945*. Washington, DC: U.S. Government Printing Office, p. 225.

———. 1961b. "The President's News Conference of May 2, 1945." In *The Public Papers of the Presidents of the United States: Harry S. Truman, Containing the Public Messages, Speeches, and Statements of the President, April 12 to December 31, 1945*. Washington, DC: U.S. Government Printing Office, p. 38.

———. 1961c. "The President's News Conference of January 3, 1946." In *The Public Papers of the Presidents of the United States: Harry S. Truman, Containing the Public Messages, Speeches, and Statements of the President, January 1 to December 31, 1946*. Vol. 2. Washington, DC: U.S. Government Printing Office.

———. 1961d. "Message to the Congress on the State of the Union and on the Budget for 1947." In *The Public Papers of the Presidents of the United States: Harry S. Truman, Containing the Public Messages, Speeches, and Statements of the President, January 1, 1946, to December 31, 1946*. Vol. 2. Washington, DC: U.S. Government Printing Office.

U.S. Census Bureau. 1940a. *1940 Census of Population and Housing. Sixteenth Census of the United States: 1940. Population, Vol. I: Number of Inhabitants*. Washington, DC: U.S. Census Bureau. http://www.census.gov/prod/www/abs/decennial/1940.html (accessed January 15, 2013).

———. 1940b. *1940 Census of Population and Housing. Sixteenth Census of the United States: 1940. Population, Vol. II: Characteristics of the Population*. Washington, DC: U.S. Census Bureau. http://www.census.gov/prod/www/abs/decennial/1940.html (accessed January 15, 2013).

———. 1960. *Historical Statistics of the United States, Colonial Times to 1957: A Statistical Abstract Supplement*. Washington, DC: U.S. Department of Commerce, Census Bureau.

———. 1975. *Historical Statistics of the United States, Colonial Times to 1970: A Statistical Abstract Supplement*. Bicentennial Edition. Washington, DC: U.S. Department of Commerce, Census Bureau.

U.S. Congress. 1944a. *Economic Problems of the Reconversion Period*. Fourth Report of the House Special Committee on Post-War Economic Policy and

Planning. 78th Cong., 2nd sess. Washington, DC: U.S. Government Printing Office.

———. 1944b. *Post-War Economic Policy and Planning.* Fifth Report of the House Special Committee on Post-War Economic Policy and Planning. 78th Cong., 2nd sess. Washington, DC: U.S. Government Printing Office.

———. 1944c. *Year-End Report.* Senate Committee on Military Affairs, Subcommittee on Military Contracts. 78th Cong., 2nd sess. Washington, DC: U.S. Government Printing Office.

———. 1945a. *Report to Accompany S. 380.* House Committee on Expenditures in Executive Departments. 79th Cong., 1st sess. Washington, DC: U.S. Government Printing Office.

———. 1945b. "Hearings on S. 380." Senate Committee on Banking and Currency, Subcommittee on Full Employment. 79th Cong., 1st sess., pp. 79–83. Washington, DC: U.S. Government Printing Office.

———. 1945c. "Hearings before the Committee on Expenditures in the Executive Departments." House of Representatives. 79th Cong., 1st sess. Washington, DC: U.S. Government Printing Office.

———. 1946. *The Employment Act of 1946.* P.L. 304. 15 U.S.C. § 1021. Washington, DC: U.S. Government Printing Office.

———. 2007. "Hearings on the Conduct of Monetary Policy under the Humphrey-Hawkins Full Employment and Balanced Growth Act, July 17." U.S. Congress. House Committee on Financial Services. Washington, DC: U.S. Government Printing Office.

U.S. Department of Commerce. 1943. June, complete issue. *Survey of Current Business* 23(6): 1–32, S-1–S-36. http://www.bea.gov/scb/pdf/1943/0643cont.pdf (accessed January 16, 2013).

U.S. Senate. 1944. *The Problem of Post-War Employment and the Role of Congress in Solving It.* Special Committee on Post-War Economic Policy and Planning. 78th Cong., 2nd sess. Washington, DC: U.S. Government Printing Office.

Wagner, Robert. 1945. *History of the Employment Stabilization Act of 1931.* U.S. Congress. Senate. Committee on Banking and Currency. Report to Committee. 79th Cong., 1st sess., Senate Committee Print No. 3, July 30. Papers of Sen. Robert Wagner, Georgetown University, Washington, DC.

Walker, Donald Edwin. 1982. "The Congressional Career of Clare E. Hoffman, 1935–63." PhD diss., Michigan State University, East Lansing, MI.

Wall Street Journal. 1942a. "Heavy Government Spending, Taxes Seen in Post-War Economy." *Wall Street Journal,* January 29, p. 6.

———. 1942b. "Industry Can Make the Plans." November 25, 1942, p. 8.

———. 1942c. "Mixed Economist Too." July 13, p. 4.

———. 1944. "U.S. Steel Head Says Industry Has Ability to Reconvert Quickly." December 6, p. 3.

Wallace, Henry A. 1945. "Jobs for All." *New Republic* 112(5): 138–140.

Warken, Philip W. 1979. *A History of the National Resources Planning Board, 1933–1943*. New York: Garland.

Washington Post. 1945. "Says Wartime Spirit Can Win Peace and Assure Prosperity." January 29, p. 6.

———. 1950. "GOP Offer 5-Point Prosperity Program." April 6, p. 2.

Weir, Margaret. 1992. *Politics and Jobs: The Boundaries of Employment Policy in the United States*. Princeton, NJ: Princeton University Press.

Williams, William Appleman. 1961. *The Contours of American History*. Chicago: Quadrangle Books.

———. 1972. *The Tragedy of American Diplomacy*. New York: Dell.

Wonnacott, Thomas H., and Ronald J. Wonnacott. 1977. *Introductory Statistics*. New York: John Wiley and Sons.

World Top Incomes Database. 2012. *The Database*. Paris: Paris School of Economics. http://g-mond.parisschoolofeconomics.eu/topincomes/#Database: (accessed October 9, 2012).

Zinn, Howard, ed. 1966. *New Deal Thought*. Indianapolis: Bobbs-Merrill.

Author

Ruth Ellen Wasem is a specialist in domestic social policy at the Congressional Research Service, U.S. Library of Congress. In that capacity, she has researched, written, and testified before the U.S. Congress on immigration and social welfare policies. Congressional committees and offices have released many of her reports, which are widely cited. She is also an adjunct professor of public policy at the Lyndon B. Johnson School of Public Affairs, University of Texas, where she teaches courses on immigration policy as well as legislative policymaking. Wasem had been a Public Health Service Fellow in the Office of Population Affairs, U.S. Department of Health and Human Services, as well as a senior research associate at the United Way of America.

Wasem earned her master's and doctoral degrees in history from the University of Michigan. While at Michigan, she held a graduate research assistantship at the Institute for Social Research's Center for Political Studies and a teaching/research fellowship from the American Institutions Program. She also directed the G. Mennen Williams and Nancy Quirk Williams Oral History Project, 1980–1982, at the Michigan Historical Collections, Bentley Historical Library. Wasem received her baccalaureate degree in history, political science, and psychology from Muskingum University in New Concord, Ohio.

Index

The italic letters *f, n,* and *t* following a page number indicate that the subject information of the entry heading is within a figure, note, or table, respectively, on that page. Double letters, e.g., *nn,* indicate more than one such feature.

About the Institute

The W.E. Upjohn Institute for Employment Research is a nonprofit research organization devoted to finding and promoting solutions to employment-related problems at the national, state, and local levels. It is an activity of the W.E. Upjohn Unemployment Trustee Corporation, which was established in 1932 to administer a fund set aside by Dr. W.E. Upjohn, founder of The Upjohn Company, to seek ways to counteract the loss of employment income during economic downturns.

The Institute is funded largely by income from the W.E. Upjohn Unemployment Trust, supplemented by outside grants, contracts, and sales of publications. Activities of the Institute comprise the following elements: 1) a research program conducted by a resident staff of professional social scientists; 2) a competitive grant program, which expands and complements the internal research program by providing financial support to researchers outside the Institute; 3) a publications program, which provides the major vehicle for disseminating the research of staff and grantees, as well as other selected works in the field; and 4) an Employment Management Services division, which manages most of the publicly funded employment and training programs in the local area.

The broad objectives of the Institute's research, grant, and publication programs are to 1) promote scholarship and experimentation on issues of public and private employment and unemployment policy, and 2) make knowledge and scholarship relevant and useful to policymakers in their pursuit of solutions to employment and unemployment problems.

Current areas of concentration for these programs include causes, consequences, and measures to alleviate unemployment; social insurance and income maintenance programs; compensation; workforce quality; work arrangements; family labor issues; labor-management relations; and regional economic development and local labor markets.